KU-249-811

The Techniques of
CUT and SEW

To Desmond, for his help, encouragement and tolerance

Also published by this author

Cut & Sew: Working with Machine-Knitted Fabrics (Batsford 1985)

The Techniques of
CUT and SEW

Pam Turbett

B. T. BATSFORD LTD

Acknowledgements

My very grateful thanks to Peter Welsh (Sewing Machine Supplies and Swiftknitters, Portsmouth) who goes on answering my questions and inspires me with his technical know-how; to Christopher Thomson of Bogod Machine Co. Ltd, John Viles of Riccar (UK) Ltd, B.J.W. Wareing of Singer Industrial Products, and Howard Evans of Husqvarna Ltd, all of whom have helped with technical details and illustrations; to Pat Carlow of Butterick Fashion Marketing Co. (UK) Ltd and Susan Haigh of the Vilene Organisation; also to Tootal Craft, Mölnlycke Sewing Thread, Coats Domestic Marketing Division, Perivale Gütermann Ltd, Jencott Shoulder Padding Co, and Kinross Supplies; to Anne Smith for permission to reproduce pictures of garments previously shown in *Machine Knitting Monthly (colour plates 5 and 11 and back jacket)*; to Michael Chevis of Midhurst, for his imaginative and painstaking photography, and to Michelle Berry of Petworth, who braved some very chilly weather to model the clothes.

My thanks, too, to my students in both dressmaking and cut-and-sew classes, from whom I constantly learn something new!

All photography by Michael Chevis, ABIP, AMPA, Midhurst, Sussex, except where otherwise credited.

All other work by the author except where otherwise stated.

FIRST PUBLISHED 1988

ISBN 0 7134 55314

TYPESET BY LASERTEXT LTD., LONGFORD TRADING ESTATE, STRETFORD, MANCHESTER M32 0JT.
AND PRINTED IN GREAT BRITAIN BY
ANCHOR BRENDON LTD., TIPTREE, ESSEX
FOR THE PUBLISHERS B.T. BATSFORD LTD
4 FITZHARDINGE STREET, LONDON W1H 0AH

Contents

Introduction

This large lady marched up to my stand at a crowded convention. 'Your cut-and-sew book explained *some* things, but you left out such a lot!' she boomed. She was not aggressive: machine-knitters, on the whole are an amazingly pleasant level-headed lot. She was, however, very cross. The zip insertion, which I had so blithely informed her could be made in a knitted skirt, had gone wrong; the skirt was unwearable and she was not impressed.

I mumbled something about my publisher limiting the amount of space, but I had to agree with her in principle. Without trying to excuse my own shortcomings, probably no book on how-to-do any craft is ever really adequate; there are always some questions left unanswered.

So, here is my attempt at a belated recompense to the large lady and any other frustrated cut-and-sew enthusiasts. Where *Cut and Sew: Working with Machine-Knitted Fabrics* (Batsford, 1985) finished, this book begins. My aim is to explain *how*, when using knitted fabrics, you set about attaching a collar, piping a seam, setting in sleeves — and inserting a zip!

This is a text book to be kept with your sewing-equipment, to be worked with rather than to be read in bed. Refer to it when you need practical help with a particular part of sewing a garment, and then follow the directions step by step — just as you do with a cookery book in the kitchen.

It could be argued that so many pages dedicated to one process, such as attaching a waistband, is making far too much of the whole thing. I have tried not to bore the reader with too much detail, but my experience in teaching Adult Education students has shown me that anything left out will inevitably cause someone a headache... 'you didn't actually *say* that in the instructions!'

At the time of writing, it is exactly three years since I presented my first cut-and-sew book to Batsford. Not only have I made many more clothes and talked to hundreds of machine-knitters about this aspect of their craft, but there have been a number of new developments in the relevant machinery and haberdashery; so I have included a final chapter which aims to explain some of these changes.

Dear large lady, I hope I am forgiven!

Abbreviations

C.B. Centre Back
C.F. Centre Front
R.S. Right Side
W.S. Wrong Side
tog. together

Note Specific numbers of dressmaking patterns are not included because delay between preparation and publication inevitably means that many will no longer be available.

▲

Chapter one

DARTS

I am devoting a short chapter entirely to the subject of darts because I have found, during the course of many years of teaching dressmaking, that they can so often go wrong. A 'poke' at the end of a dart is such a common complaint and yet such an easy one to cure. When using knitted fabrics, it is especially important to get it right.

You simply have to understand that a dart is usually there to shape the fabric over a curved area of the body and that that area is either a *convex* shape (e.g. over the hip or over the shoulder — see Fig. 1a, b, c.) or a *concave* shape (e.g. from waist or hip level, up to and under the bust; or from the shoulder, rising up the curve of the neck — see Fig. 2a, b.). *Therefore the sewing-line of the dart is a curved line and not a straight one.*

Part of the trouble arises because, on most paper patterns, darts over the hip and stomach are frequently printed as straight lines and beginners naturally assume that they should follow the stitching lines exactly. Occasionally, even darts for concave shapes are shown as straight lines, although this is much less common.

Fig. 1 Darts over convex shapes

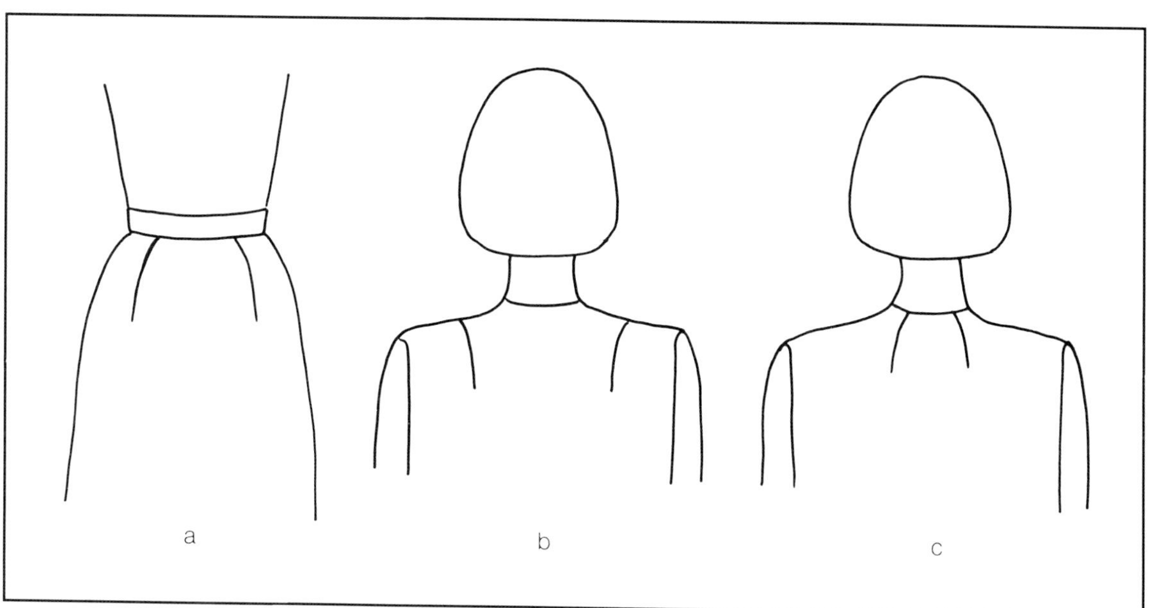

Fig. 2 Darts over concave shapes

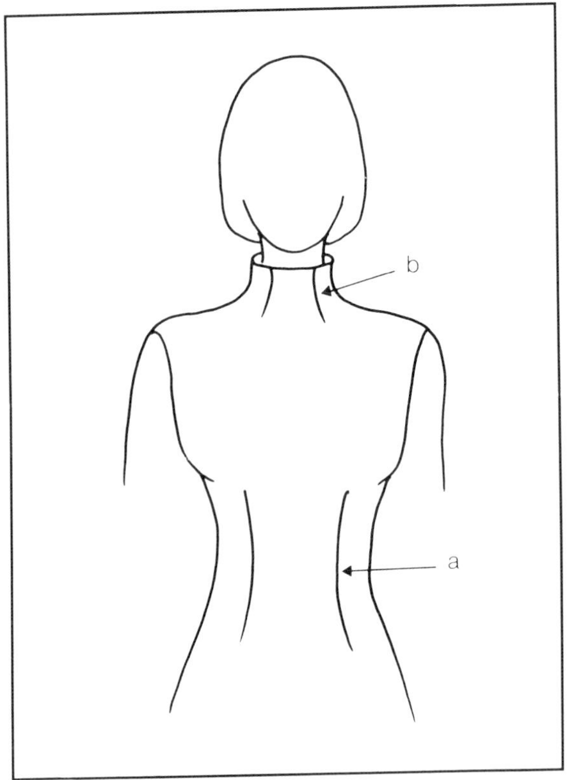

Fig. 3 Darts sewn for convex shape

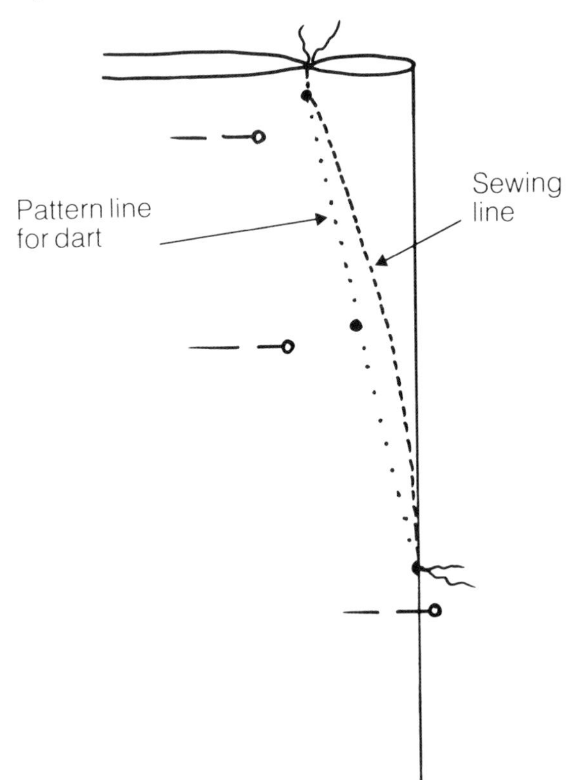

To sew a dart for a convex shape (*Fig. 3*)

Transfer all pattern lines for the dart to the fabric. Fold the fabric, matching the marks at the top of the dart, and pin as shown. Stitch from the wide end to the point, moving out towards the fold rather earlier than is indicated by the pattern lines, and then taper off very gradually so that the stitching merges into the fold without any kind of 'peak'. The last few stitches should be barely on the edge of the fold.

To sew a dart for a concave shape (*Fig. 4a, b*)

Transfer pattern marks and pin as shown. Stitch, following the pattern lines, but make sure the widest part of the dart is smoothly curved and that the end (or ends) are tapered off very gradually.

The length of the dart depends very much on your own individual contours, but generally waist darts over the stomach are shorter than waist darts at the back. When trying out a new pattern, always machine-tack the darts before trying on for fitting (using a loose needle-tension so that the stitching can be pulled out easily); then be prepared to shorten or lengthen the darts as necessary.

Bust darts

There is one kind of dart which should not usually be curved: this is any dart which runs towards the bust from the upper side seam, the armhole, the shoulder, the neck, the C.F. seam (*Fig. 5a*), or from a vertical bodice seam (*Fig. 5b*). This is just because a 'poke' is actually needed there to cope with the outward thrust of the bust.

Fig. 4 Darts sewn for concave shapes

Fig. 5 Darts which can be sewn as straight lines

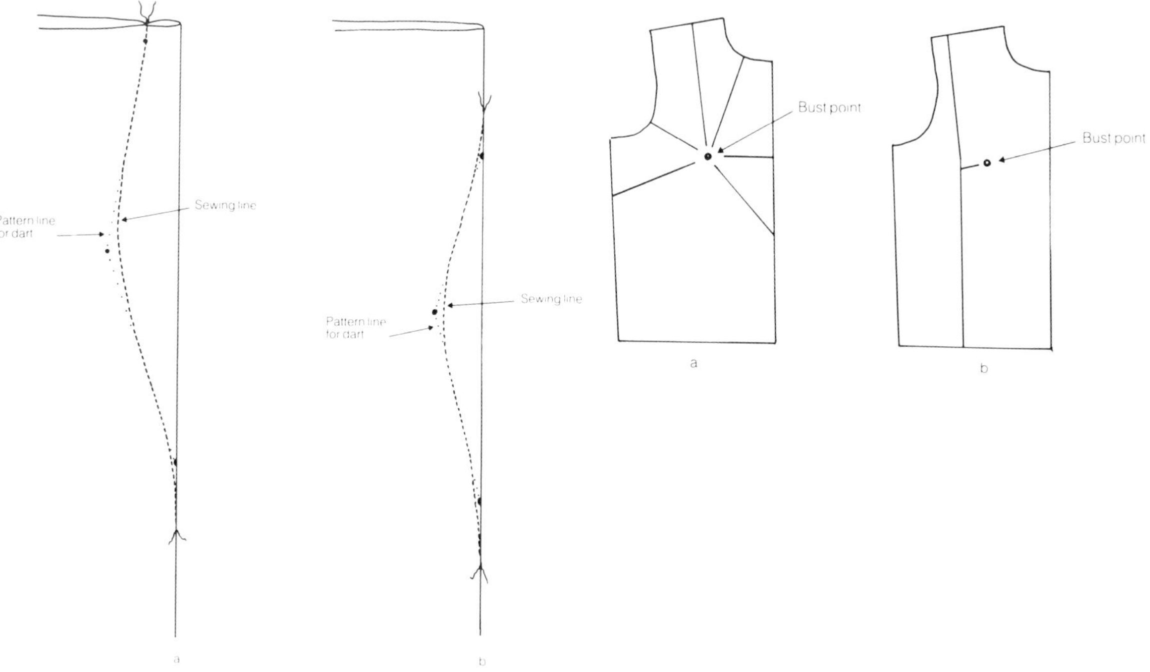

Pressing darts

On the W.S. of the fabric, horizontal darts should generally be pressed downwards and vertical darts should generally be pressed towards the centre of the body. When lining a garment, however, press the darts on the lining the opposite way to those on the garment in order to avoid unnecessary bulk. If you are using a rather bulky knitted fabric, it may be wise to split the dart down its fold and press it open flat.

Note For advice on enlarging a bust dart (for those who take C, D or DD-cup bras) turn to pp. 77–79 of *Cut and Sew: Working with Machine-Knitted Fabrics* (Batsford, 1985).

For cut-and-sew work, it is often possible to eliminate darts by simply easing in the fullness which the dart aims to remove. You could always try easing first, to see if you like the effect, and then return to the dart if you don't.

Chapter two

PIPING

I mentioned piping in *Cut and Sew: Working with Machine-Knitted Fabrics* as both a decorative method of trimming and an excellent way of stabilising some of the seams and edges of cut-and-sew clothes. I did not, however, because of lack of space, enlarge on the subject; as a number of readers have asked for more detail I am including it in this book.

Piping can draw attention to seams where you want to display their line, for example, the seamline of a yoke, or where a raglan sleeve joins the body. These can often get lost in the texture of the knit, especially when it is patterned; but when piping is inserted, the shapes immediately become obvious (*Fig. 6*).

Piping also stabilises those seams in which it is inserted, simply because the piping cord cannot stretch — a good reason for adding it not only to yokes and raglan armholes, but also to pocket tops (*Fig. 7*), neck edges (where there is no collar) and the front opening edges of coats and jackets. Having thus stabilised the edges, facings can be cut from the same knit as the rest of the garment.

Suitable fabrics for pipings

Piping can be purchased ready-made but I find that I can ill-afford the time involved in searching for just the right shade and thickness. It is usually much easier (and often cheaper) to find a suitable woven fabric which can be bias-cut into strips and then used to cover plain cotton piping cord.

A length of 20 to 40cm ($\frac{1}{4}$ to $\frac{1}{2}$yd) by whatever the width, between selvedges, happens to be, will be sufficient for most purposes; the smaller the piece, the more joins you will have to make. With practice and experience you will find that you can obtain an amazingly long strip from quite small odd pieces; if you have already combined a woven fabric with the knit elsewhere on the garment, use the leftover pieces of that — providing the texture is suitable.

Avoid thick, bulky or loosely-woven fabrics for covering piping cord; in fact, avoid anything which will not stand up to a fair amount of friction. Velvet is not generally suitable unless the pile is very short and dense. Suede-cloth, on the other hand, works beautifully. So do poly/cotton poplin or gingham, fine linen-type mixtures of natural and synthetic fibres, polyester linings or polyester satin. Small candy-stripes can make very effective piping on plain knits; Fig. 8 shows a blue and white striped poly/cotton seersucker used for a hat band as well as for the piping in the seamline.

I have used fine (purchased) jersey fabrics successfully for covering piping cord but have not so far used knitted fabrics made on a domestic knitting machine; I think this might work providing the texture and tension are sufficiently fine.

Fig. 6 A piped seamline; close-up of armhole seam in colour picture 2

Fig. 7 Piped pocket top; close-up of pocket in skirt on back jacket

Fig. 8 Piping inserted in hat seamline to match hatband

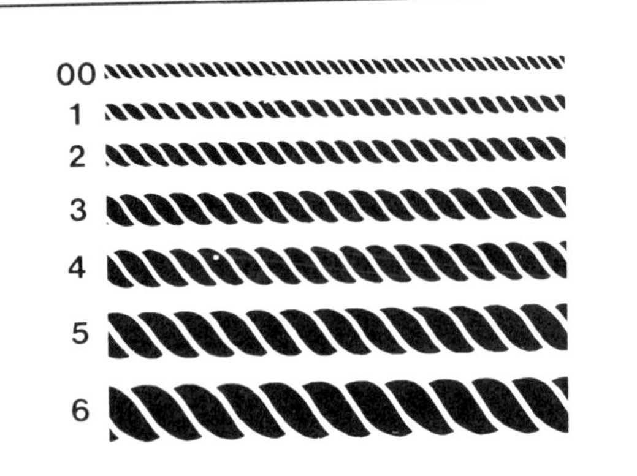

Fig. 9 Sizes of piping cords (Tootal)

The piping cord

Tootal make excellent piping cord in seven different thicknesses (*Fig. 9*). Choose the right thickness to complement the garment; I find that I mostly use sizes 1 and 2, though I might use size 3 for a rather bulky knit.

This cord is made from pure cotton, so buy rather more than you actually need because it must be made to shrink before use. Put it into a saucepan, cover with water and bring to the boil. Drain and allow to dry before using.

It is possible to find piping cord made from polyester and this does not require pre-shrinking.

To make the piping

If you have never done this before, do have a trial run before actually trying to do it on a garment; your results will improve enormously after a modicum of practice!

1 Cut and join bias strips, following the directions on pp. 83–5. But note that the width of the strips has to be decided according to the thickness of the piping cord to be used: i.e. the circumference of the cord plus twice the width of the seam allowances. For a size 1 cord (and allowing for 1.5cm [$\frac{5}{8}$in] seam allowances) strips 3.8cm ($1\frac{1}{2}$in) wide are about right; thicker cord will require wider strips.

2 Fit a presser foot which will accommodate the piping cord to your sewing machine, instead of the normal presser foot. At present, comparatively few manufacturers (known exceptions are Bernina and Husqvarna) produce a specially designed foot for this purpose, and even these are optional extra purchases (see *Cut and Sew: Working with Machine-Knitted Fabrics*, pp. 29–30). In the case of the majority of sewing machines, the zipper foot has to be used; adjust this, if possible, so that the needle can penetrate the fabric as close as possible to the cord without actually catching it in.

3 Fold the bias strip in half lengthwise, R.S. out, fitting it over the cord and lining up the raw edges together (*Fig. 10a*). Pin in position if necessary, and then machine stitch as close as possible to the cord, using a short stitch length (about $1\frac{1}{2}$).

To apply the piping

Note Always stitch the piping first to whichever of the two garment pieces appears to be the more stable. For example, on a neckline, where the facing has been interfaced with Vilene, stitch the piping first to the facing rather than to the garment, which is more likely to stretch during the process.

1 Place the prepared piping on the R.S. of the garment piece, as shown in Fig. 10b, so that the stitching line on the piping lies exactly on the seamline of the garment. If you judged the width of the strips correctly, it means that all three raw edges will lie exactly together. Pin in position, taking great care to see that neither the knitted fabric nor the piping are unduly stretched out. Do this flat on a table, not in your lap!

Machine stitch again precisely on the previous line of stitching, still using the zipper or piping foot.

Note To carry the piping round a corner, snip into the seam allowances of the piping at a point exactly where you will pivot to turn the corner; snip almost right up to the stitching line (*Fig. 11a*). The corner will be slightly rounded rather than a sharp right angle. To cope with more gentle curves, make more snips in the seam allowances (*Fig. 11b*).

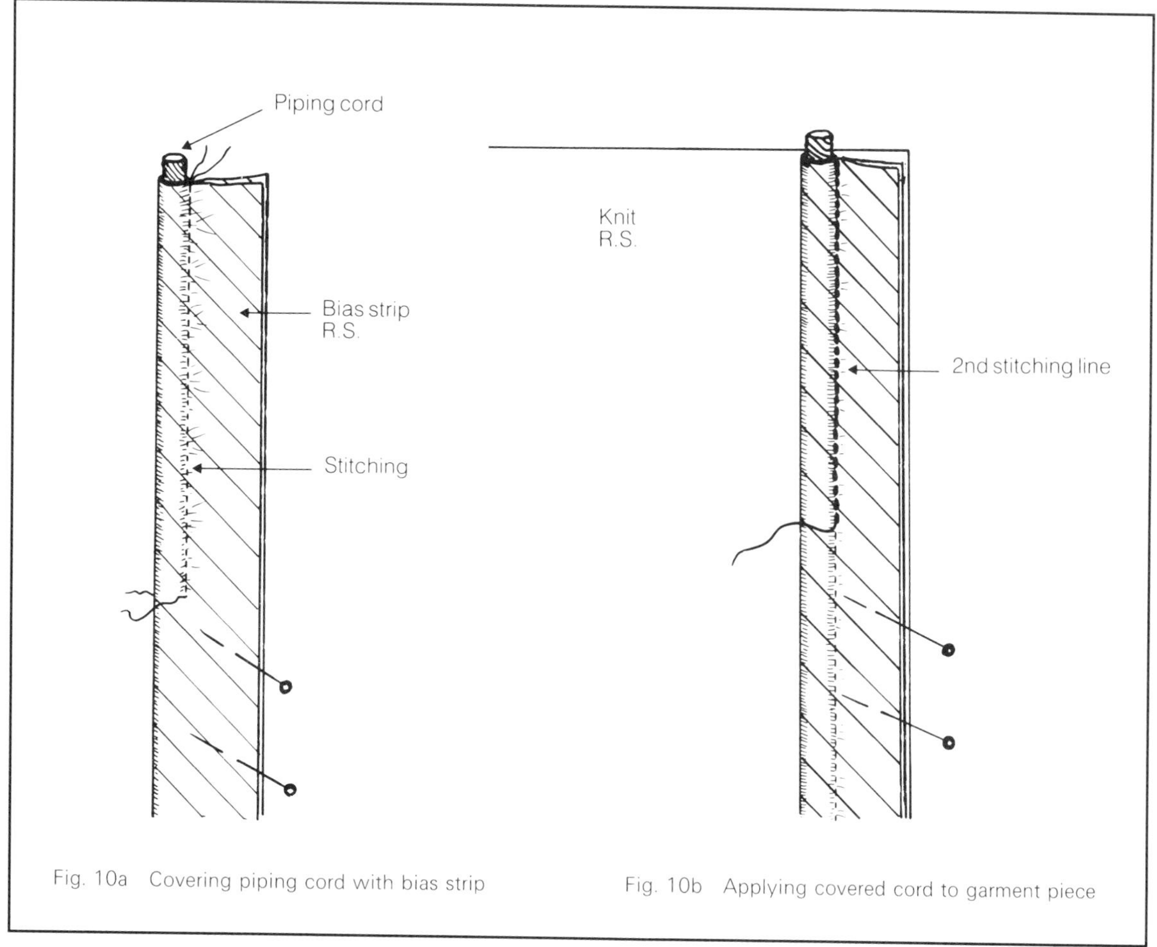

Fig. 10a Covering piping cord with bias strip

Fig. 10b Applying covered cord to garment piece

2 Take the piece of fabric to which the piping is now attached and turn it over so that the W.S. is uppermost. Place it on the appropriate garment piece, R.S. tog, so that the raw edges are lined up. Machine stitch again, still using the zipper or piping foot, exactly on the line of stitching already there.

3 Trim back the seam allowances by about half and snip them wherever you have concave curves. Turn through to the R.S.

4 Secure the seam allowances in place by under-stitching (p. 101. *Cut and Sew: Working with Machine-Knitted Fabrics*) or by top-stitching through all seam allowances on one side of the seamline.

Note To avoid bulk where the ends of the piping are enclosed in seams, pull out and cut off sufficient cord to leave the casing empty where it lies within a seam.

Piping a continuous edge

To pipe a continuous edge, such as a neckline or a sleeve end, where there is no opening, start at a point where the join will be least obvious — perhaps the C.B. Remove the cord from the first 2cm ($\frac{3}{4}$in) of piping and fold the empty casing towards the raw edges, as shown in Fig. 12a.

Start the machine-stitching just before the folded edge of the casing. When you have completed the circle, stop the stitching exactly where you started and stitch in reverse for 1.2cm ($\frac{1}{2}$in). Cut off the remaining piping strip 2.5cm (1in) from the end of the stitching and remove the cord from this loose end. Turn it towards the

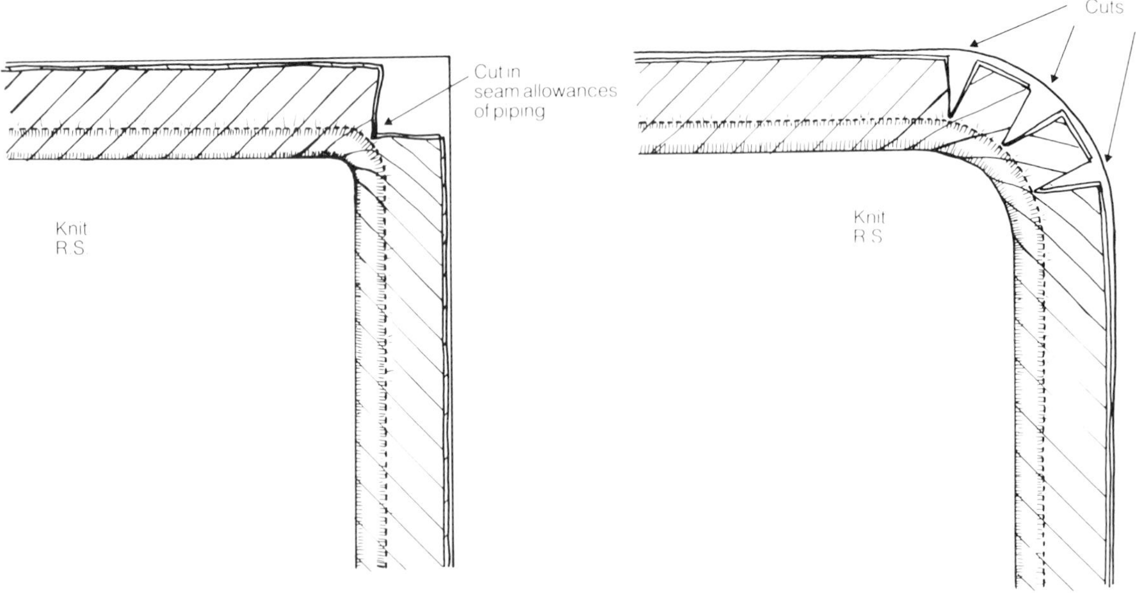

Fig. 11a Carrying piping around corners

Fig. 11b Carrying piping around curved edges

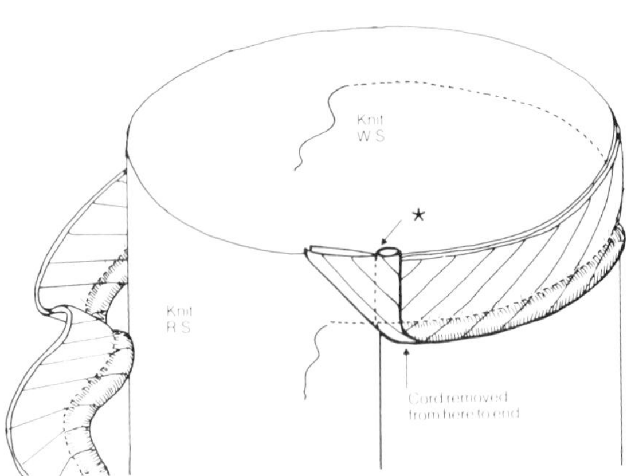

Fig. 12a Piping a continuous edge: starting

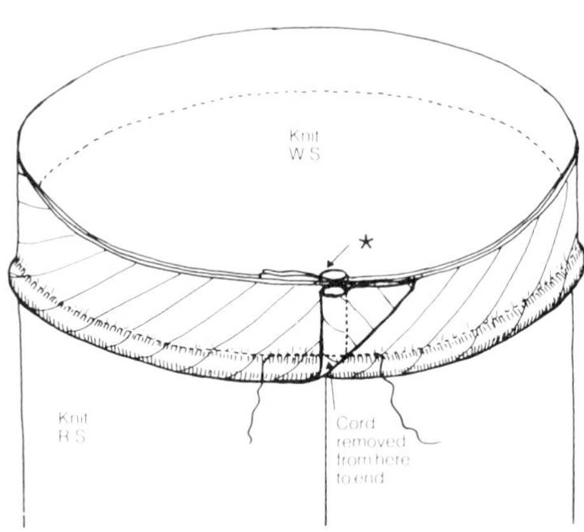

Fig. 12b Piping a continuous edge: finishing

raw edges as shown in Fig. 12b. Stitch in position.

If you have done this correctly, the covered ends of the piping cord meet without overlapping, so that no excess bulk occurs. You can slip-stitch the ends together invisibly with needle and thread.

▲

Chapter three

COLLARS

Collars can vary so widely that a whole book could be devoted to this one subject. Anyone who wants to pursue the study of collar shapes and the principles of collar fitting should read the relevant chapters in Natalie Bray's *Dress Pattern Designing* (Crosby Lockwood Staples, London).

For the purposes of this book, in which I am concentrating mainly on the use of commercial paper patterns, it might be sufficient to say that you should choose the design you want, purchase the pattern in the correct size for your figure (see Chaps. 8 and 9, *Cut and Sew: Working with Machine-Knitted Fabrics)* and then simply follow the pattern instruction sheets.

However, the application of a collar to a garment can cause more headaches than almost any other process in its completion. You can get away with errors in other parts, but a badly fitting collar simply looks like home-dressmaking at its worst! In cut-and-sew work, the added hazard of using a stretchy fabric increases the chances of getting it wrong; so, start by anticipating the possible problems and take positive steps to avoid them.

Planning the collar

Check the fitting of the collar if you are in any doubt about that; some people know in advance that the collar is going to be their particular fitting problem! It might be worth cutting the collar in a piece of old sheeting and simply trying it on to see how it fits and whether or not you actually like its shape.

Fitting problems in collars usually occur only when the pattern has been purchased in the wrong size. However, if you happen to have a neck which is larger or smaller than average for your size and also want a buttoned-up collar to fit perfectly, it is worth checking the actual length of the neck seamline between the C.F. marks on the collar and then comparing it with your own measurement. Take care to see that you measure your neck exactly where the neck seamline will come — not higher or lower. Then make the collar longer or shorter accordingly, by adding to, or subtracting from, the paper pattern; divide your alterations so that you make small differences to front, back and each side of the collar, rather than just adding or removing a large chunk at C.B.

If an adjustment has been made to the collar, the garment neckline must be altered to fit it. Lowering it slightly will enable it to accommodate a longer collar; raising it slightly will enable it to accommodate a shorter collar. Check the lengths of the two neck seamlines, between the C.F. marks, to make sure that they are identical.

Stabilise the collar so that neither it nor the neckline of the garment can possibly stretch. This can be done in one of several ways.

1 When both layers of the collar are cut from knitted fabric, one of them can be interfaced with

Fig. 13a Collar, yoke facing and front-buttoning band cut from woven fabric to tone with the knit from which the rest of the garment is cut

Fig. 13b Collar cut from woven fabric to contrast with the knit. The double-breasted, buttoned opening is faced with the same woven fabric. Yoke lined with polyester lining fabric (close-up of colour picture 5)

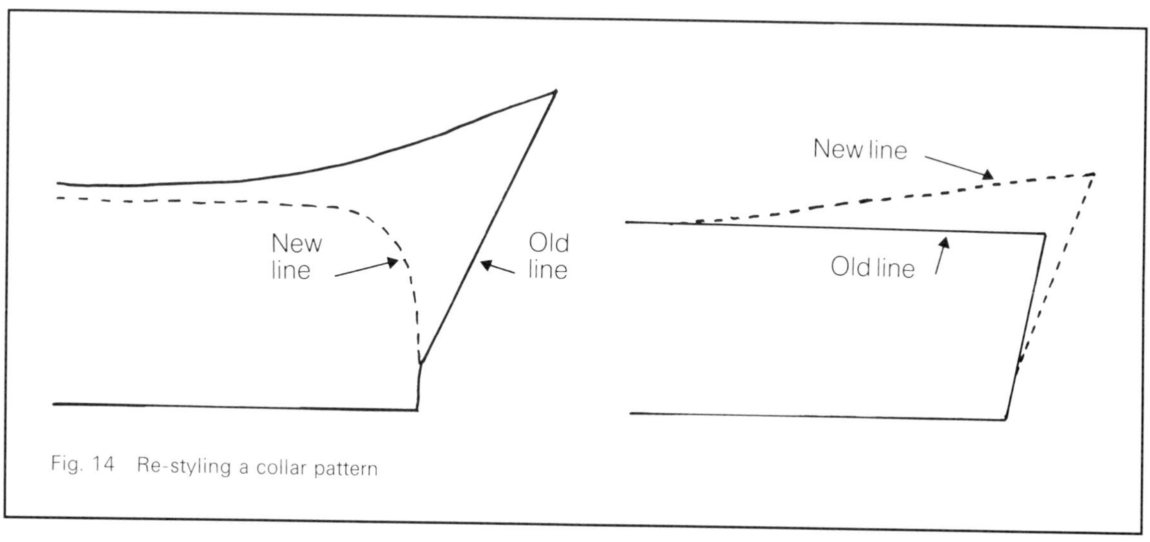

Fig. 14 Re-styling a collar pattern

a non-stretch, woven interfacing such as fusible cotton muslin, or sewn-in lawn or organza. Remember that a non-woven interfacing, such as fusible knitted nylon, or any of the Vilenes, can still stretch a little.

2 The upper layer of the collar can be cut from knitted fabric and the under layer (the collar facing) can be cut from a woven fabric chosen to match, tone or contrast with the knitted fabric. A fusible or sew-in interfacing can be used as well if necessary.

3 Both layers of the collar can be cut from woven fabric as above. Examples of this are shown in Figs. 13a, b.

4 A collar can be made from a single layer of knitted fabric; for an example of this, look at the draped collar of the grey two-piece in colour picture 6 and 84. To stabilise the neck in this case, the neck facing was cut from woven lining fabric, which was then interfaced with Vilene Ultrasoft lightweight to make it a little firmer, without adding bulk.

Cutting and making-up the collar

There are several aspects of making collars which are worth studying briefly; some understanding of these will not only provide a foundation of extra background knowledge which is not generally provided in pattern instruction sheets, but will also help you to solve problems when they inevitably occur.

For instance, you can, with safety, always alter the shape of the outer edge of a collar if you wish (*Fig. 14*). As long as you have not altered its neck edge, the collar will still fit the neck of the garment. Old patterns with out-of-date collars can often be re-used in this way.

With experience you can change one type of collar for another, but always remember that the collar must be designed or adapted to fit the neckline upon which it is to be placed. This generally means that the seamline on the neck edge of the collar must be adjusted so that it becomes precisely the same length as the neck seamline on the garment, between the points where the ends of the collar should be placed.

Sewing the two layers of a collar together

Note For ease of description, 'collar' refers to the top layer, the one which will be on view when the garment is complete; 'collar facing' refers to the underpart of the collar which is usually hidden when the garment is complete, and 'interfacing' refers to the stiffening and/or stabilising fabric which lies between the collar and the collar facing.

A problem occurs when making shirts and dresses because the collar and collar facing, which are sewn together before being applied to the garment, are usually both cut from the same pattern piece. This leads to some difficulty in getting the finished collar to roll properly, with the seamline on its outer edge rolled neatly just underneath, rather than showing on the edge — or, even worse, actually rolling up and over on to the upper side of the collar. *In fact, to achieve a neatly rolled effect, the collar facing needs to be slightly smaller than the collar.*

The following process solves the problem.

Note Instructions are for dressmaking; tailoring is different (see p. 22–4).

1 If interfacing is required, add it to the collar. It should be cut on the same pattern piece so that the edges match exactly — not, as some pattern instructions suggest, with the seam allowances removed; it needs to be included in the seam when this is machined.

2 Draw the pattern markings (notches, dots, C.B. line, C.F. marks, etc.) onto the interfacing,

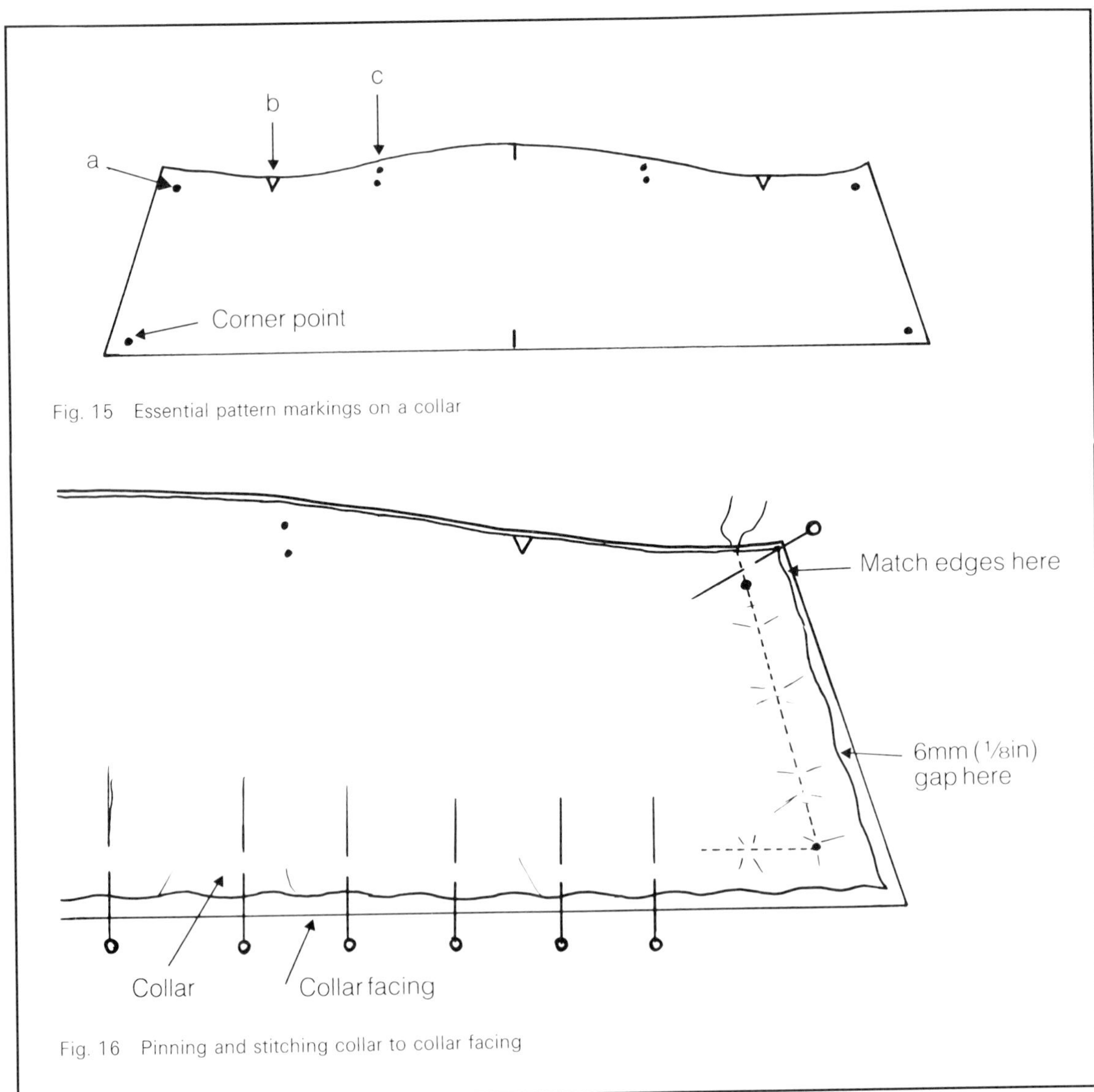

Fig. 15 Essential pattern markings on a collar

Fig. 16 Pinning and stitching collar to collar facing

using a sharp soft lead pencil or a dressmarking pen. Mark, also, the points at the outer corners of the collar, where you will actually be turning the corners when sewing (*Fig. 15*). A clearly marked dot here will help tremendously when the work is under the machine presser foot.

3 Place the collar on top of the collar facing, R.S. tog., carefully matching the ends of the collar pieces at the neck edge. Pin these points exactly together.

4 Pin the remaining outer edges of the collar to the corresponding edges of the collar facing, as shown in Fig. 16, *with the collar pushed slightly inwards, making it pucker a little and creating a gap of approximatey 3mm ($\frac{1}{8}$in) between the two pieces.* Do this all around the outer edges of the collar, easing it slightly (and stretching the collar facing a little) to make it fit. Leave the neck edge alone.

Note If the fabrics are very thick and bulky, you may need to increase the gap to 6mm ($\frac{1}{4}$in).

Use plenty of pins to hold the two layers together securely; one every 1.2cm ($\frac{1}{2}$in) is not excessive.

5 Machine along the collar seamlines. Sew with the collar on top and the collar facing underneath. (Having the interfaced piece immediately under the presser foot helps to reduce stretching problems.) Use a small stitch length because you will have to reduce the seam allowances to a minimum before turning the collar; large stitches would allow the knit to fray.

Check, after stitching, that there are no faults in the seam. It is all too easy to make little tucks accidentally; if this has happened, simply unpick about 2.5cm (1in) either side of the fault, re-arrange the fabrics, and re-stitch.

6 Trim the seam allowances and turn the collar to the R.S.

7 Push the seamline out from the inside with a large knitting needle, taking care not to pierce through. Press the collar carefully and thoroughly, rolling the seam on the outer edge so that it is just hidden on the underside of the collar.

When making coats and jackets, the order of assembly is slightly different. A tailoring method is used whereby the collar facing is attached to the coat, the collar attached to the facings and only then are the two outer edges of the collar sewn together. At this stage, it is advisable to use the same technique of pushing the collar further in than the collar facing, even if you have actually been given a separate, slighty smaller pattern for the collar facing, simply because of the thickness of the knit.

Attaching collars

In general, follow your pattern instructions for attaching collars, but I do want to emphasise three simple rules for ensuring success, whatever the style. Follow them and your collars will always look professional.

Rule 1

Look for, and transfer to the fabrics, all the pattern marks on the neck edge of the garment and on the neck edge of the collar; i.e. all dots, circles and notches. Also mark the C.B. line on both collar and garment.

These marks are vitally important and cannot be safely ignored! They have been carefully placed in position by the pattern-maker precisely to within a millimetre of where they should be, so you must be equally precise about transferring them to the fabrics. Look again at Fig. 15 where these marks are illustrated.

a The mark on the front neck edge of the garment where the finished ends of the collar are to be placed.

b The notches on the neck edge of the garment and the corresponding notches on the neck edge of the collar.

c The dots, on the neck edge of the collar, roughly halfway between C.B. and the collar ends, which indicate the shoulder-line. These have to be positioned exactly on the shoulder-line of the garment when the collar is attached. (*Note* Your garment could possibly have a dropped shoulder seam, in which case there will be a mark on the garment neck edge indicating where the true shoulder-line lies.)

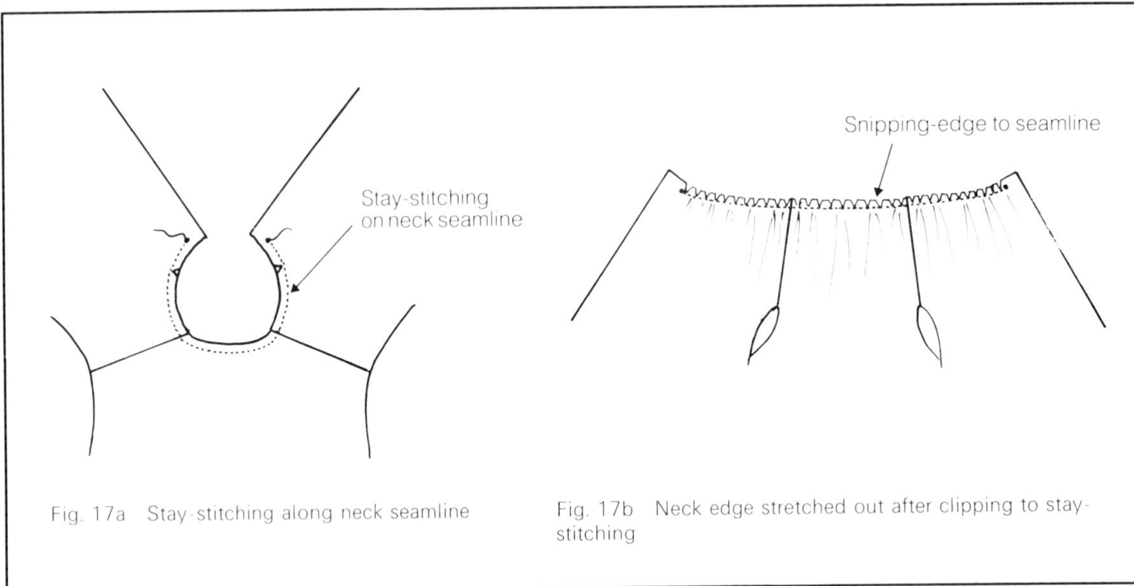

Fig. 17a Stay-stitching along neck seamline

Fig. 17b Neck edge stretched out after clipping to stay-stitching

Rule 2

Stay-stitch the neck seamline on the garment and then snip the neck seam allowance all round, cutting almost to the stay-stitching (*Fig. 17a, b*).

'Stay-stitching' means straight machine-stitching on a very short (1–1½) stitch length; it is usually mentioned in the pattern instructions but that paragraph is all too frequently either ignored or misinterpreted! The reason for stay-stitching is simple — it stops the knit from fraying when the snipping is done. The reason for the snipping may not be quite so obvious, but you have probably already discovered that when the neck of the garment is a definite concave curve and the neck edge of the collar is either straight or even a convex curve, the neck edge of the collar often appears to be too long for the neck edge of the garment. Snipping the seam allowance on the neck edge of the garment enables you to stretch it out into a straight line and so fit the collar on quite easily.

Rule 3

Match all the dots, notches and C.B. lines precisely when pinning the collar to the neck edge of the garment. Also make sure that the edges of the seam allowances lie exactly together; it is all too easy to let one of them slip down.

Funnel collars

This is a type of collar which can very easily be added to any circular neckline, and it works particularly well with knitted fabrics. You can even rejuvenate old sweaters by removing the old collar and adding a new funnel collar, in the original yarn if you still have some, or in a contrasting shade or texture. (Collars like this are, in fact, selling well in the boutiques, at present, as separate items which can be worn over any sweater, dress, coat, etc., without being sewn on at all. The same idea, but cut deeper, becomes a 'wimple' which can be pulled up right over the head.)

No interfacing is used. Do some experimenting before committing yourself because a lot can depend on the thickness and texture of the knit; you also need to try out the effect to see if it actually suits you.

To make a funnel collar

1 Draw out a pattern in the shape of a rectangle. *See Fig. 18a.*

A–B equals the measurement of the neck seamline on the garment.

B–C can be whatever depth of collar you want. (It could be quite shallow, or it could rise up

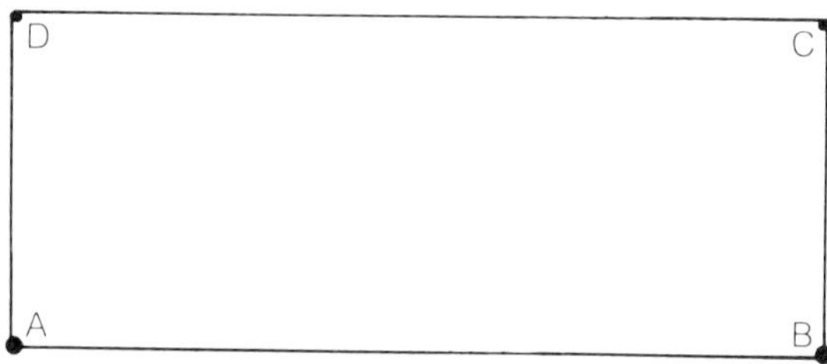

Fig. 18a Rectangle drawn for funnel collar

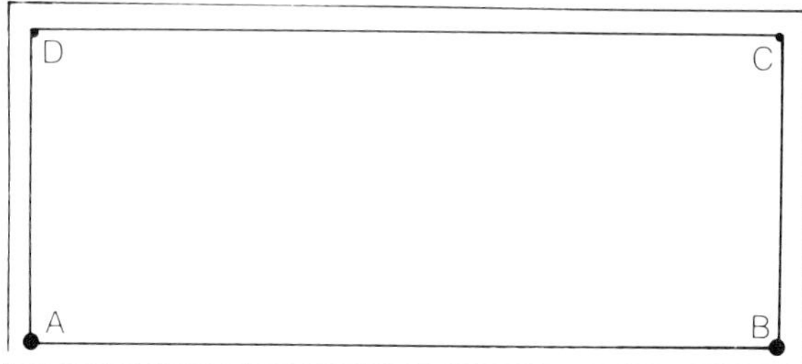

Fig. 18b Seam allowances added to complete pattern for funnel collar

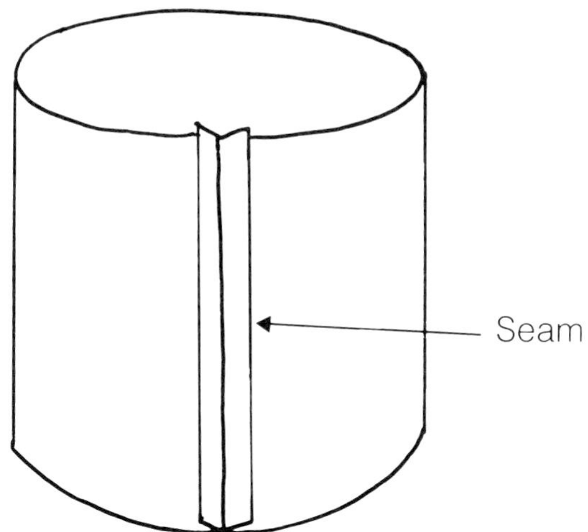

Fig. 19 Joining back seam of funnel collar

the neck and then turn over and down, once or even twice, depending on the thickness of the knit.)

See Fig. 18b.

Add seam allowances to all four sides of the rectangle. Mark the straight grain line as shown.

2 Cut the collar from the knitted fabric using this paper pattern.

3 Sew up the vertical seam, A–D to B–C, R.S. tog. (*Fig. 19*). (In practice, this seam would have to be neatly finished.)

4 Turn in and hem the top edge of the collar, or neaten it with the help of an overlocking machine. Take care not to stretch it out too much, but also aim at a finish which will allow it to stretch out a little if necessary.

5 Holding both the garment and the collar W.S. out, place the collar inside the neck of the garment, so that the seam in the collar is placed at C.B. of the neck and the raw edges of the neck seam allowances lie exactly together.

Note The W.S. of the collar must face the R.S. of the garment.

6 Pin and stitch the collar to the garment as shown in Fig. 20. Neaten the seam allowance with over-edge stitching, or overlocking, but take care not to stretch out the neck seam any more than you can help. If it does stretch badly, thread a double length of fine shirring elastic through the neatened seam allowances.

7 Turn the collar upwards from the neck (Fig. 21) and then roll the top edge to the R.S., down over the seamline.

Here are several variations on this idea. You can probably invent more.

a The neck edge of the collar can be placed on the R.S. of the garment, R.S. tog, and stitched; the top edge of the collar is then turned over to the W.S. of the garment and hemmed in place over the seam allowances. This collar is now of double thickness and can either rise straight up the neck, or, if cut deeper, can rise up, turn over and fall down to the R.S. like a polo-neck.

b The collar, cut as a much more shallow rectangle and made up as in **1** above, could take the form of quite a narrow band, and this could be stiffened, if required, by the addition of interfacing.

c The collar can be cut in two sections, shaped as in Fig. 22a; line A–B is exactly half the measurement of the neck seamline. The two seams are sewn up and the collar is attached to

Fig. 20 Joining funnel collar to neck edge of garment

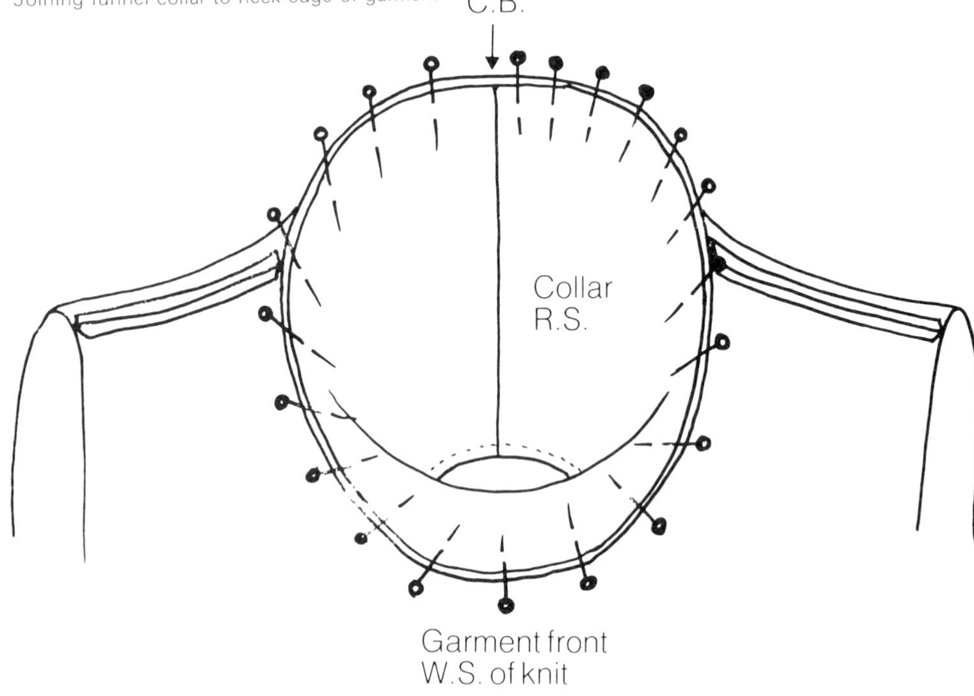

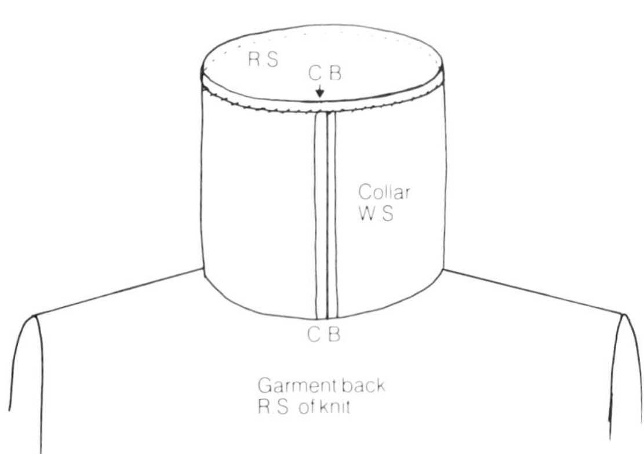

Fig. 21 Collar pulled out to R.S. of garment

the garment as shown in Fig. 22b, with one seam lined up with each side of the neck. This produces a softer collar which falls lower on the garment.

d Making the neck edge of the collar slightly larger than the neck edge of the garment, and then easing it on to the seamline, also makes for a softer, more draped collar.

Tailored collars

Collars on tailored coats and jackets are constructed by special tailoring methods. A good dressmaking pattern should give sufficient detail to enable you to get them right, but if you are left in doubt, consult the chapter on tailoring in the *Readers Digest Book of Sewing*, or the *Vogue Sewing Book*. In these cases, the collar facing should be interfaced, rather than the collar itself. Use a non-stretch, iron-on fabric such as fusible cotton muslin. It is possible nowadays to obtain fusible tailoring canvas, but this can sometimes make a cut-and-sew garment rather heavy.

To ensure that the finished collar is going to be neatly rolled and well-shaped, the collar facing and the interfacing shoud be pad-stitched together along the lines shown in Fig. 23, in the following order.

1 You should find that the roll-line of the collar is marked on the paper pattern for the collar facing. Transfer this line from the pattern to the interfaced collar facing, using a cloth-marking pen or a soft lead pencil (*Fig. 23a*).

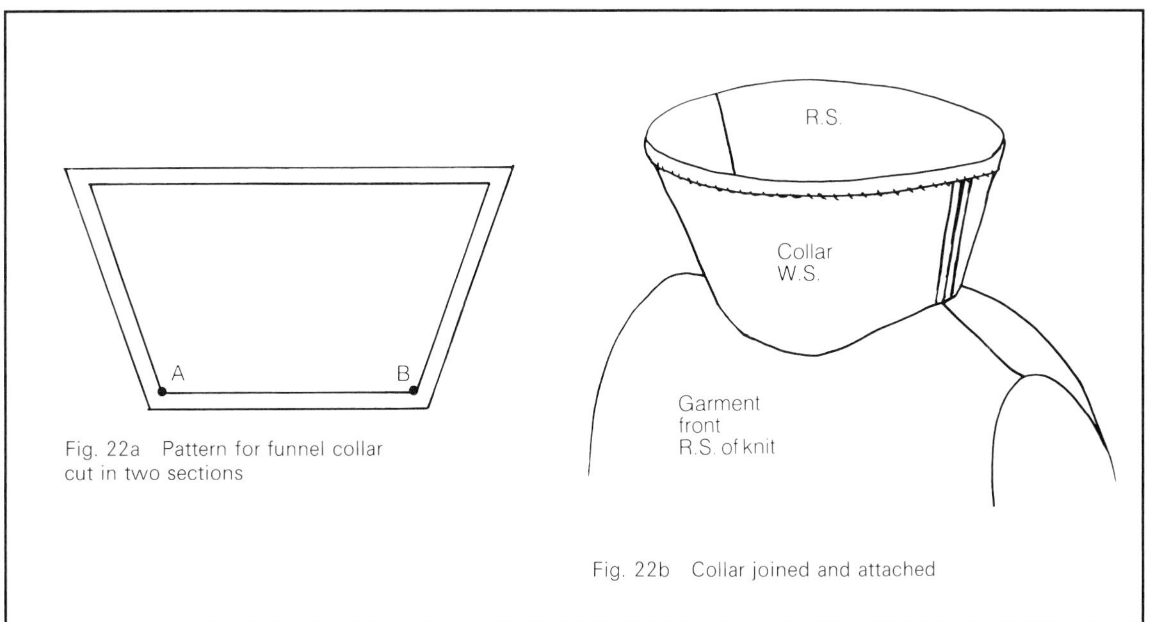

Fig. 22a Pattern for funnel collar cut in two sections

Fig. 22b Collar joined and attached

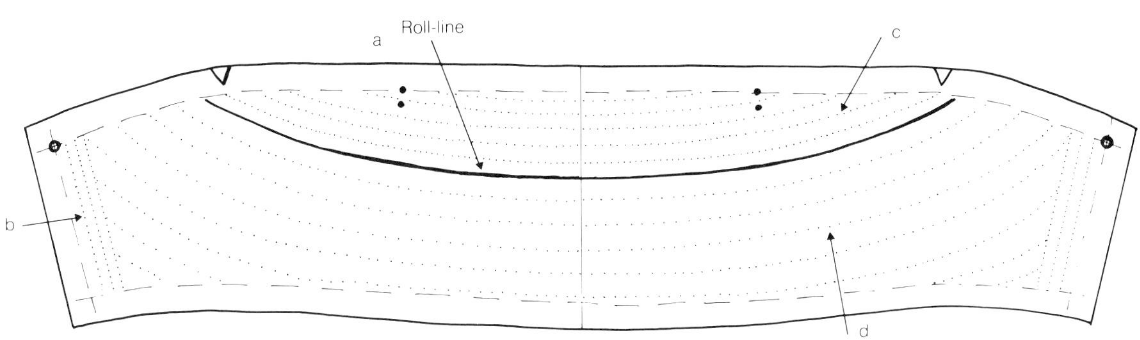

Fig. 23 Pad-stitching lines for tailored collar

2 Pad-stitch along the marked roll-line. To do this, hold the collar, interfacing on top, curving it over the fingers, and take small stitches which cross the line at right angles. Use a thread which matches the collar facing fabric exactly. These stitches should sew into but not right through the collar facing fabric.

3 Make three lines of small pad-stitching parallel with the collar ends (*Fig. 23b*).

4 Fill in the area between the roll-line and the neck edge with small pad-stitching, and the area between the roll-line and the outer edge of the collar with larger pad-stitching, following the lines drawn on the interfacing (*Fig. 23c, d*).

Note For small pad-stitching, the needle should pick up about 3mm ($\frac{1}{8}$in) of fabric and the gaps between stitches shoud be about 6mm ($\frac{1}{4}$in).

For larger pad-stitching, the needle should still pick up only 3mm ($\frac{1}{8}$in) but the gaps between stitches can be 1.2cm ($\frac{1}{2}$in) or more.

Sew firmly but not too tightly; you should aim at a curved shape, not a crinkled or tucked one.

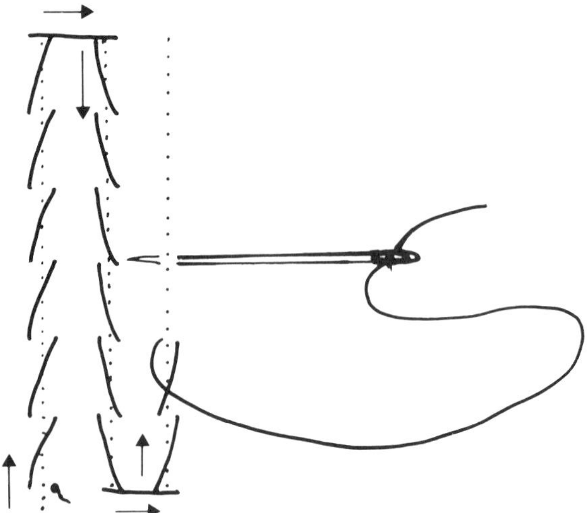

Fig. 24 Detail showing how to pad-stitch

Stitch down one line, then take a stitch sideways and continue stitching up the next line, and so on (*Fig. 24*). Do not take the pad-stitching over into the seam allowances.

1 Quilted patchwork jacket

2 Yellow and grey jacket

▲
Chapter four

SLEEVES

Sleeves which are cut as part of the body of the garment, such as raglan or dolman sleeves, necessarily have to be there when you do your first fitting, and are then fairly easily adjusted — providing your pattern was the right size in the first place. The troubles which usually beset home dressmakers arise when sleeves are cut separately and then set in on an armhole seamline; mistakes in this area can label the finished article as home-made.

Checking the armhole seamline

First, some warning notes!

1 Always try the garment on *after* the bodice has been completed (including the neckline) but *before* you make any attempt to set in the sleeves.

Tacking the sleeves in before this fitting is generally a complete waste of time because you simply do not know where the upper end of the armhole seamline should actually be. My own experience of fitting clients and students has proved to me that most women need to have the top of the armhole seamline moved in a little towards the neck.

2 The neckline needs to be finished first, because the addition of the collar, and/or neck facing, stops any outward stretching there.

3 For cut-and-sew purposes, shoulder seams should always be taped when sleeves are to be set in. Failure to do this will result in the shoulder seam being stretched down by the weight of the sleeve, and consequent dropping of the sleeve head down over the arm.

4 The style of the garment has to be taken into account before you decide on the best position for the top of the armhole seamline. If in doubt, read the designer's description, which should be included with other details on the back of the pattern envelope, and/or study the illustrations on the front and in the instruction sheets.

Here are some general guidelines.

a Wearing the garment, tuck a thin book under the armpit and hold it in place there while you look in a mirror. An imaginary line continuing straight up from the book is where the armhole seamline should normally be (*Fig. 25a*).

b Plain set-in sleeve (Fig. 25b) Mark the imaginary line with a line of pins, graduating from where the seamline already lies at the underarm curve, to the shoulder-line. Continue the pin-line over the back shoulder, merging back into the original seamline where necessary; take care not to make the back too narrow.

c Puffed sleeve (Fig. 25c) The line should come a little further in towards the neck, so that the top of the arm will help to support the gathered top of the sleeve.

d Exaggeratedly square shouders (Fig. 25d) The shoulder seam will be rather longer than usual, extending outwards to meet the sleeve-head, beyond the normal set-in sleeve-line. The shoulder seam may also be higher than usual at

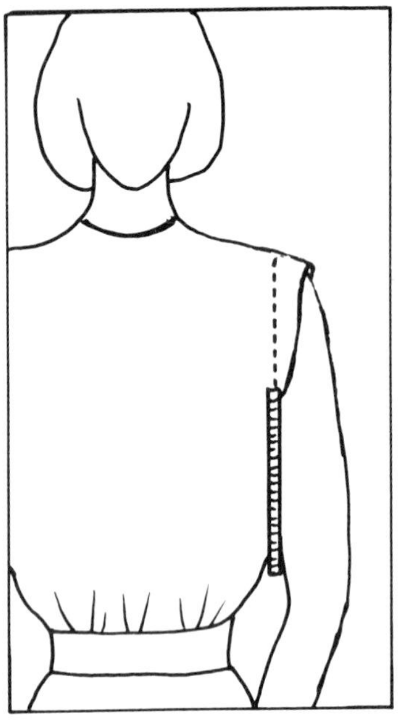
Fig. 25a Book under arm to indicate armhole seamline

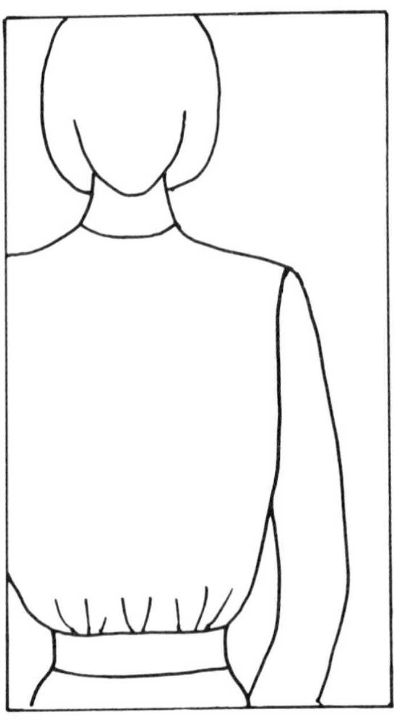
Fig. 25b Line for set-in sleeve

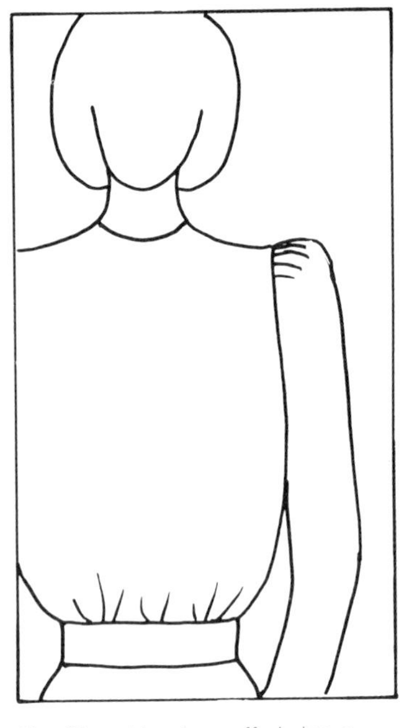
Fig. 25c Line for puffed sleeve

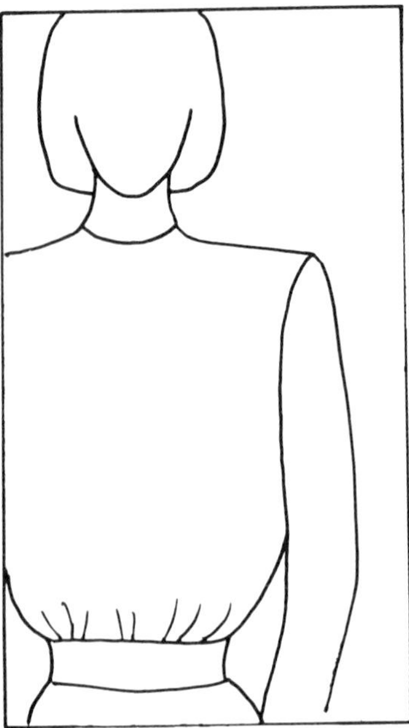
Fig. 25d Line for squared or extended shoulder

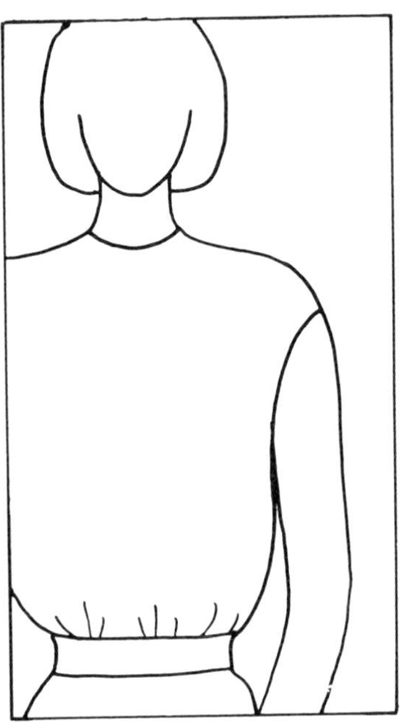
Fig. 25e Dropped shoulder line

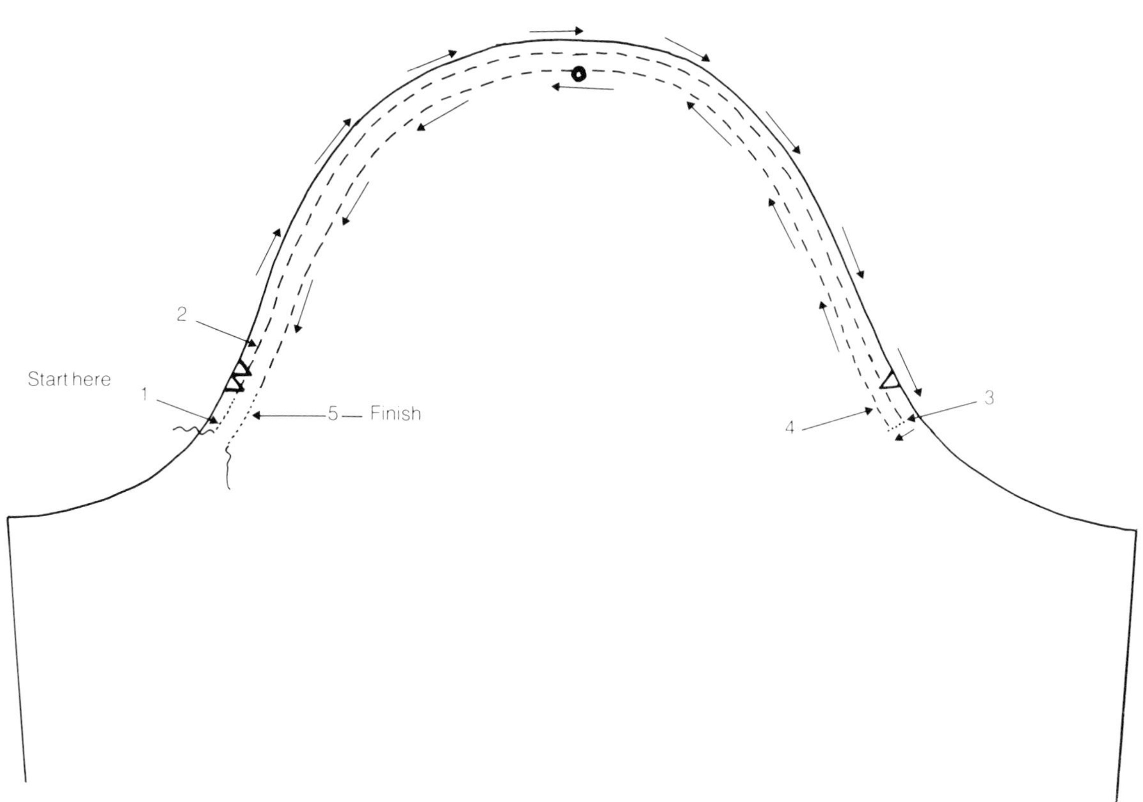

Fig. 26 Ease-stitching lines for top of sleeve

the outer end in order to accommodate the necessary shoulder-pad. If you really feel that this kind of shoulder shape does not suit you, you will probably need to lower the outer end of the shoulder seam slightly and also bring the top of the armhole seamline inwards.

e Dropped shoulders (Fig. 25e) Here the armhole seamline is deliberately allowed to fall over the end of the shoulder, down the arm.

Whichever of these variations applies to your particular pattern, some adjustment may be needed in order to obtain a perfect fit for your particular figure.

Remember that adjustments to the armhole seamline should only be made on the armhole (on the body of the garment) and never to the top of the sleeve.

Mark the adjusted armhole seamline with a tacking thread and then trim off any excess seam allowance, leaving an exact 1.5cm ($\frac{5}{8}$in) all round.

Preparing the sleeve head

This is not always absolutely necessary when using knitted fabrics, because the armhole can easily be stretched; however, stretching it might be unwise: taping it is often advisable. The following process does help the less experienced dressmaker to overcome that old problem of trying to fit what appears to be too much sleeve into too little armhole! *See Fig. 26*.

Note It may be necessary to loosen the tension on the needle thread a little for this process to work well.

1 Starting at the inner curve on one side of the sleeve head, 6mm ($\frac{1}{4}$in) in from the edge and parallel with it, make a few very small machine stitches.

2 Change to the longest straight-stitch your machine can do and stitch around the sleeve head, keeping 6mm ($\frac{1}{4}$in) from the edge, until you reach the inner curve on the other side.

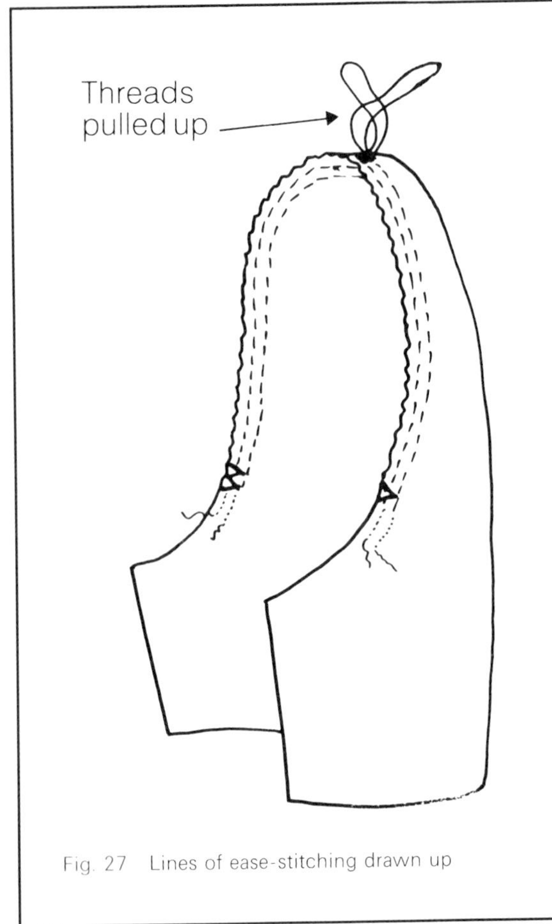

Fig. 27 Lines of ease-stitching drawn up

3 Change back to a very small stitch length, turn and stitch inwards until the seamline is reached.

4 Change to the longest straight-stitch and stitch along the seamline until you get back to your original starting-point.

5 Finish off with a few very small stitches.

6 (*Fig. 27*) Hook up *either* the bobbin threads *or* the needle threads (whichever are the tighter) at the top point of the sleeve, using a pin, and ease them gently out into two loops. The outer line of the stitching will need to be pulled up rather more than the inner line. Keep pulling and easing until you have a nicely shaped top to your sleeve without producing pleats or gathers.

Do not tie the loops because you may need to adjust the easing later. If the sleeve is actually intended to be gathered into the armhole, of course the loops will have to be pulled up much further.

Checking the length

Once the sleeve head has been prepared, the length should be checked by placing the arm in the sleeve, with the top in its correct position on the shoulder. If you are going to use shoulder pads, slip them in position now as these will alter the length of the sleeve. Shorten, by cutting off from the lower end, if necessary, but check that you can bend your elbow easily. If, despite careful planning, you find that it is going to be too short, you can then plan a cuff, or lengthen any cuff which has already been planned.

A sleeve which is to have a buttoned cuff will need an opening at the lower end.

Making a sleeve opening

Any opening at the lower end should be made at this stage because it is so much easier to do *before* the sleeve seam is sewn up than after. In case you are designing your own garment, remember that the opening should usually be on the back quarter of the sleeve (*Fig. 28*).

Here are two methods of finishing these openings which work well on knitted fabrics. The first is very simple and the second slightly more complicated, but both require careful and accurate machine-stitching — and that comes with practice! In both cases, a finely woven fabric (e.g. cotton gingham, linen, poly/cotton poplin, polyester lining, etc.) is used to give a firm and secure finish to the knit without adding too much bulk.

Method A (see finished example in *Fig. 29.*)

1 *Fig. 30a.* Mark the position of the opening on the R.S. of the sleeve.

2 *Fig. 30b.* Cut a rectangle of woven fabric approximately 6cm ($2\frac{1}{2}$in) wide, by 4cm ($1\frac{1}{2}$in) longer than the required length of the opening. Oversew the raw edges on three sides as shown.

3 *Fig. 30c.* Centre the woven fabric piece over the marked position on the knitted sleeve, R.S. tog., and pin in place. Draw the line of the opening on the W.S. of the fabric piece.

4 *Fig. 30d.* With the stitch length set at very small (about 1 to 1½), stitch around the pencilled line, keeping about 9mm (⅜in) away from it at the lower end and making a narrow U-shaped bend (*not* a sharp point) at the top.

5 *Fig. 30e.* Cut carefully between the lines of stitching, right up to the stitching at the top, stopping only just short of it.

6 *Fig. 30f.* Turn the woven fabric piece through to the W.S. of the sleeve, rolling the seamline slightly to the W.S. so that it is invisible from the R.S. Press well. Tack the lower edges of the woven fabric piece to the lower edges of the knitted sleeve on both sides of the opening. Blind-hem the top of the woven fabric piece to the knit to hold it in place.

Method B

1 *Fig. 31a.* Mark the position and length of the opening on the W.S. of the sleeve.

2 *Fig. 31b.* With the stitch length set at very small (about 1 to 1½) stay-stitch around the marked line, as in Method A–**4.**

3 *Fig. 31c.* Cut as in Method A–**5.**

4 *Fig. 31d.* Cut a straight-grain strip of woven fabric, 3.75cm (1½in) wide, by twice as long as the proposed opening. This is your binding strip.

5 *Fig. 31e.* Open the cut slit out into a straight line and lay it, W.S. down, onto the R.S. of the binding strip. Keep the stay-stitching line parallel with the edge of the binding strip. Pin in position and then machine again *exactly on the stay-stitching line.* Take care to avoid catching in the folds of the knitted sleeve when you reach the middle of the line.

6 *Fig. 31f.* Turn the free edge of the binding strip to the W.S. and then roll the folded edge towards the R.S. of the sleeve until it just barely covers the stitching line. Pin and top-stitch in place. To finish (*Fig. 31g*), turn one side of the bound opening to the inside of the sleeve; *which* side depends upon which sleeve you are working on. Remember that the front of the sleeve should overlap the back.

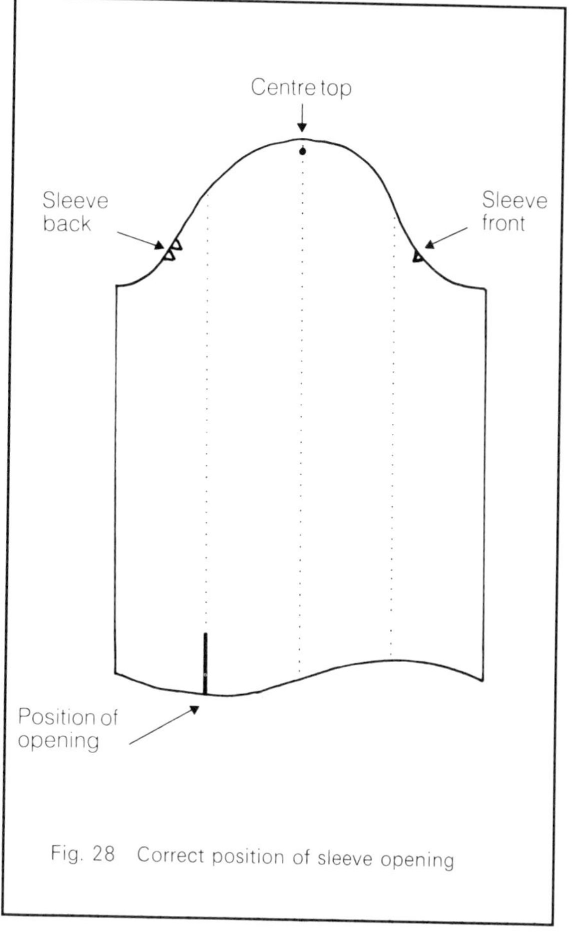

Fig. 28 Correct position of sleeve opening

When the opening is completed, the sleeve seam can be sewn up and pressed. The cuff should then be attached.

Cuffs

Cuffs come in many forms and you probably have adequate instructions for making them in the instruction sheets given with the pattern you are using, but, in case you are designing your own garment, here are some simple guidelines.

Making a buttoned cuff

A shirt-type cuff can be made of knitted fabric which has been interfaced to make it stable and

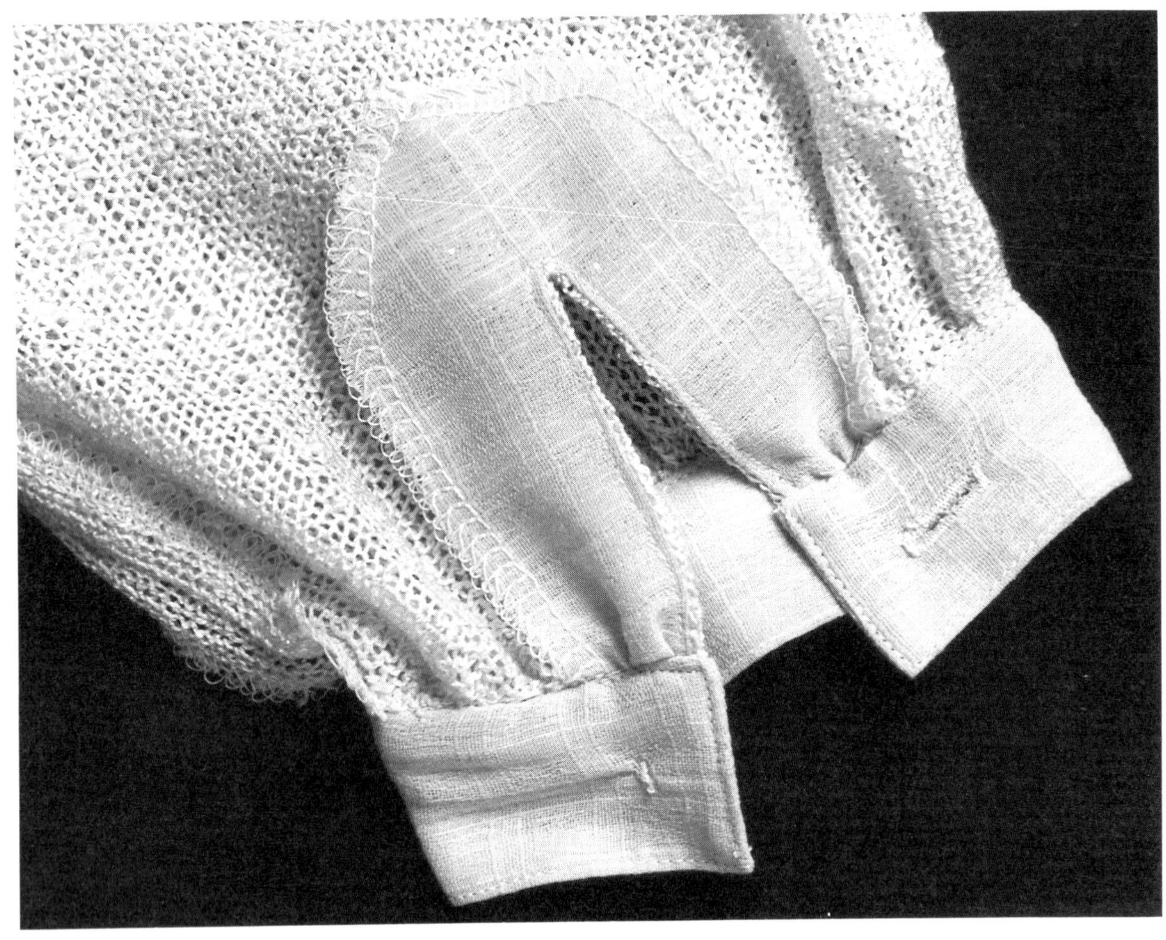

Fig. 29 Detail of faced sleeve opening W.S. (upper end of facing, in this case, has been rounded off)

reasonably firm — but do beware of ending up with something which is far too bulky. A possible solution to this probem is to make a cuff in two parts — the outside layer of the knit and the inside (the cuff facing) of lining fabric or some other thin woven cloth. Alternatively, consider making the cuff entirely of woven fabric, perhaps matching the collar, the front buttoning band and the binding used for the sleeve opening. (See Figs. 32a and b, and also the photograph of the cuff on p. 48 of *Cut and Sew: Working with Machine-Knitted Fabrics.*)

(Combining woven fabrics with knits in this way is both practical and attractive; a variety of effects can be achieved by mixing the textures and the colours — rough with smooth, plain with pattern, matt with shine, etc.)

There are a number of different methods of constructing cuffs but here is a very simple one for a one-piece cuff which you could cut in woven fabric, or perhaps a thin knit.

1 Cut two identical rectangles. *Note* 'length' = measurement of wrist, plus a total of 8cm ($3\frac{1}{4}$in) for ease, overlap and seam allowances; 'depth' = twice the desired depth of the finished cuff, plus 3cm ($1\frac{1}{4}$in) for seam allowances.

2 Mark a foldline along the centre of the cuff lengthwise.

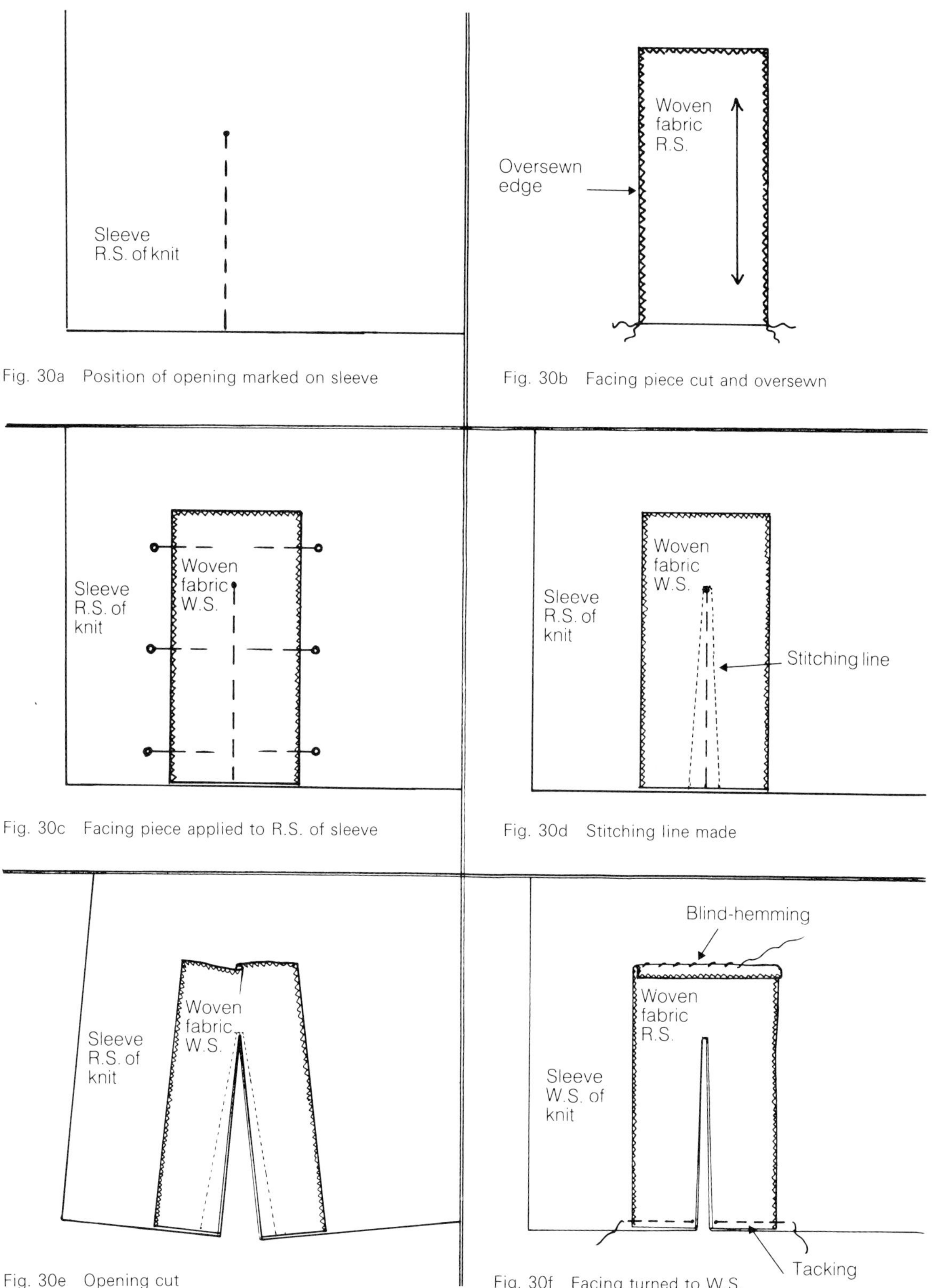

Fig. 30a Position of opening marked on sleeve

Fig. 30b Facing piece cut and oversewn

Fig. 30c Facing piece applied to R.S. of sleeve

Fig. 30d Stitching line made

Fig. 30e Opening cut

Fig. 30f Facing turned to W.S.

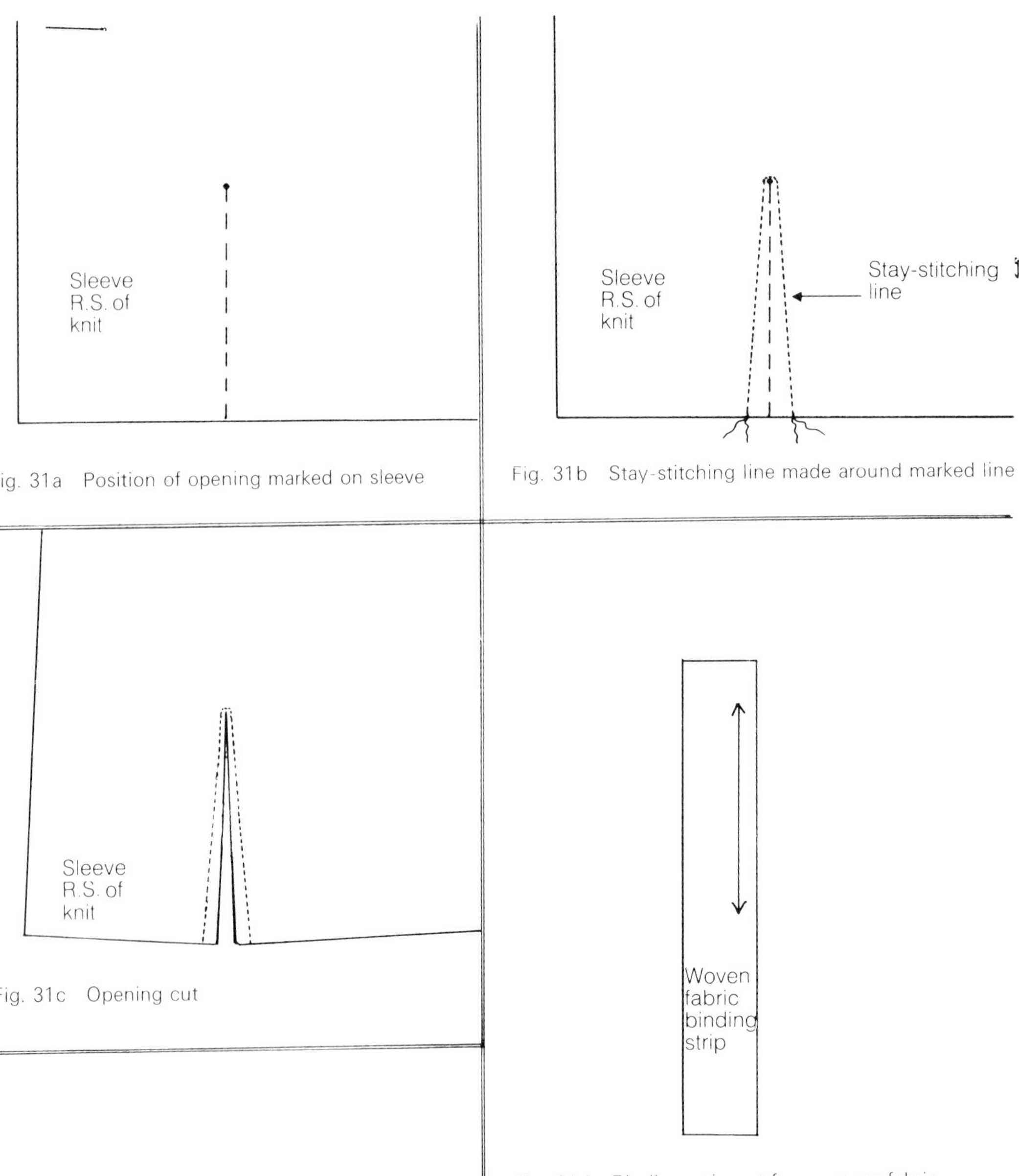

Fig. 31a Position of opening marked on sleeve

Fig. 31b Stay-stitching line made around marked line

Fig. 31c Opening cut

Fig. 31d Binding strip cut from woven fabric

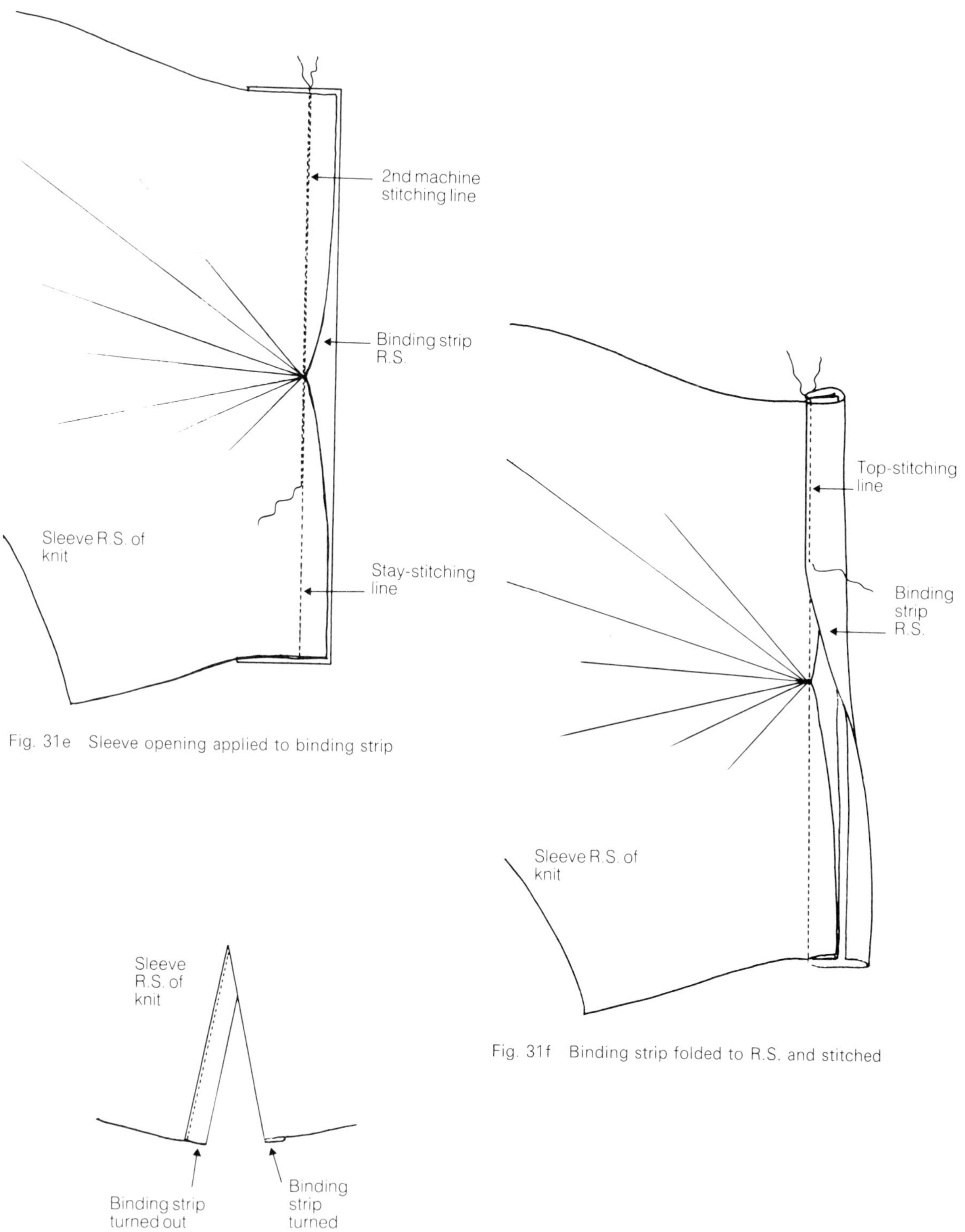

Fig. 31e Sleeve opening applied to binding strip

Fig. 31f Binding strip folded to R.S. and stitched

Fig. 31g Finishing the opening

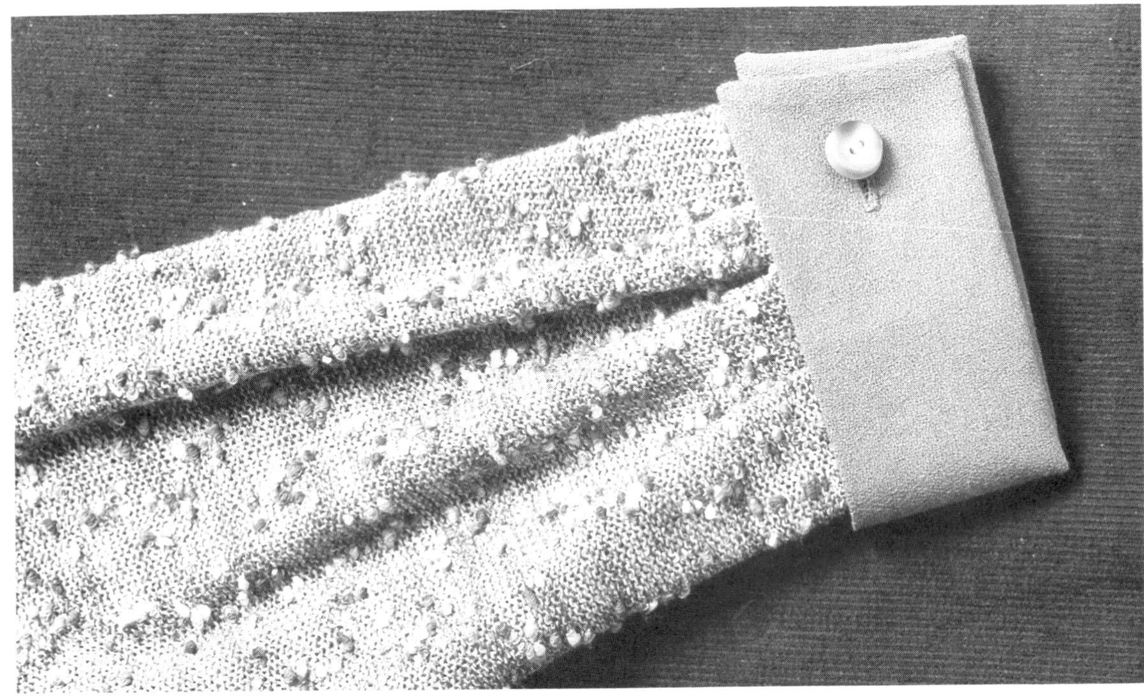

Fig. 32a Cuff cut from woven fabric to match collar in Fig. 13b

Fig. 32b Cuff cut from woven fabric to match collar in Fig. 13a

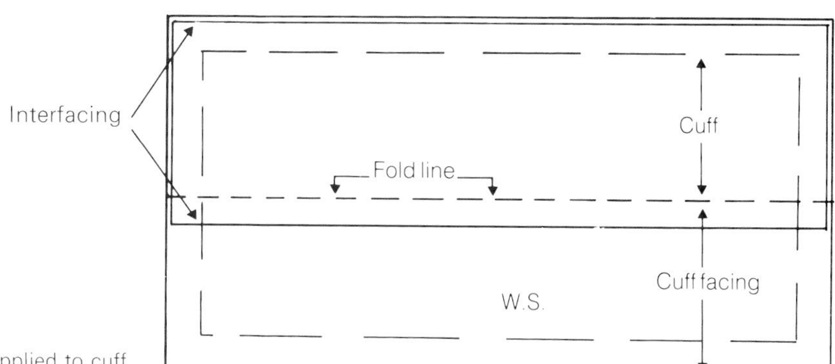

Fig. 33a Interfacing applied to cuff

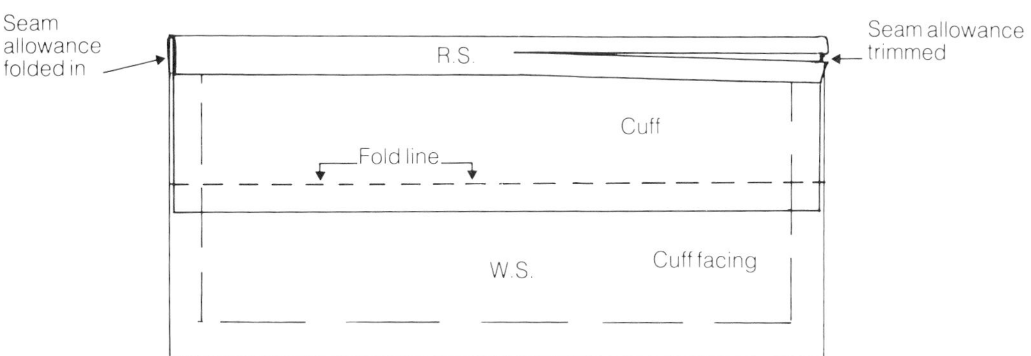

Fig. 33b Cuff seam allowance pressed to W.S. and trimmed

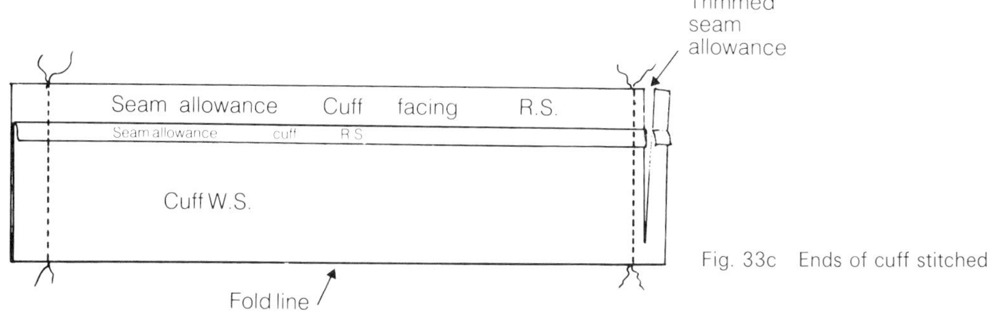

Fig. 33c Ends of cuff stitched

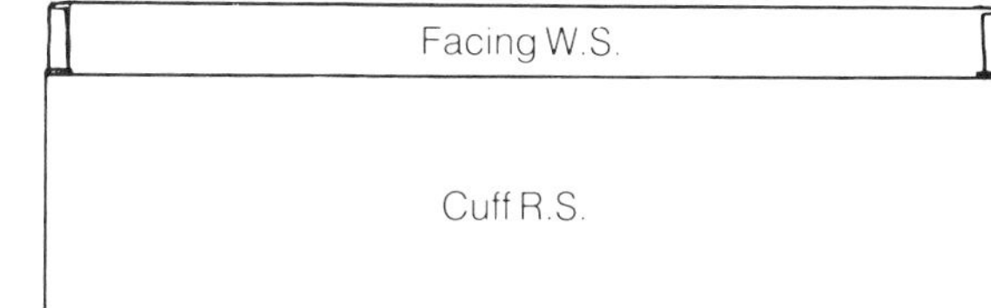

Fig. 33d Cuff turned to R.S.

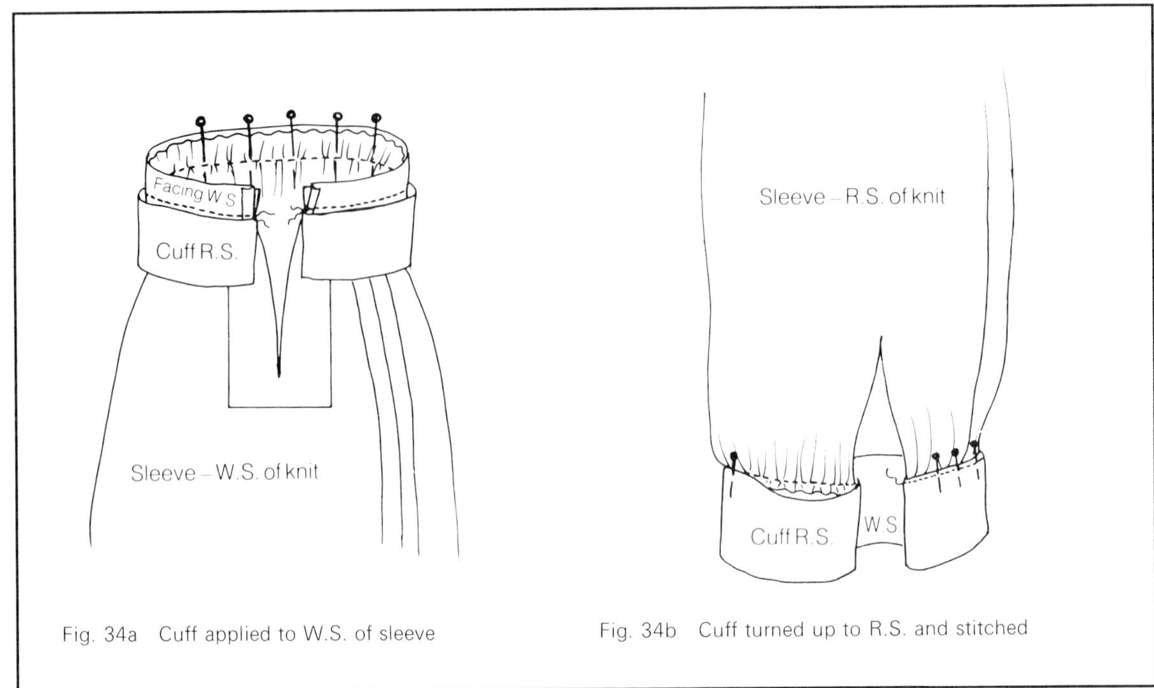

Fig. 34a Cuff applied to W.S. of sleeve

Fig. 34b Cuff turned up to R.S. and stitched

3 Cut and apply interfacing to fit just over half the cuff, so that it extends approximately 1.2cm ($\frac{1}{2}$in) over the marked foldline (*Fig. 33a*). *Note* that the part which is completely interfaced is termed *the cuff* and the rest is termed *the cuff facing*.

4 Press the interfaced seam allowance of the cuff to the W.S. Tack if necessary and then trim to 6mm ($\frac{1}{4}$in) (*Fig. 33b*).

5 Fold the cuff, R.S. tog., along the foldline. Stitch the end seams, using a fairly short stitch length, and trim the seam allowances to 6mm ($\frac{1}{4}$in) (*Fig. 33c*).

6 Turn the cuff to the R.S., pushing out the corners gently. Press (*Fig. 33d*).

Note A cuff made in two fabrics (knitted and woven) would, of course, have to be cut in two halves with a seamline between cuff and cuff facing, where I have illustrated a foldline.

Attaching a cuff to a shirt-type sleeve

1 Turn the sleeve inside out.

2 Apply the R.S. of the seam allowance on the cuff facing to the W.S. of the seam allowance on the sleeve end, matching the edges of the seam allowances. Line up the cuff ends with the edges of the sleeve opening. Pin carefully, as shown (*Fig. 34a*), adjusting the gathering (or pleating) on the sleeve to fit the cuff. Tack if necessary. Machine-stitch (small stitch length) and trim the seam allowances to 6mm ($\frac{1}{4}$in).

3 Turn sleeve and cuff to R.S. and pin the turned-in seam allowance of the cuff to the sleeve, so that it just covers the previous seamline (*Fig. 34b*). Top-stitch in place, carrying the stitching right round the entire cuff edge if desired.

Note If a plain finish, with no visible stitching on the R.S., is required, attach the cuff to the R.S. of the sleeve first and then hem the facing to the W.S. by hand.

Other types of cuff

Cuffs which will stretch, and therefore do not need an opening in the sleeve above them, can be cut from purchased ribbing available from some haberdashers. This is cut to the correct length to fit comfortably around the wrist, sewn into a circle, stretched out to fit the lower end of the sleeve and sewn with zigzag stitching and overlocking. (See the illustration on p.23 of *Cut and Sew: Working with Machine-Knitted Fabrics.*)

Similar cuffs can be made from your knitted fabric providing it still has a fair degree of stretching quality after pressing, and is not too bulky.

1 Cut a strip across the knitted fabric, keeping straight along one row.

Note 'Length' = long enough to fit comfortably around the wrist (or wherever on the arm the sleeve is intended to finish) and for the hand to pass through, plus two seam allowances; 'depth' = twice as deep as the desired depth of the finished cuff plus two seam allowances. (Interfacing is not needed here because you need to retain the stretch quality of the knitted fabric.)

2 Stitch the ends of the strip, R.S. tog., to form a circle.

3 Fold the circle in half lengthwise and stitch the raw edges together with a zigzag stitch, keeping 6mm ($\frac{1}{4}$in) from the edges.

4 Pin the raw edges of the cuff to the R.S. of the sleeve end, stretching out the circle to fit. (If the sleeve is very full it may need to be gathered first.) Sew with zigzag stitching, trim the seam allowances and oversew or overlock. Turn the cuff down.

An elasticated cuff can be made by turning up a hem allowance at the bottom of the sleeve, approximately 5cm (2in) to 7.5cm (3in) deep, and dividing this hem into several channels by making lines of straight machine-stitching parallel with the lower edge; a length of elastic to fit the wrist is then inserted into each channel (*Fig. 35*).

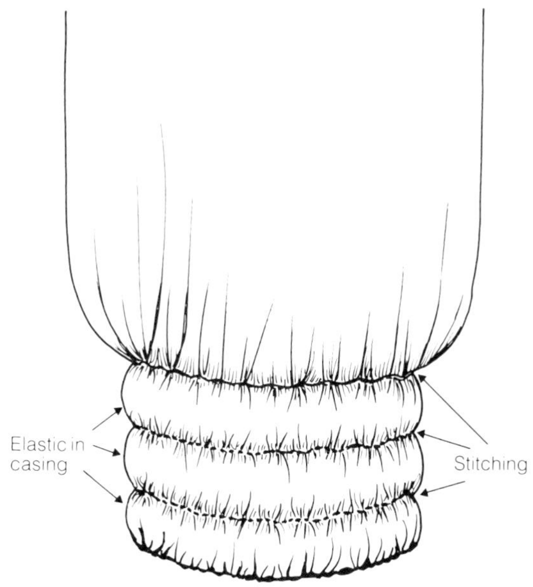

Fig. 35 Elasticated cuff

Inserting the sleeve into the armhole

Helpful hints

Work with the sleeve towards you, not the armhole.

Place all the pins *across* the seamline, not parallel with it. Take care to keep the edges of the two seam allowances exactly together.

It may be necessary either to loosen or tighten the ease-stitching on the sleeve head to make it fit the armhole, but remember that a plain set-in sleeve should have no visible gathering or pleating (*Fig. 36*). In the case of a puffed sleeve, aim to keep most of the gathering within about 7.5cm (3in) either side of the shoulder line.

Work in the following order (*Fig. 37*)

1 Turn the garment W.S. out and the sleeve R.S. out.

2 Pass the sleeve through the armhole until the top edge of the sleeve meets the armhole edge of the garment.

3 Match and pin the underarm points.

4 Match and pin the dot at the centre top of the sleeve to the shoulder seam (or shoulder-line) of the garment.

5 Match and pin the one notch at the front of the sleeve to the one notch at the front armhole, and the two notches at the back of the sleeve to the two notches at the back armhole.

6 Continue pinning until the sleeve is held in place all round the armhole.

Fig. 36 Plain set-in sleeve (detail from colour picture 5)

7 *Either* machine-stitch the seam, removing the pins just before they go under the presser foot, *or* hand-tack, using fairly small stitches so that the fabrics will not slip, and follow this with machine-stitching.

Use a fairly small straight-stitch when machining; alternatively, if the seam is likely to need to stretch a lot, use a small zigzag stitch.

If you actually want to prevent this seam stretching, you should apply 6mm ($\frac{1}{4}$in) pre-shrunk cotton tape to the armhole seamline before sewing the seam.

8 Trim the seam allowances around the underarm back to about 9mm ($\frac{3}{8}$in). Leave the seam allowances around the top of the armhole intact but trim off any stray ends.

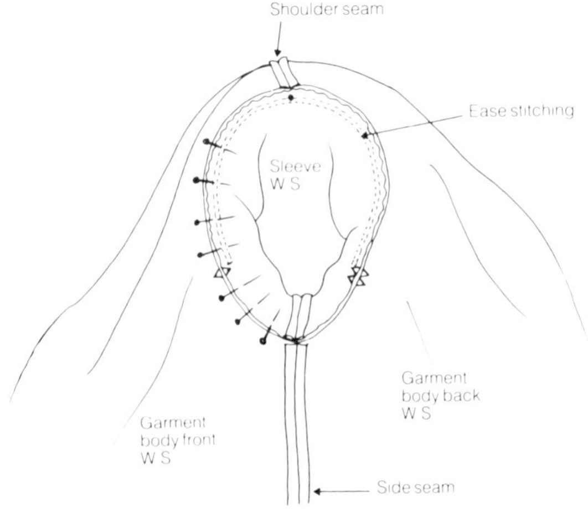

Fig. 37 Setting a sleeve into an armhole

9 Oversew or overlock the two seam allowances together, all round the armhole.

Note The armhole seam allowances are usually turned out towards the sleeve, but you should check this with your pattern instruction sheets in case there are any design variations.

Neatening the armhole seamline

In the case of a dress or shirt, simply oversewing or overlocking the armhole seam allowances will probably be sufficient.

If you are making a coat or jacket, where the inside could be on display, you may want to make a neater job of it. Consider binding the trimmed seam allowances with a bias-cut strip of matching lining fabric, or perhaps silk or poly/cotton. (See Chapter 10 of this book for instructions on binding.) Consider also, perhaps, knitting a matching narrow strip for binding.

The armholes can be sewn with felled seams which are top-stitched on the R.S. (see pp. 93–94 *Cut and Sew: Working with Machine-Knitted Fabrics*).

The armhole seamline can be made on the R.S. of the garment, the seam allowances pressed open flat and then trimmed back to 6mm ($\frac{1}{4}$in); flat braid is then applied to cover the seamline and seam allowances, carefully eased to fit around the curves.

▲

Chapter five

SHOULDER PADS

Shoulder pads are an essential part of the current fashion scene but are far removed from the cumbersome affairs made of horsehair which gave us the military look (or, in some cases, the 'spiv' look!) during World War Two. Many women, however, are now reluctant to use shoulder pads, fearing that they may look like an escapee from an American soap opera; this is a pity because the average British rather pear-shaped figure is generally enormously improved by making the shoulders appear wider and straighter.

I suggest, therefore, that whenever you make a garment you simply try out the effect of padding out the shoulders with anything handy — spare fabric, tissues, a skein of wool — and then look at the result in a good mirror. If your dressmaking pattern was designed for shoulder pads (check on this in the instruction sheets) then you actually have a gap there which should either be filled with a pad, or removed by taking in the outer end of the shoulder seam and moving the armhole seamline inwards towards the neck. Even if no shoulder pad is suggested in the instructions, a small one usually improves the line tremendously. Just try it.

Until now, home dressmakers have had difficulty in finding shoulder pads in the variety of shapes and sizes demanded by the pattern designers, but, at the time of writing this, we do at last have a good selection available in specialist dressmaking shops and haberdashery departments (*Figs. 38a and b*). (Note that Vilene also produce an excellent 'sleeve head' which is sewn into the top of the armhole seamline, and gives a firm base to the sleeve top in coats and jackets.)

Alternatively you can make your own; Vogue and Butterick sell excellent paper patterns for shoulder pads in a wide range of styles.

Whether you buy pads or make them, be careful to select the correct shape for the garment you are sewing. A pad designed for a set-in sleeve simply will not work in a raglan sleeve!

Remember that shoulder pads sewn into a garment which is going to be dry cleaned should be suitabe for dry-cleaning; likewise, if the garment is to be washed, the pads must also be washable.

Purchased pads made of polyester foam with no outer covering need to be covered with some kind of fabric before being sewn into a garment, otherwise they simply get torn by the needle and thread. If they are going to lie between the main fabric of the garment and a lining, they can be covered with virtually anything which is soft, flexible and thin: butter muslin, nylon tricot or even fabric cut from the wide end of an old pair of nylon tights. If the garment is to be unlined then the pads must match the main knitted fabric as closely as possible, so you should cover them with your knitted fabric.

Purchased pads which already have a fabric covering of some sort, or which are constructed of some material into which you can sew, will need no further covering if they are going to be hidden by the garment lining. If they are going to be visible they should be covered with matching knitted fabric.

Covering shoulder pads

For a set-in sleeve

1 *Fig. 39a.* Take a sufficiently large square of fabric (cut straight with the grain) and mark a diagonal line on the W.S. from one corner to the opposite corner.

2 Place the thicker edge of the pad along the marked diagonal line.

3 *Fig. 39b.* Fold the fabric over and pin the two layers together all around the rounded edge of the pad, as shown. Because the covering fabric

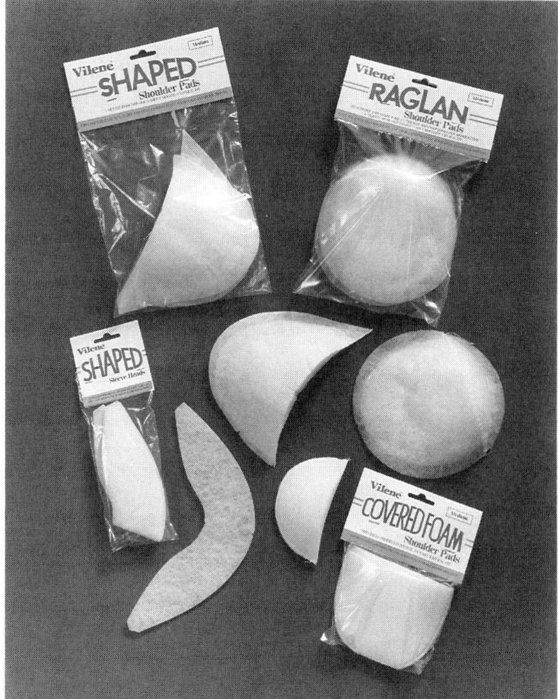

Fig. 38a A selection of shoulder pads and sleeve heads (*photo: The Vilene Organisation*)

Fig. 38b Selection of shoulder pads (*Jencott Shoulder Padding Co.*)

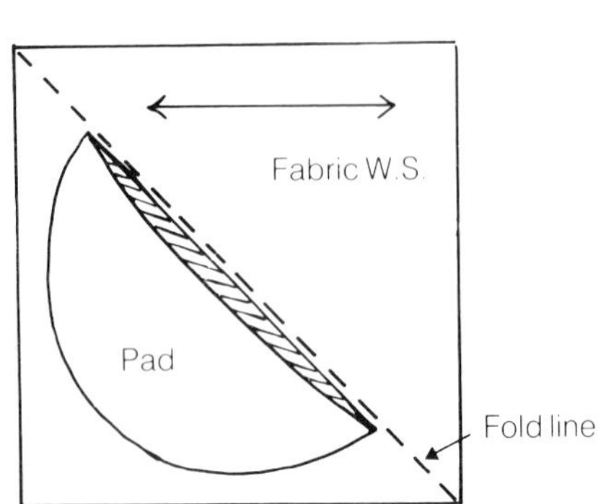

Fig. 39a Pad placed on covering fabric

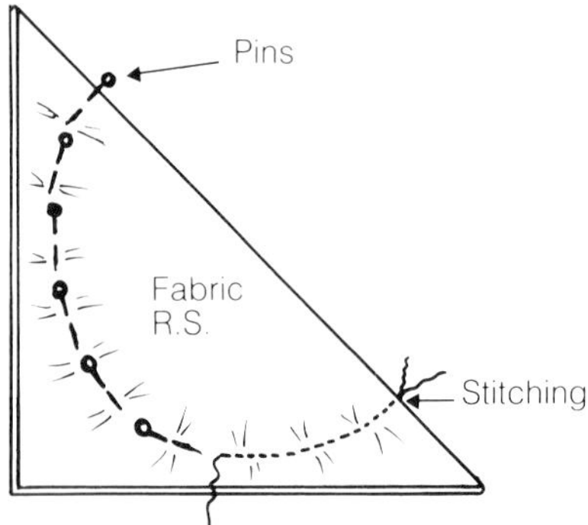

Fig. 39b Fabric pinned over pad

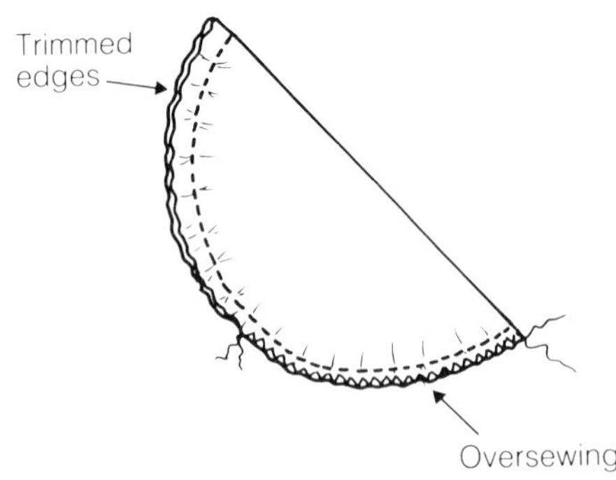

Fig. 39c Covering fabric stitched and trimmed

is now on the bias grain you can mould it to fit the pad closely. Take care to retain the curved shape of the pad — don't flatten it. It is a good idea to pin just fractionally inside the edge of the pad so that the stitching which follows will catch in the pad, and so that it will not eventually be left floating around loose inside the cover.

Machine-stitch where the pins lie, removing each pin as you get to it.

4 *Fig. 39c.* Trim off the surplus fabric leaving a small seam allowance. Oversew or overlock the raw edges together.

For a raglan or dolman shaped sleeve

Follow the same procedure as for the set-in sleeve pad, but you may well have to cut two separate pieces of fabric for each pad — one (or possibly two seamed together) for the top and one for the under surface — in order to get the shaping correct. You must still cut them on the bias grain, and you will, of course, now have a seam all round the pad.

Sewing in shoulder pads

Note Always sew in (or, at least, pin in) your shoulder pads *before* finishing the ends of the sleeves, because the pads will raise the sleeves a little.

For a set-in sleeve

1 Mark a line on the *upper* side of the pad, exactly along the centre, from the outer (thick) end to the inner (thin) end (*Fig. 40*). Use pencil, pins or thread.

2 On the inside of the garment, place this marked line exactly along the shoulder seam*, *with the thick end of the pad extending 1.5cm ($\frac{5}{8}$in) out into the sleeve head.* If you have left the full 1.5cm ($\frac{5}{8}$in) armhole seam allowance, you will find that the thick end of the pad lines up neatly with the edge of the seam allowance.

*If you have no shoulder seam, or you have a 'dropped' shoulder seam, you must line the centre of the pad up with the shoulder-*line* (you will find that this is marked on your paper pattern). You then have to catch the pad to the garment wherever you can do so invisibly.

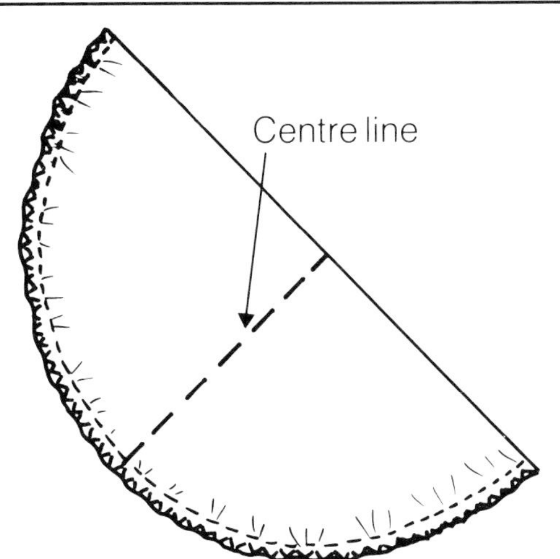

Fig. 40 Centre line marked on pad

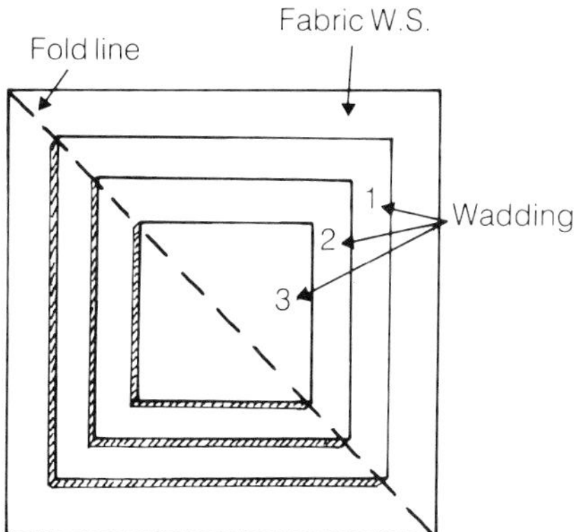

Fig. 41a Fabric and polyester wadding cut and positioned for home-made shoulder pad

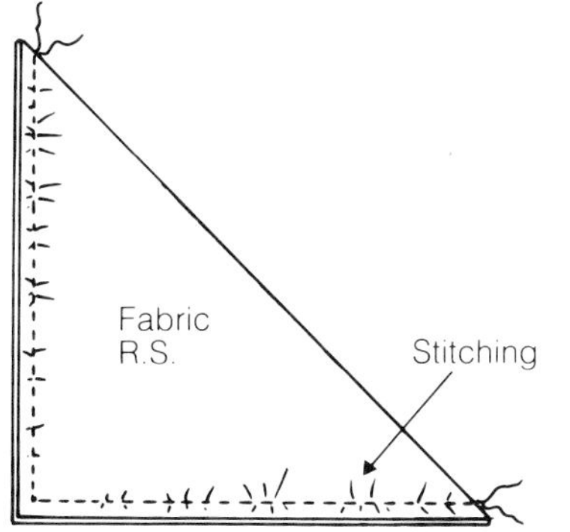

Fig. 41b Pad completed

3 Try the garment on to check that the padding looks right. Adjust if necessary. The front and back ends of the pad can be attached to the armhole seamline if you feel the need, but it is often better to leave them to 'float'.

For a raglan or dolman sleeve

To find the point where the outer end of the pad should go, try on the garment in front of a mirror. The centre line of the pad should be attached to the shoulder seam. If there is no shoulder seam, the pad should be placed so that its centre line lines up with the shoulder-line, and sewn to the garment wherever it can be done invisibly.

Alternatives

Simple home-made shoulder pad

Fig. 41a. This is made with a square of knitted fabric (or lining fabric) and three squares of polyester wadding, graded in size as shown. The layers should be loosely tacked to each other and to the fabric square, to keep them in place.

Fold diagonally and stitch along the two straight sides, as shown in Fig. 41b. The same kind of pad can be made by cutting oval or circular shapes.

Remember that pads filled with polyester wadding must never get involved with heat pressing, because that flattens the wadding irretrievably.

Other ways of padding a sleeve top

There are numerous ways of making little sausage-shaped bags and stuffing them with wadding or yarn or small bits of knitting, etc., and any of these may be perfectly suitable for supporting the head of a sleeve without actually padding the shoulder line. Any kind of puffed or gathered-top sleeve can be helped this way.

Fig. 42 Support for puffed sleeve made from petersham

Another way of supporting a gathered sleeve head is to take some fairly stiff petersham ribbon (about 2.5cm [1in] wide) and pleat it into a slightly curved shape, about 10cm (4in) long (*Fig. 42*). Machine-stitch along the shorter edge, and then sew this to the top of the armhole seamline, with the fanned-out pleats extending out into the top of the sleeve.

This can also be made from Vilene firm interfacing, or even stiff tulle or organza.

▲

Chapter six

POCKETS

Some people don't like pockets and never seem to need them. I feel positively deprived if I do not have a pocket somewhere around my person to give me instant access to my reading glasses, handkerchief, car keys, etc. However, pockets are not always utilitarian; they can be an aesthetically pleasing part of the style and shape of the garment even if they are never actually used.

It is rarely safe to assume that you can simply slap a pocket on at a late stage in the making up process; they need careful planning and, depending upon the type of pocket, some degree of expertise in their execution. The dressmaking pattern you are using will probably give you sufficient instruction in how to cut and apply the particular kind of pocket used in the design, but as you will have the additional problem of coping with knitted fabrics, these instructions may not be adequate. Here are several general points which it may be helpful to consider.

1 Check the position of the pockets by pinning the pattern for the pocket to the pattern for the garment front. Hold this up against you (lining up the shoulder- and C.F. lines correctly) and have a look in a mirror. Is it at the right level for you? Is it perhaps just where it will make your worst feature look even worse? Is the opening wide enough for your hand to enter comfortably? Do you like it? If there is anything you need to alter, do it now, to the paper pattern, before starting to cut the knit.

2 Consider whether the weight of the pockets is likely to stretch the knit to which they are going to be sewn; this is a definite possibility, for instance, where a patch pocket is going to be lined and interlined, and therefore becomes heavier than the main fabric. In this case, the front of the garment will probably have to be interlined to give it strength and stability, either over its whole area, or simply over the part where the pockets are to be attached.

3 A patch pocket could be made of the knit alone, unlined, but care must be taken to see that the upper (opening) edge does not then stretch out of shape. The top of the pocket could be faced on the inside with woven fabric, or it could be finished with a band of woven fabric on the outside (*Fig. 43*). It could be interfaced with Vilene Fold-a-Band or it could be bound with straight-cut binding or with ribbon (*Chapter 10*).

4 A patch pocket made of the knit alone could possibly get baggy if it is going to be used much. Consider this and decide to line it if necessary.

5 Any part of the pocket which is hidden away inside the garment should be cut from a thin but stable woven fabric such as polyester lining, cotton poplin or strong calico; this helps to limit the bulk and make a harder-wearing pocket.

6 Jetted or welt pockets, which are made rather like very large button holes, must have firm

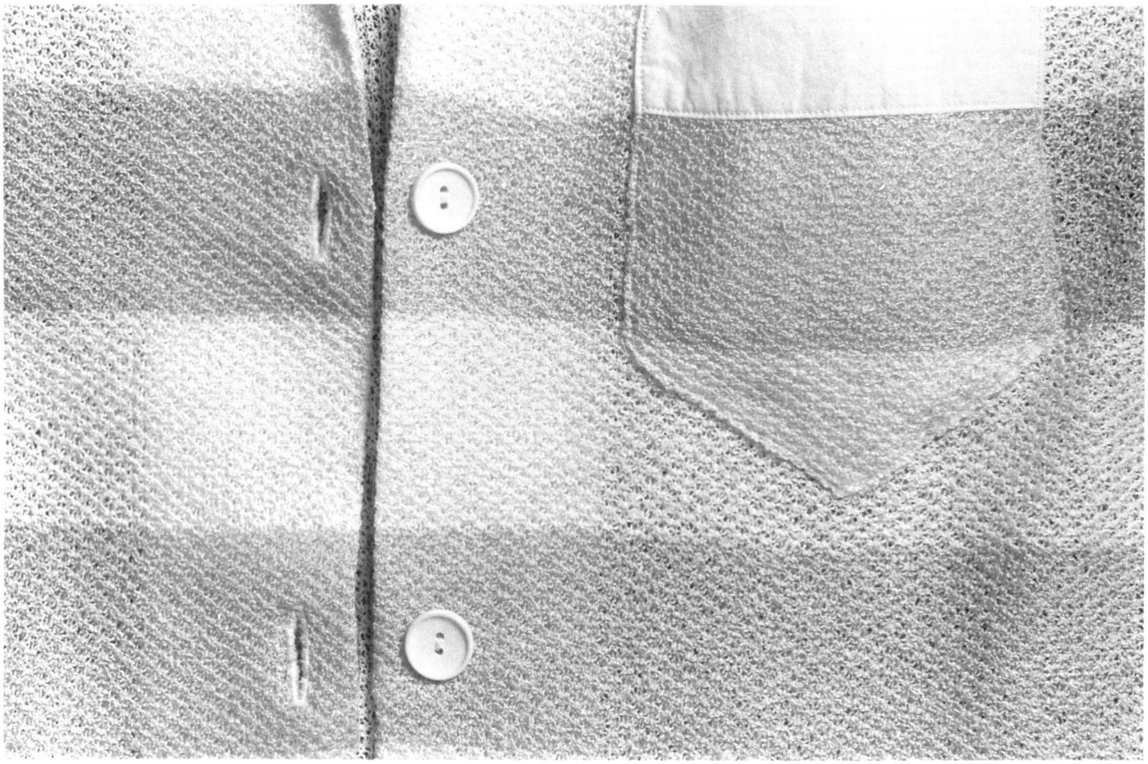

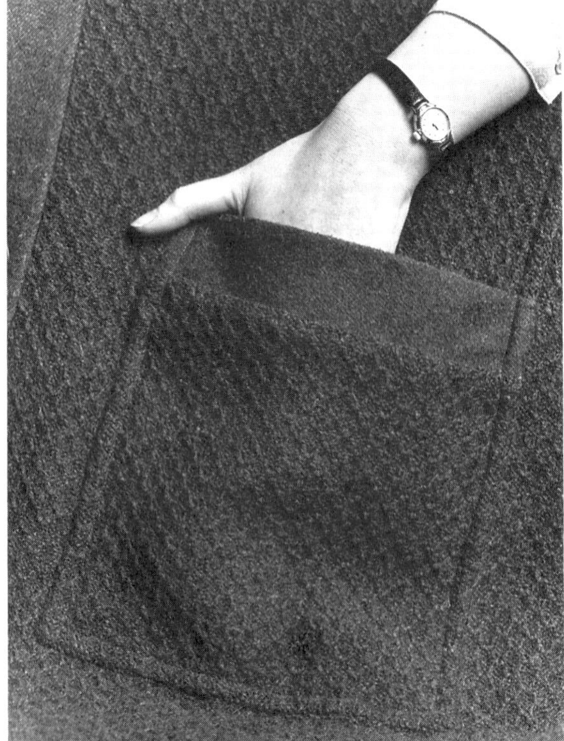

Fig. 43 a & b Pockets; tops banded with woven fabric (detail from colour pictures 3 and 4). Also shows vertical buttonholes made in the knitted fabric

interfacing behind the area of knit where they will be constructed. A fusible non-woven interfacing should be used so that the knit is prevented from stretching.

This interfacing has two added advantages:

a All the tiny thread ends which could otherwise fray when the pocket slit is cut, are firmly stuck down.

b The pattern lines, dots, circles, etc., which are your guidelines in constructing this kind of pocket, can all be drawn on the interfacing with a sharp pencil and a ruler.

Cut the binding strips (the lips of the pocket) from a firm woven fabric rather than attempting to make them from knitted fabric (*Fig. 44*). After folding the binding strip lengthwise, stick the two layers together with Wundaweb: they are then much easier to handle without danger of fraying.

Fig. 44 Welt pocket using woven fabric for the lips of the opening

Fig. 45 Lined and interfaced patch pocket

Fig. 46 Pocket in side seam (detail from colour picture 8)

Patch pockets, and bag-shaped pockets hidden behind seams are the two types you are most likely to want to add to any garment when you do not actually have a pattern to help you, so I am incuding detailed instructions for these. As with all cut-and-sew processes, it is wise to have a dummy run first, using odd pieces of fabric. See the examples of these in Figs. 45 and 46.

Lined and interfaced patch pockets

1 Draw and cut out a paper pattern for your pockets as shown in the diagram in Fig. 47a.

The dimensions are your own choice but should be in correct proportion to the garment to which the pockets wil be applied; if in doubt, cut paper to what you think should be the size and shape of the *finished* pocket and pin it to the garment; then check on how it looks. I have drawn a pocket with rounded corners but of course they could be square if you choose. Draw the finished shape first, add the pocket facing at the top (this is roughly a quarter of the depth of the finished pocket), and then add 1.5cm ($\frac{5}{8}$in)

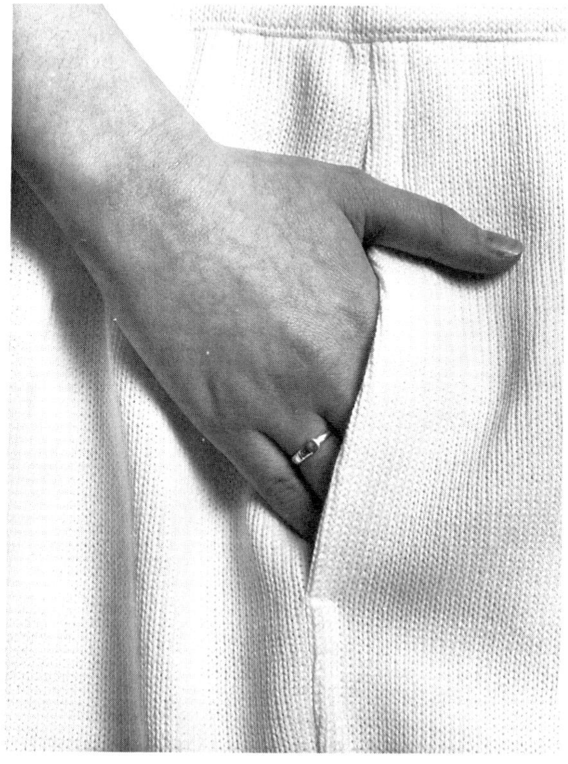

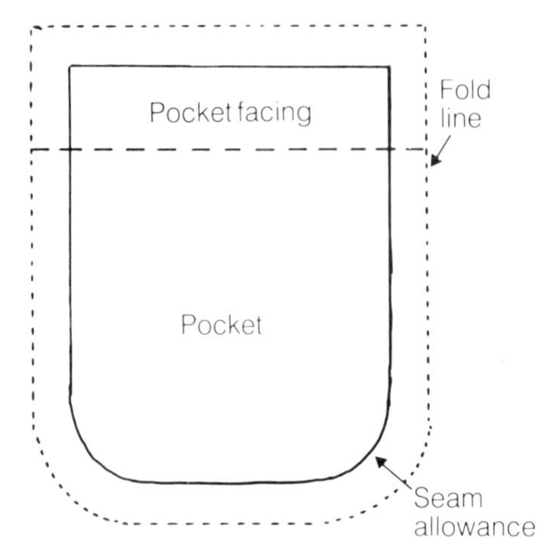

Fig. 47a Pattern for patch pocket

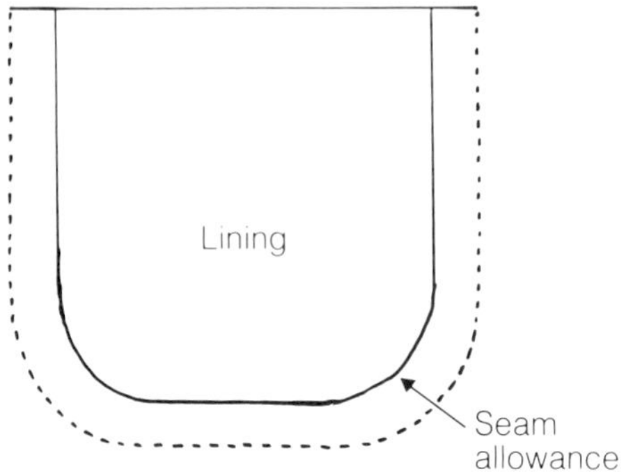

Fig. 47b Pattern for pocket lining

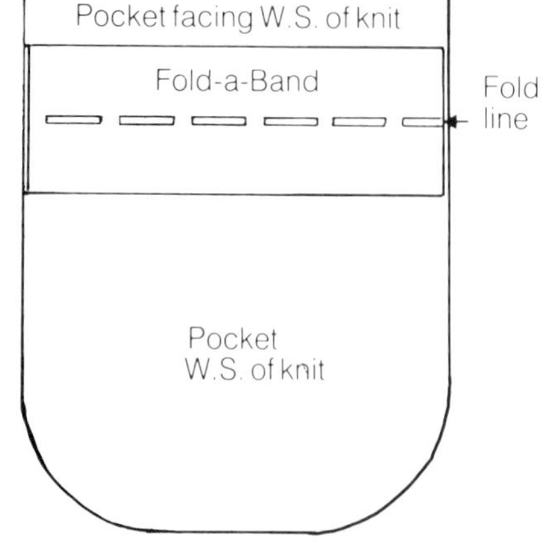

Fig. 48 Interfacing the foldline

seam allowances all round. Be very accurate — use a ruler and measure to the nearest millimetre. Rounded corners can be drawn around a wine glass or a saucer.

2 Draw and cut out a paper pattern for the pocket lining (*Fig. 47b*). This is exactly the same as the pocket pattern but does not have the pocket facing area above the foldline.

3 Cut out your pocket pattern in the knitted fabric and your lining pattern in a lining fabric. When doing this, take great care to keep the grainlines straight, e.g. the rows of knitting parallel with the pocket top and the stitch lines parallel with the pocket sides. Any mistakes here will show up badly on the finished garment! Draw the foldline on the W.S. of the pocket fabric.

4 Interface the pocket. This could mean covering the entire area of the pocket, including the facing, with a fusible interfacing such as knitted nylon, Vilene Ultrasoft in an appropriate weight, or cotton muslin. As the lining will do the job of eliminating the stretch factor, you might consider interfacing only the facing area. Alternatively, Fold-a-Band (light-weight or medium weight) placed along the foldline could possibly be sufficient. Fig. 48 shows the latter method.

5 Pin the top edges of the pocket and the lining, R.S. tog., and stitch on the 1.5cm ($\frac{5}{8}$in) seamline *leaving a 5–8cm (2–3in) gap in the stitching* as shown in Fig. 49a. This is the gap through which you will turn the pocket right side out later on.

6 Pull the lining downwards until the fold at the top of the pocket comes exactly on the foldline (or on the slits in the Fold-a-Band). Press the seam allowances downwards, as shown in Fig. 49b. Make sure that the lining is lying straight and flat on the pocket and then trim off any excess lining fabric, so that the edges are exactly even all round.

7 Turn the pocket over so that the knit side is on top and push this slightly *inwards*, pinning as you go, so that the edge of the lining projects about 3mm ($\frac{1}{8}$in) beyond the edge of the knit (*Fig. 49c*). The effect of this is to make the pocket fabric slightly larger and looser than the lining fabric; the seamline around the pocket

3 *(inset)* Purple Shetland wool coat
4 Yellow and white shirt

5 *(inset)* Blue dress
6 Grey lace knit two-piece

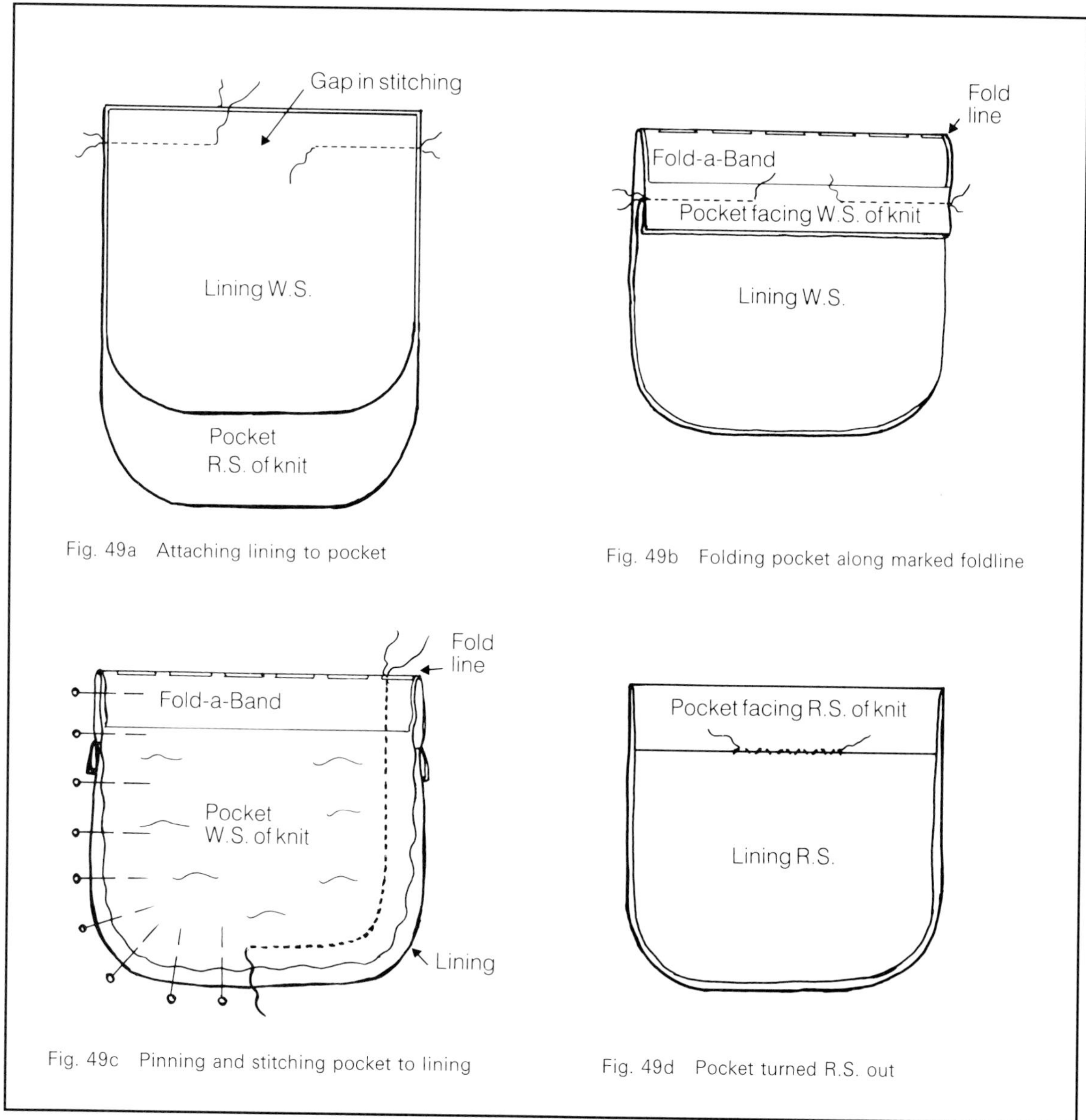

Fig. 49a Attaching lining to pocket

Fig. 49b Folding pocket along marked foldline

Fig. 49c Pinning and stitching pocket to lining

Fig. 49d Pocket turned R.S. out

edge will then roll neatly to the underside when the pocket is complete.

Machine-stitch, using a short stitch length, 1.5cm ($\frac{5}{8}$in) from the edge of the knit, around the three sides as shown. Trim the seam allowances back to 6mm ($\frac{1}{4}$in).

8 Turn the pocket through the gap to the R.S. Using blunt scissors or a large knitting needle, push out the corners and the seam all round from the inside. As the lining is now a little smaller than the pocket, the seam should have rolled well to the lining side of the pocket. Press well, using steam and a pounding block if necessary. With a needle and matching thread, slip-stitch the lining to the facing where the gap was left (*Fig. 49d*).

9 If an inner top-stitching line is required, do this now before attaching the pocket to the garment. Stitch about 1–1.2cm ($\frac{3}{8}$–$\frac{1}{2}$in) from the outer edge.

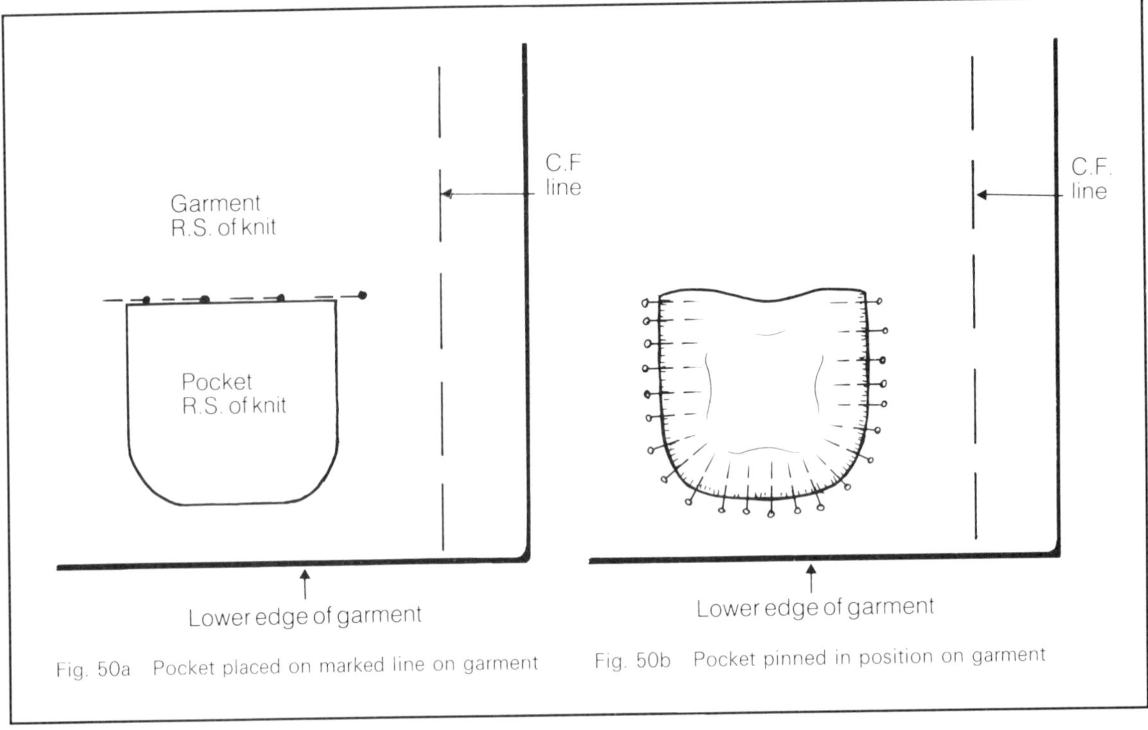

Fig. 50a Pocket placed on marked line on garment

Fig. 50b Pocket pinned in position on garment

10 Pin-mark a line on the garment to show where the top of the pocket should be. In most cases the pockets sits squarely on the garment, so this marked line will be exactly at right angles to the C.F. line. Place the pocket on the marked line (*Fig. 50a*). The pocket edge nearest to the C.F. line should be exactly parallel with the C.F. line, and the lower edge of the pocket should be parallel with the hem. Depending on the shape of the garment, the remaining side of the pocket might (or might not) be parallel with the side seam.

11 Pin the pocket to the garment as shown in Fig. 50b, *pushing the edge of the pocket inwards a little*, so that it is just slightly 'cupped'. It must not lie absolutely flat on the garment fabric. The reason for this is simple when you think about it. The garment is going to fit around the body — a convex curved surface — and therefore the outer layer of fabric (the pocket) must be slightly larger than the under layer (the garment). If you sew your pocket flat on to the garment, there will be puckers in the fabric behind the pocket when you wear it.

12 Stitch the pocket to the garment, as it is pinned. This can be done by hand from the W.S. of the garment front, by back-stitching securely into the seam allowances, so that no stitching shows on the R.S. Alternatively, you can top-stitch the pocket in position by machining on the R.S., 3mm ($\frac{1}{8}$in) from the pocket edge, removing each pin in turn as it comes up to the presser foot.

Note It may be necessary to tighten up the tension on the needle thread of your sewing machine when executing this top-stitching because of the collective thickness of the several layers of fabric. If in doubt, try out the top-stitching for a short distance, remove the work from the machine and look at the underside; if there are loops there, you need to tighten the top tension.

To match precisely the pocket position on the other half of the garment front, place the two halves W.S. tog., matching all the edges exactly; push pins straight through at the two top corners of the pocket and mark where these come through on the other side.

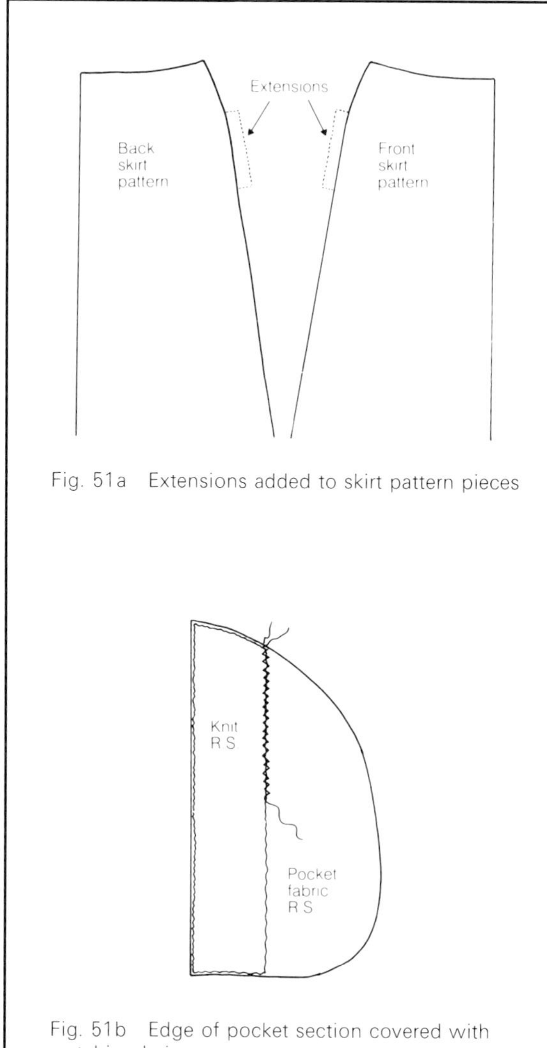

Fig. 51a Extensions added to skirt pattern pieces

Fig. 51b Edge of pocket section covered with matching knit

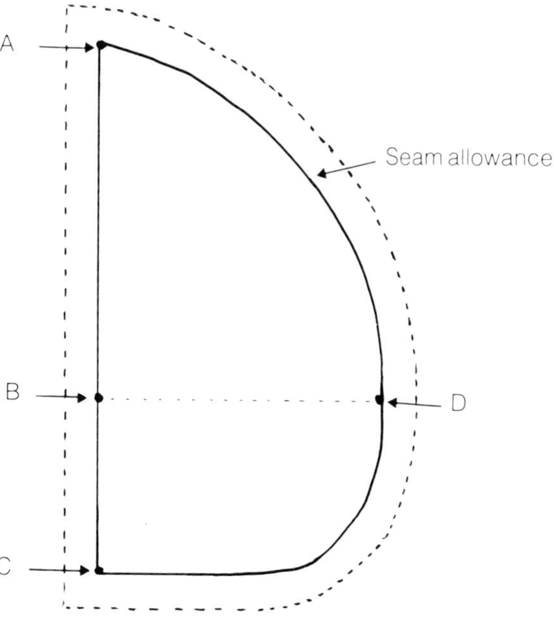

Fig. 52 Pattern for pocket pieces

Pockets in side (or side-front) seams

These can be used in any dress, skirt, coat or jacket. By unpicking the appropriate seam, you can even add them, as an afterthought, to a finished garment.

General notes

1 Use woven fabric for the pocket pieces rather than the knit used for the rest of the garment; the woven fabric then stabilises the knitted fabric around the pocket opening so that it cannot stretch out of shape. It should match the colour of the knitted fabric as closely as possible, and should be strong without being thick or bulky. Polyester lining fabric is generally good for this purpose.

2 A problem can occur: the pocket fabric may show inside the opening when the garment is worn, especialy if it fits fairly closely. If you have used a woven fabric elsewhere in the outfit, for collar, cuffs, etc., you could use the same fabric for the pockets and their visibility might then be acceptable. Otherwise, you should aim to avoid the problem by a bit of planning at the cutting-out stage; simply allow an extension to each garment piece where the pocket will be attached (*Fig. 51a*). The width of the extension should be about 4.5cm ($1\frac{3}{4}$in) and the length 11cm ($4\frac{1}{4}$in) longer than the required opening. If you have already cut out, or you are adding pockets to a finished garment, you will have to cover the straight edge of each pocket section with a strip of the knit about 5cm (2in) wide; this should be stitched on flat (not turning in the edges), using a short-length, full-width, zigzag machine-stitch (*Fig. 51b*).

3 The illustrations which accompany the following instructions show pocket extensions cut in one with the right front and right back sections of a skirt. This allows for one pocket in the right side seam. Adapt the instructions for adding a similar pocket to the left side seam, if required.

To cut and apply a side-seam pocket

1 Draw and cut out a paper pattern for the pocket pieces as shown in Fig. 52.

A–B is the measurement of the pocket opening and so must be long enough to allow the hand to slip through with ease.

B–C is the depth of the pocket 'well'; about 7.5cm (3in) is usually sufficient.

B–D is approximately 12.5cm (5in).

Add 1.5cm ($\frac{5}{8}$in) seam allowances all round. Draw a straight-grain line parallel with line A–B–C.

2 Cut out two pocket sections, from the woven fabric, using this paper pattern.

3 Place the pocket pieces on the skirt extensions, R.S. tog., matching the straight edges. Pin and then machine-stitch as shown in Fig. 53a.

4 Turn the pocket sections outwards over the seam allowances, as shown in Fig. 53b. Press the seams.

5 Place the two skirt sections R.S. tog., matching the top and lower ends of the side seam, and the pocket edges. Pin and machine-stitch as shown in Fig. 53c.

6 Trim the seam allowances around the curved edge of the pocket and oversew or overlock them together (*Fig. 53d*).

Snip the back skirt seam allowance, as shown, at both ends of the pocket opening, so that both seam allowances there can be pressed towards the pocket, whereas the seam above and below the pocket can be pressed open flat.

7 On the R.S., using machined satin stitch (as for one side of a buttonhole), stitch from the seamline towards the skirt front, for about 1.2cm ($\frac{1}{2}$in), through all thicknesses (*Fig. 53e*). This stitching not only holds the pocket in position towards the front of the skirt, but also strengthens the ends of the pocket opening.

Here is one other kind of pocket which I have found useful in cut-and-sew projects such as anoraks, or in fact in any casual clothes where a zipped-up pocket is an asset. You could add these to any child's pullover you have already made, as a safe place to keep lunch money or a bus ticket. You do not need matching yarn but you will need a 10–15cm (4–6in) zip, and a small piece of fairly thin but strong woven fabric for the pocket bag (*Fig. 54*). Do a practice one,

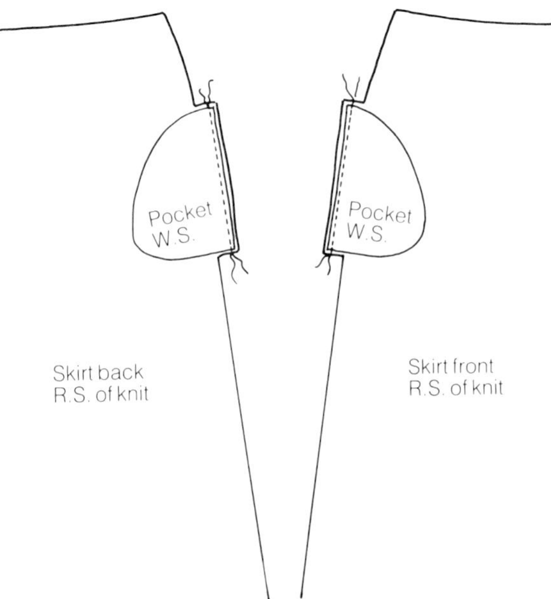

Fig. 53a Pocket sections sewn to skirt extensions

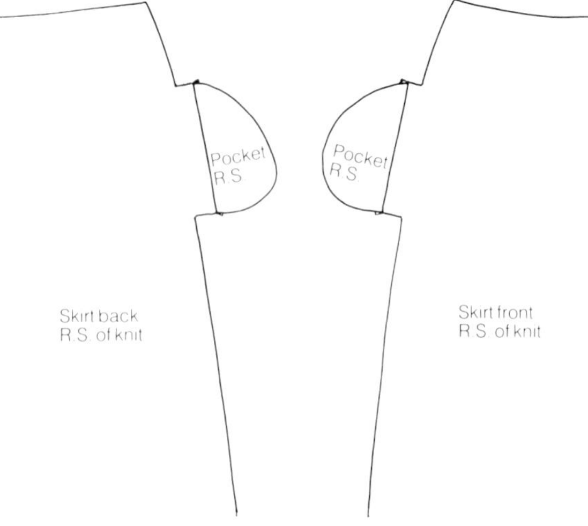

Fig. 53b Pocket sections pressed outwards

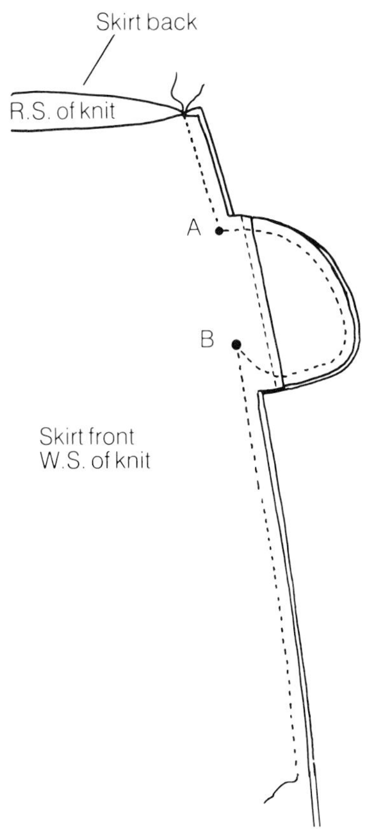

Fig. 53c Skirt front and back sewn together to include pockets

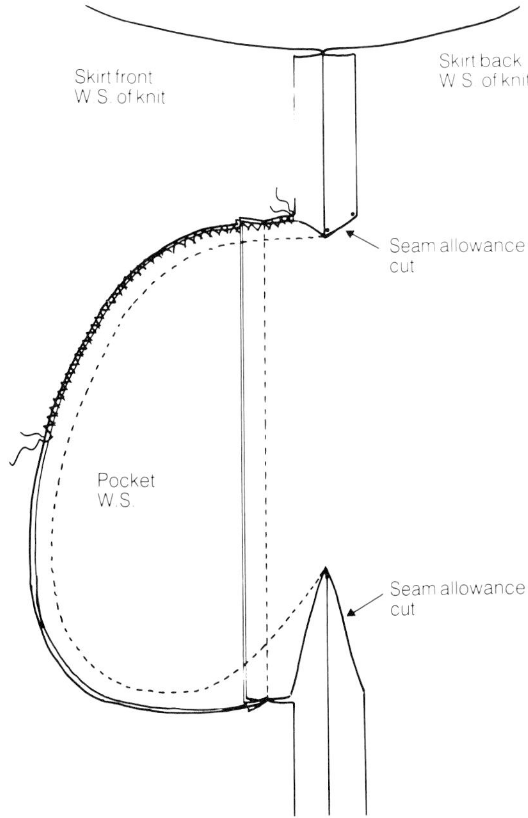

Fig. 53d Pocket edges oversewn and seam allowances, on skirt back, cut to stitching line

using an old tension square, before operating on a real garment.

Zipped pocket in knit where no seam exists

1 Mark the proposed position of the pocket opening on the garment. The length of the opening will be exactly the length of the zip you will be using to close it (not including the zip tape extensions). The line can be straight with the grain of the knitted fabric or it can be at any other angle you choose. (See the examples in Fig. 55a, b and c.) If you decide to make it parallel with either the rows or the stitch lines, be accurate; it must be really parallel.

2 Cut two identical pieces of the woven fabric for the pocket bag. The shape is indicated in the examples shown in Fig. 56a, b and c. Mark the

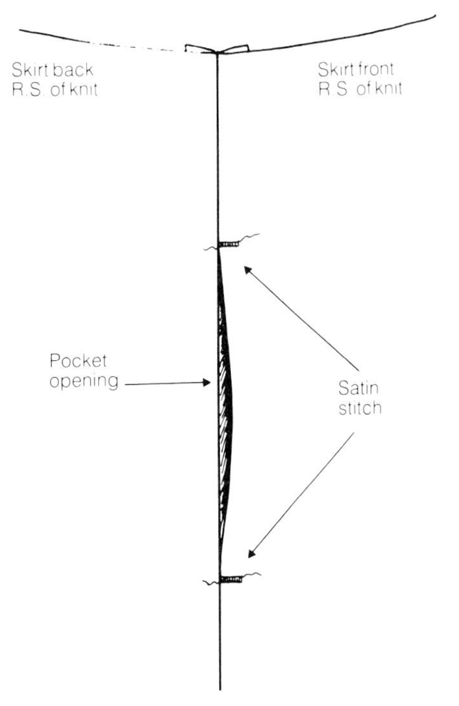

Fig. 53e Ends of pocket opening secured on R.S. with satin-stitch

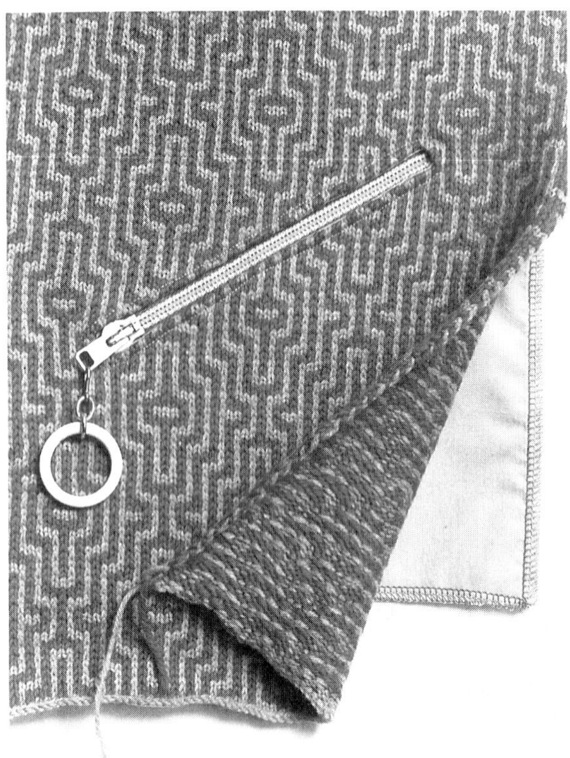

Fig. 54 Zipped pocket placed in knitted fabric

line of the pocket opening with a pencil and a ruler, on the W.S. of one of the pocket pieces, making it the same length as the marked line on the garment. There should be about 4cm ($1\frac{1}{2}$in) of fabric around the marked line on the opening end of the pocket; the depth of the pocket is your own decision.

3 Place the pocket piece which has the opening line marked on it, on the garment, R.S. tog., so that the marked lines lie exactly together. Pin in position, keeping the pins clear of the marked line, as shown in Fig. 57a.

4 Machine-stitch, using a very short stitch length (about 1) all around the marked line (the very short stitch length is vital in order to sew all the fibres down firmly so that fraying will not occur when the slit is cut). You will be sewing a rectangular shape, the short sides of which will touch the ends of the line; the long sides should be parallel with the line and a fraction more than

Fig. 55 Marking position for zipped pocket

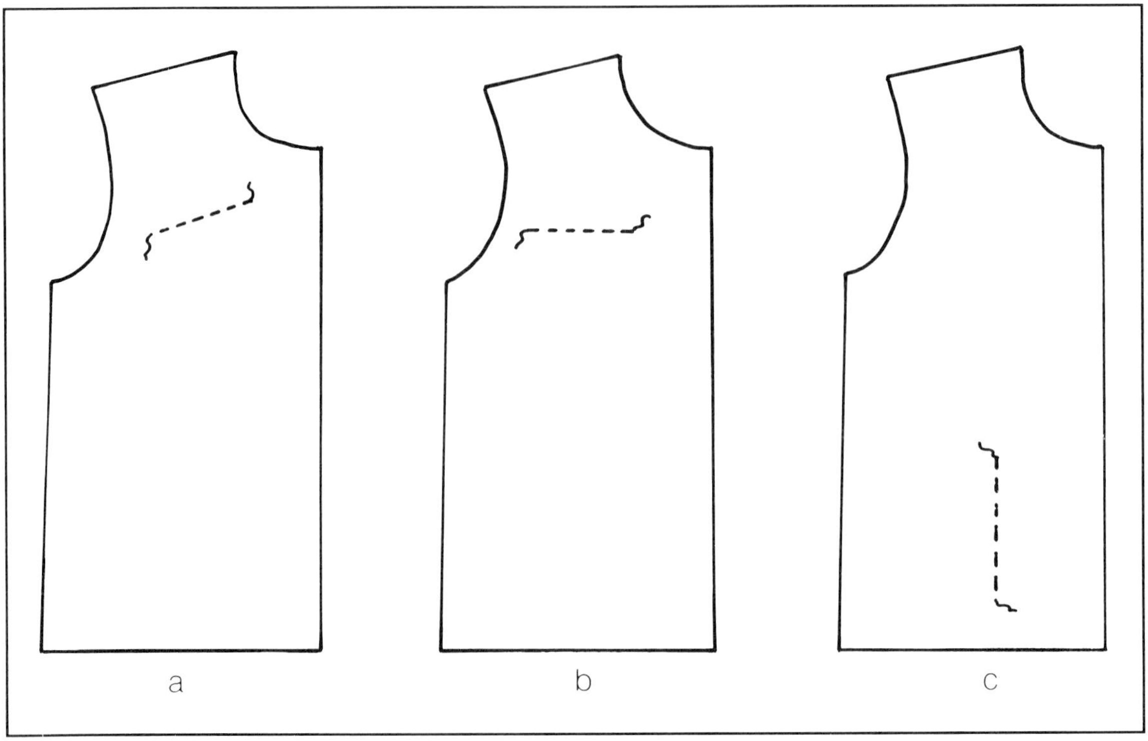

a b c

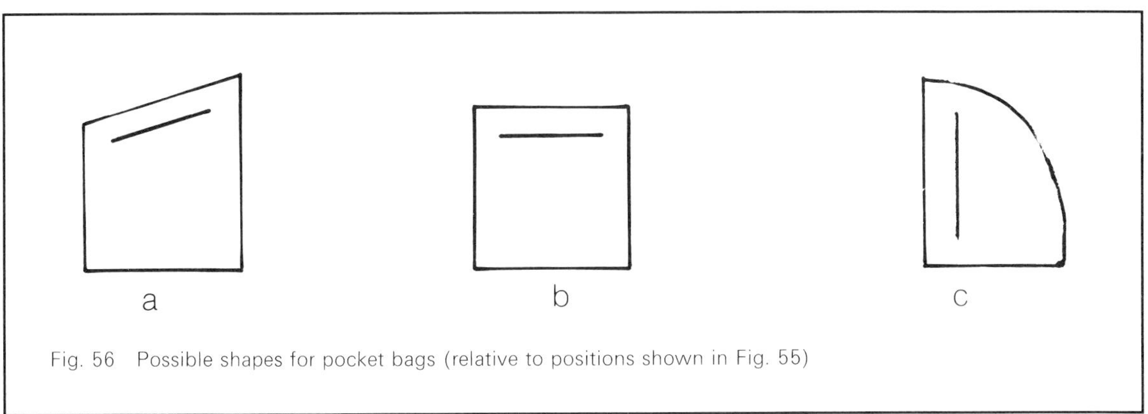

Fig. 56 Possible shapes for pocket bags (relative to positions shown in Fig. 55)

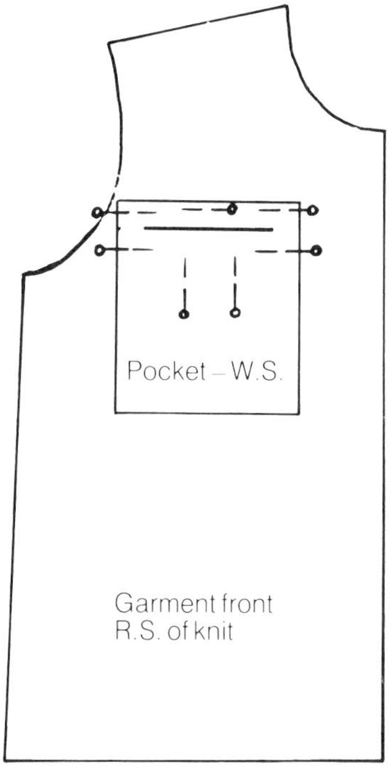

Pocket – W.S.

Garment front
R.S. of knit

Fig. 57a Pocket piece positioned on garment front

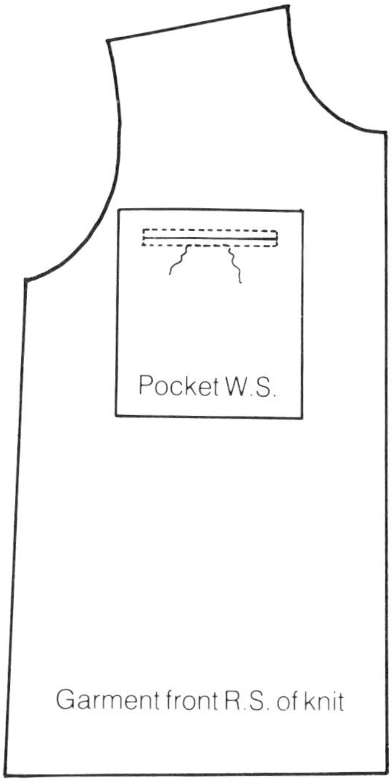

Pocket W.S.

Garment front R.S. of knit

Fig. 57b Stitching around marked line

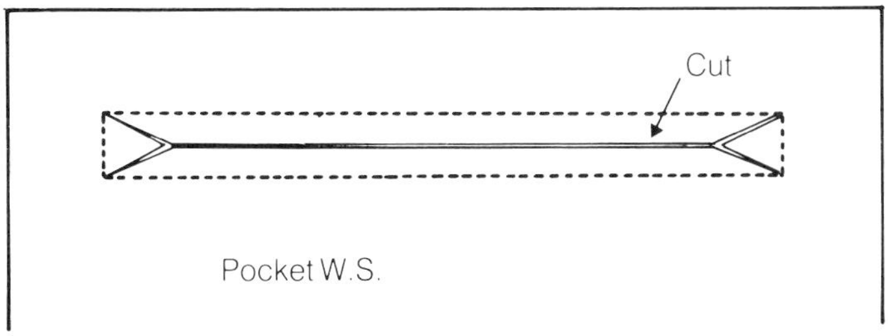

Cut

Pocket W.S.

Fig. 57c Cutting the pocket opening

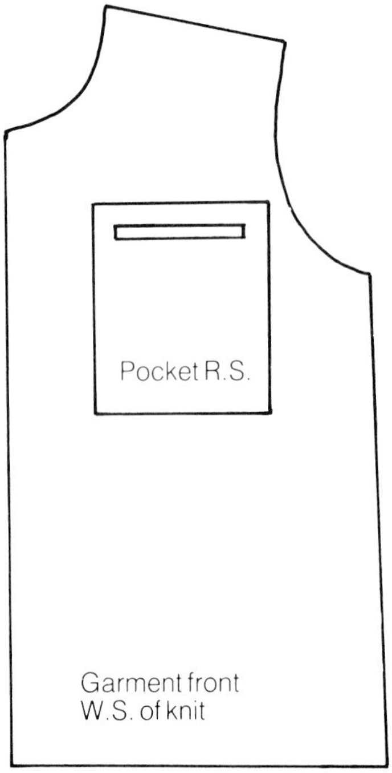

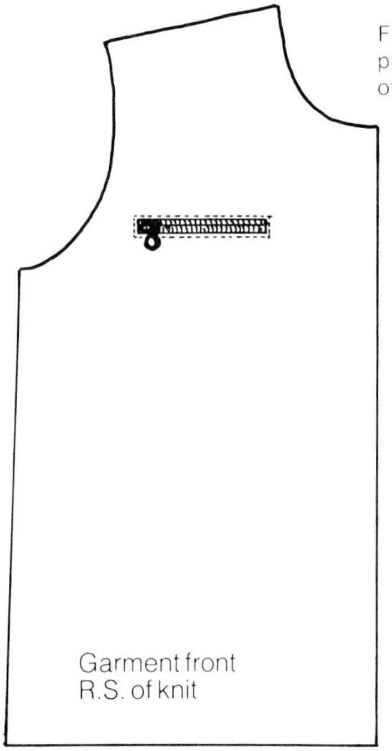

Fig. 57d Pocket piece pulled through to W.S. of garment

Fig. 57e Pocket opening stitched around zip

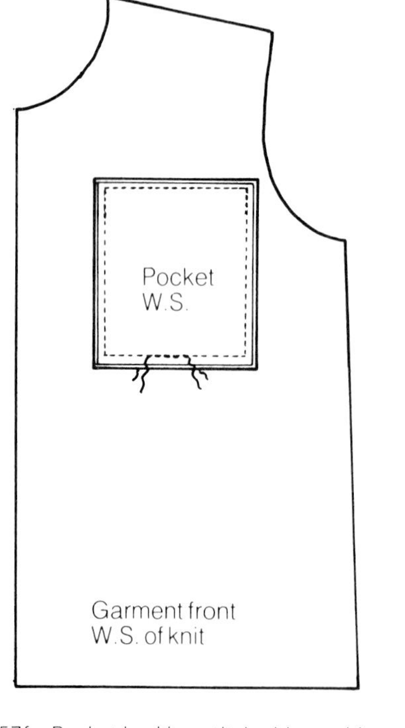

Fig. 57f Pocket backing stitched in position

half the width of the zip teeth away from it. Start the stitching at some point on one of the long sides, and overlap this when you have completed the circuit (*Fig. 57b*).

5 Cut straight up the marked line, exactly in the middle of the two long lines of stitching, and out to each corner as shown in Fig. 57c. You must cut *right up to* the stitching in the corners or the pocket will not turn neatly through to the W.S. of the garment.

6 Pull the pocket section through to the W.S. of the garment (*Fig. 57d*). Push out the seams from the inside so that they lie straight and parallel; press thoroughly.

7 Position and sew the opening around the zip in the same way as directed on pp. 71–3. The only difference is that you will now be making a complete circuit of the zip instead of only three sides (*Fig. 57e*).

8 Place the remaining pocket section onto the first, R.S. tog., matching all edges exactly. Pin the two pocket sections together and machine-stitch 1.2cm ($\frac{1}{2}$in) from the edge all round. Trim and oversew or overlock (*Fig. 57f*).

Chapter seven

BUTTONS AND BUTTONHOLES

In order to produce a garment which looks professionally made, and expensive at that, great care and thought has to be given to choosing just the right buttons, because more often than not, they are the focal point. The buttonholes, too, demand precision both in their placement and in their execution.

Planning

Choosing the size of the button

If you have designed your own garment, you will have marked in the C.F. line. Decide *either* the width of the overlap between C.F. line and edge, *or*... the diameter of the buttons you are going to use. As a general rule these two should be the same: one depends upon the other (*Fig. 58*). If they are not roughly the same, the buttons tend to look out of proportion to the overlap width.

Always try out the effect that buttons of different sizes will have on a garment. Avoid very large buttons if you are on the small side.

If you have used a dressmaking pattern, the proposed size of the buttons will be indicated in the 'Notions' section on the back of the pattern envelope; the C.F. line will be clearly shown and the exact positions and size of the buttonholes drawn on the paper pattern. Remember, however, that if you have had to alter the body-length in the area of the buttoned fastening, this will affect the spacing of the buttonholes. In this case, it would be wise to postpone marking the button-hole positions until after the first fitting, or even to leave marking until the garment is otherwise complete.

Determining the position of buttons and buttonholes

Generally, the C.F. line determines where buttons should actually be, because that, in the majority of clothes, is the centre of the complete over-lap (when one side is fastened over the other [*Fig. 59*]).

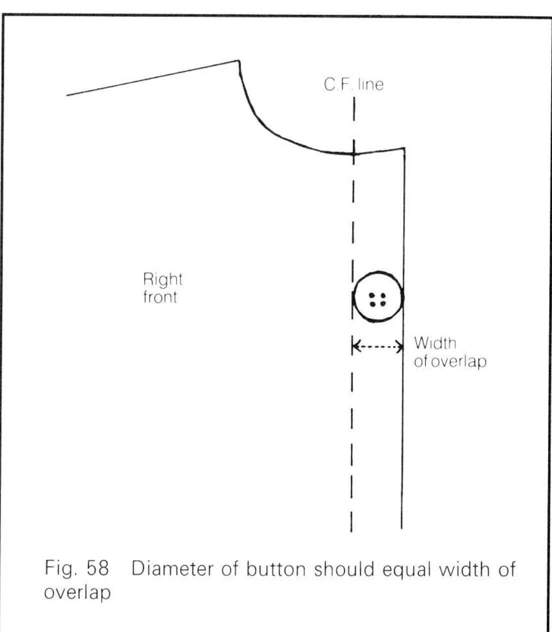

Fig. 58 Diameter of button should equal width of overlap

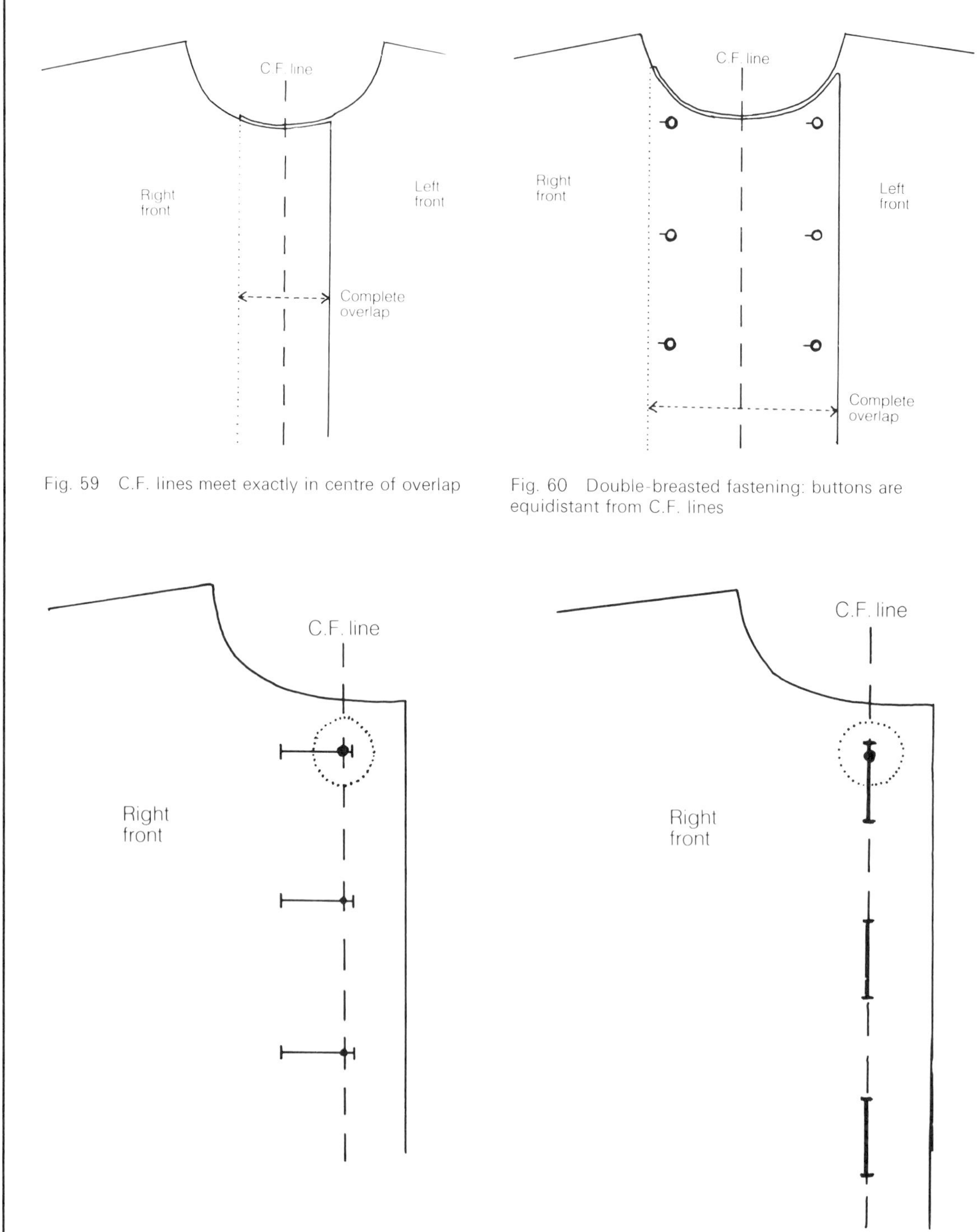

Fig. 59 C.F. lines meet exactly in centre of overlap

Fig. 60 Double-breasted fastening: buttons are equidistant from C.F. lines

Fig. 61a Positioning for horizontal buttonholes

Fig. 61b Positioning for vertical buttonholes

Where, however, garments fasten at the back, on the side or asymmetrically, the centre line of the complete overlap is, again, the deciding factor. In double-breasted garments, the two lines of buttons must be equidistant from the C.F. line (*Fig. 60*).

Note In order to make the following instructions clearer, we will assume that the garment is fastened at the C.F.

Remember two important points:

1 Buttons should be positioned exactly on the C.F. line.

2 The position of the button*holes* is determined by the position of the buttons.

If the buttonholes are to be horizontal, the line for each hole should start on the side of the C.F. line nearest to the edge of the overlap, leaving just enough room for the shank of the button where it is to be sewn exactly on the C.F. line. This is usually about 6mm ($\frac{1}{4}$in) but may be more for very thick fabrics. They should finish sufficiently far away on the other side of the C.F. line to enable the buttons to slip through the buttonholes with ease (*Fig. 61a*).

If the buttonholes are to be vertical, they should lie precisely on the C.F. line, starting approximately 6mm ($\frac{1}{4}$in) above the button mark and ending sufficiently far below the button mark to enable the button to slip through the hole with ease (*Fig. 61b*).

Note If the edge has an attached band (as in a tailored shirt) the buttonholes *must* be vertical so that they lie exactly in the centre of the band and parallel with it. If there is no attached band, the buttonholes can be either vertical or horizontal.

Determining the distance between the buttons

1 First decide where you want the top button and mark this position with a pin; if the garment is to be buttoned right up to the top, this point is generally half the diameter of the button below the finished top edge.

2 Decide, and pin-mark, where the bottom button is to be; this should never be in the hem and, as a general rule, should be about one and a half 'spaces' (the distance between buttons) above the lower edge.

3 Pin-mark the positions of the remaining buttons, spacing them out evenly between the top and bottom buttons. Bear in mind that, if the garment is not to have a belt, it might be advisable to have a button at the waistline; whereas a button placed underneath a belt could be bulky and uncomfortable. If your figure demands it, ensure that there is a button at the fullest part of the bust.

Determining the required length of the buttonhole

Measure the diameter of the button, allowing also for its thickness, and then add 6mm ($\frac{1}{4}$in) for ease.

Making the buttonholes

Interfacing

The inclusion of some kind of firm interfacing, between the main fabric and the facing is generally vital to the production of professional-looking buttonholes. This rule applies to normal dressmaking and is generally indispensable when it comes to most cut-and-sew projects. (Possible exceptions could be where the facing is cut from a firm woven fabric or from something like petersham ribbon.) The facing will probably already be interfaced but an additional strip of some interfacing, such as one of the fusible Vilenes, or fusible cotton muslin, can be added to the W.S. of the garment front to cover the area in which the buttonholes will be made. This will help to control any tendency to stretch or fray when it comes to sewing and cutting the buttonhole.

Sewing

Bound buttonholes can be difficult when using knitted fabrics, but are sometimes advisable on coats and jackets, where the thickness of the layers makes for an unsuitable situation for machined buttonholes. Well executed, they can add a wonderfully expensive-looking couture touch. In this case, I would suggest you cut the

Fig. 62 Buttonhole in knitted fabric, bound with cotton denim

piping strips from a finely woven fabric such as lightweight flannel or gabardine. In Fig. 62 the buttonhole is bound with cotton denim. Certainly do not try to use your knitted fabric for this!

There are several methods of making bound buttonholes; get in plenty of practice if you are not used to doing this, following the instructions in a good sewing manual.

Machined buttonholes are usually successful on all but very thick knits. You need to have practised the process on your sewing machine, using easily-managed woven fabrics, and to be feeling fairly confident about it. Some examples are shown in Figs. 43 and 63.

Use the following guidelines.

1 Mark the positions of the buttonholes carefully and exactly; use a marking pen or pencil (with care) or small running stitches made with a needle and a sharply contrasting thread. Tacking is useless for this purpose because it can move about when under the presser foot.

2 Read and digest the instructions for making

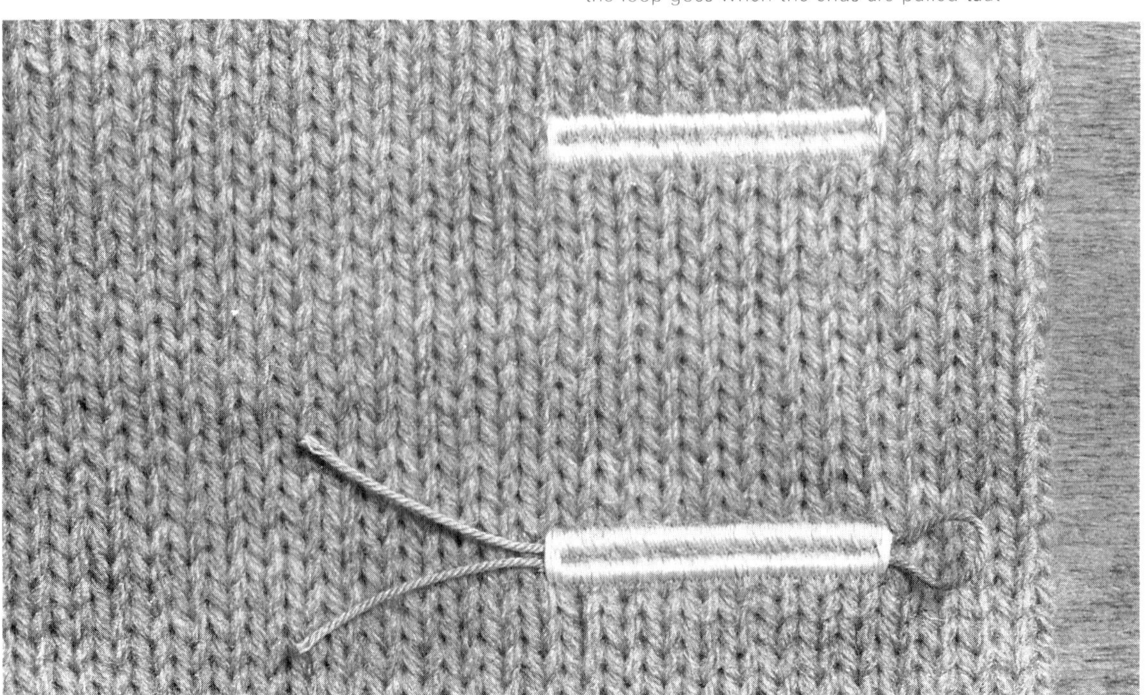

Fig. 63 Machined buttonholes in knitted fabric. The lower one has been reinforced by the addition of crochet cotton; the loop goes when the ends are pulled taut

buttonholes in your sewing-machine manual with great care.

3 Check that you have fitted the correct presser foot for sewing buttonholes.

4 Check on whether it is necessary to loosen the top-tension. On some machines, such as Bernina, the tension on the bobbin thread is increased instead.

5 Pin together the area around the buttonhole line, through all fabrics. Keep the pins sufficiently far away from the buttonhole line to ensure that they will not interfere with the presser foot.

6 Adjust the stitch length to where it should be for sewing buttonholes and then try it out on a spare piece of fabric, using the same number of layers that you will have to stitch on when actually making the buttonholes. The exact position of the stitch-length lever (or dial) will vary according to the thickness and texture of the fabric. You have to get the right balance between setting the length so long that you have gaps between the stitches, and setting it so short that you risk stopping the forward-feed mechanism. Often it is better to have slight gaps and then to sew round the buttonhole twice; in fact, stitching round the line twice actually improves the look of the finished buttonhole in most cases.

7 Cut the slit carefully between the two lines of stitching, using a sharp buttonhole knife or stitch-ripper. Cut from each end in turn towards the middle. If you try to cut straight through from one end to the other, you could have a nasty accident!

8 If the edge of the buttonhole stretches when the hole is cut, you should be using a reinforcing thread under the stitches (*Fig. 63*). Consult your manual on how to do this. Usually the buttonhole presser foot incorporates some means of guiding a thicker thread (such as a fine crochet cotton) so that the zigzag stitching is done over it. The ends of this thread can then be pulled up to get rid of the loop and to tighten the stretched edges of the buttonhole. If your sewing machine does not have this facility, try a line of short-length, straight-stitch machining, placed 6mm ($\frac{1}{8}$in) all around the buttonhole line, before starting with zigzag stitching. Alternatively, run a thread through the zigzag stitches, using a hand needle; then pull up to tighten and fasten off securely.

9 If some of the zigzag stitching gets cut accidentally, when slitting the hole, put the buttonhole back under the machine presser foot again, positioning it carefully with the hole spread slightly open. Re-stitch the damaged area.

10 Sew in, on the W.S., all thread ends.

Sewing on the buttons

Almost everyone knows how to sew on a button but it is surprising how few people know exactly *where* to sew it!

When the buttons are intended to lie in one straight line (e.g. down C.F. or C.B.) there is a simple foolproof method.

1 Place the two opening edges, W.S. together, with the top and bottom ends matching exactly and the edges level. Have the buttonholed side on top (*Figs. 64a and b*).

2 For *vertical buttonholes,* stick a pin straight through the buttonhole at a point 3mm ($\frac{1}{8}$in) below the *top* end of the hole. This should come out, on the button side of the garment, exactly on the centre line of the overlap.

For *horizontal buttonholes,* stick a pin straight through the buttonhole at a point 3mm ($\frac{1}{8}$in) inwards from the *outer* end of the hole. This should come out exactly on the centre line of the overlap.

3 Mark, with marking pen or pencil, a small dot exactly where the pin comes through, on the centre line of the overlap, on the button side.

4 Sew a button exactly on the mark. Remember to make a long enough shank to allow for the thickness of the overlapping side of the garment.

This method ensures that, in the case of vertical buttonholes, the top and bottom ends will remain level when the buttonholed side automatically slides downwards until stopped by the buttons. Similarly, in the case of horizontal buttonholes, the centre lines of the overlap will remain in line together when the buttonholed side is inevitably pulled sideways until stopped by the buttons.

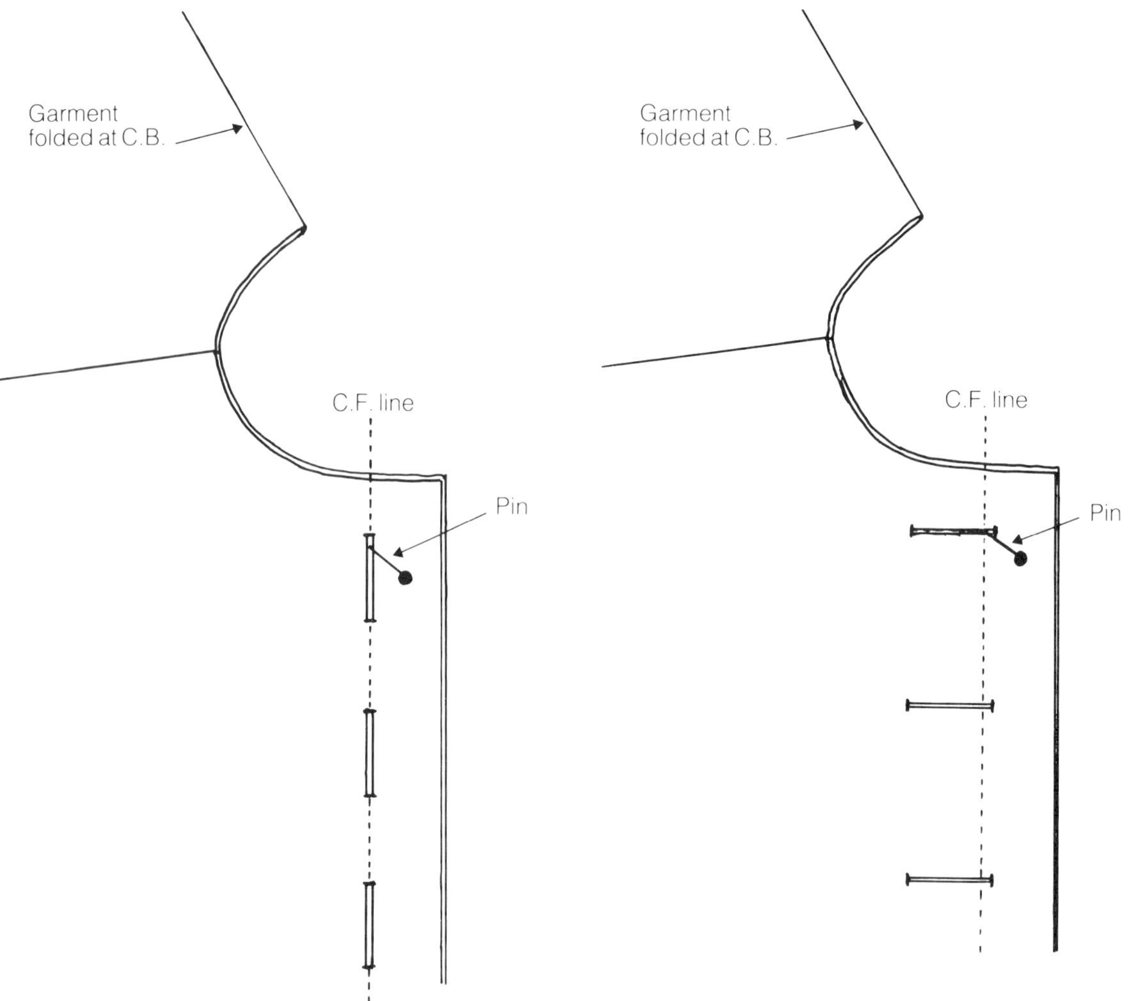

Fig. 64a Finding button position for vertical buttonholes

Fig. 64b Finding button position for horizontal buttonholes

For double-breasted or asymmetrically-buttoned garments (*Fig. 13b*) place the two parts together so that the C.F. lines match exactly; then push a pin through the upper or outer end (whichever end will be taking the strain when the garment is worn) of the buttonhole.

Adding a couture touch

On coats and jackets, reinforce each button by placing another very small button on the W.S., exactly underneath it. Both outer and inner buttons are sewn to the garment in one operation.

Try sewing four-holed buttons on in different ways (*Fig. 65*). Where suitable, use a thicker than normal thread, perhaps in a contrasting colour related to another colour in the fabric. (E.g. an emerald-green and sapphire-blue tweed knit could have matching emerald-green buttons sewn on with sapphire-blue thread.)

Making your own buttons

This is sometimes a feasible alternative to searching the shops for matching ones, or sending some of your fabric away for professional button-covering. Here are just a few ideas.

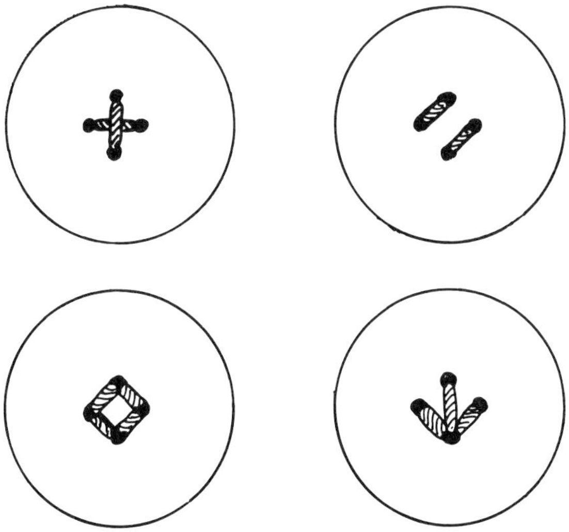

Fig. 65 Ways of sewing on four-holed buttons

1 *Purchased button-covering kits*, available from haberdashers, enable you to cover metal or plastic button-forms with your own fabric (which can be knitted, woven, or even leather) providing it is not too thick and bulky. If you intend to use knitted fabric for this purpose you will probably need a woven lining fabric as well, to prevent the metal or plastic showing through.

2 *Plastic or bone rings* (sold by haberdashers for curtain-making) can be covered with a circle of matching fabric, cut twice as large as the button. Make a line of tiny running-stitches all around the edge of the circle, put the ring in the middle, pull up the thread and fasten off securely at the back. Then make a line of back-stitching close to the inner edge of the ring through both layers of fabric (*Fig. 66*). In this case, also, avoid thick fabrics and add a lining if necessary.

3 *Dorset buttons* are made also by using curtain rings of bone or plastic. In this case, yarn is applied by buttonholing all around the ring and then filling in the centre with a network of stitches. Muriel Kent's book *A Complete Crochet Course* (David and Charles, 1984) contains beautifully clear instructions for these buttons which are so eminently suited to all knitwear.

4 *Chinese-ball buttons* can be made from purchased cord, from neatly crocheted chain or from

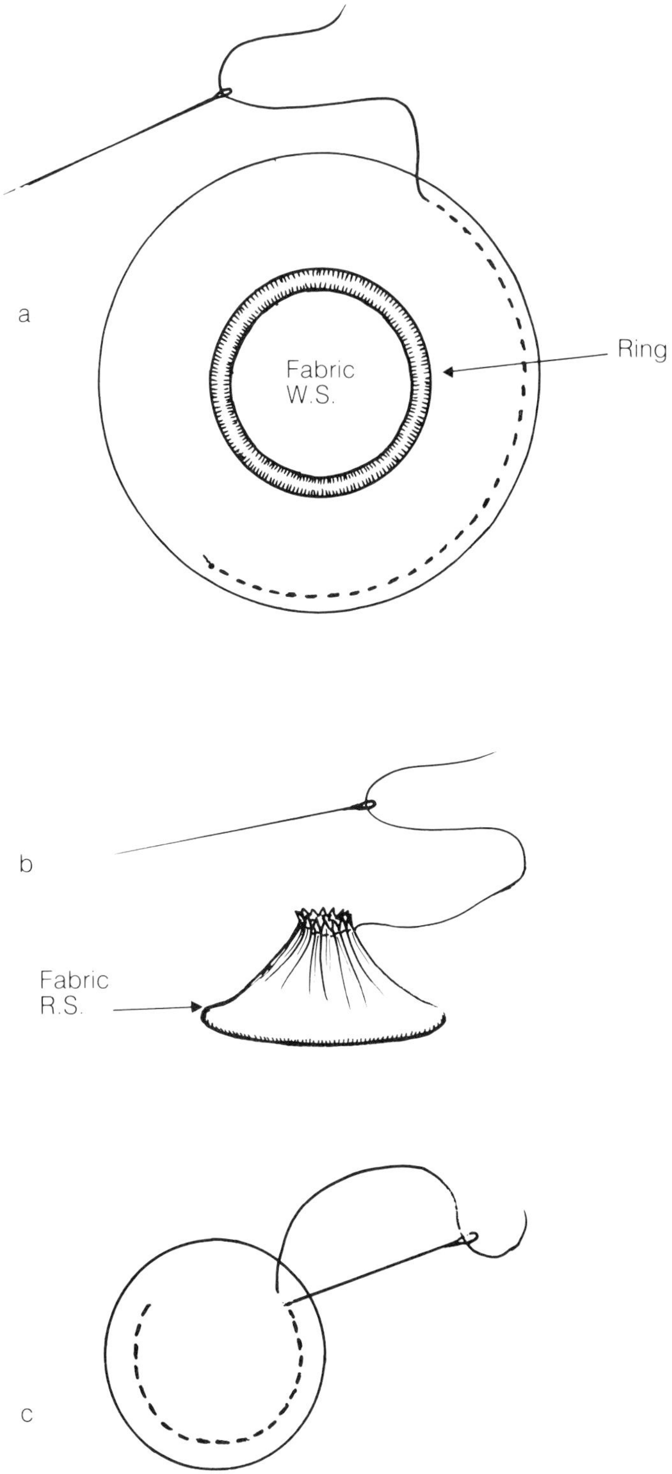

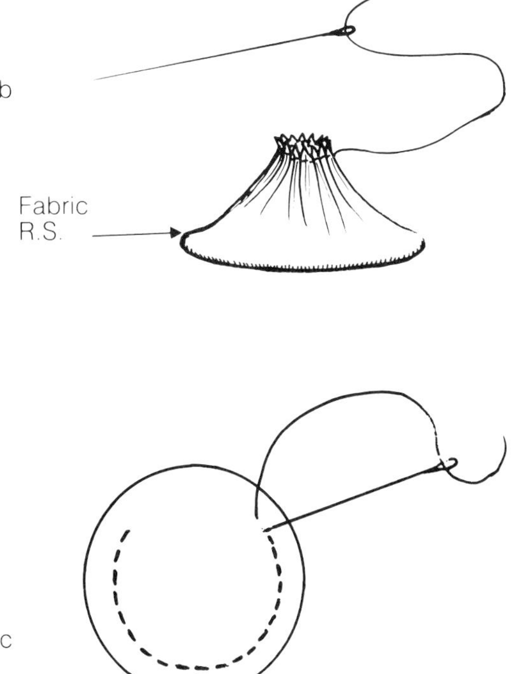

Fig. 66 Making a button by covering a ring

a length of French-knitting. There are very clear instructions for these in most comprehensive sewing primers. These are usually better combined with loops than with buttonholes.

5 *Crocheted buttons* should be made with fine yarn and a small-size hook; aim at a circular shape with a tightened-up edge. Fill with some kind of washable material such as polyester-wadding, a length of yarn, or crumpled-up fine soft fabric. Gather up the edge and fasten off securely. Fasten to the garment with a thread shank, and combine these also with loops rather than with buttonholes.

6 *Buttons and belts professionally made.* See 'Harlequin', Appendix I, for mail order details: send your own knitted fabrics for processing.

▲

Chapter eight

ZIPS

There is a school of thought on the subject of cut-and-sew which declares that zips are unnecessary in clothes made of knitted fabrics. If you are prepared to design your garments accordingly, you can of course eliminate them; but, as my angle on cut-and-sew is 'dressmaking with knitted fabrics', I find that I frequently need to sew in a zip, either because it is part of the design or for purely practical reasons.

Setting in a zip fastener so that it looks neat and professional is sometimes a considerable challenge to the average home dressmaker, and, when knitted fabrics are involved the hazards are multiplied; so it seems appropriate to sort out the difficulties for cut-and-sew enthusiasts.

Buying a zip

Nylon or polyester zips are lighter and more flexible than metal ones and are certainly just as strong. I also feel that they are more suited to knitted fabrics. The zip tapes should also be made from nylon or polyester as this is stronger and more stable than cotton. They are available in a reasonably wide variety of colours but a perfect match is not always possible.

If you want your zip to be near-invisible, look for the one which has the smallest and flattest head, i.e. the part you pull. The thickness of the head can vary from 5 to 10mm ($\frac{3}{16}$ to $\frac{6}{16}$in), and although this does not sound like a great difference, the thinner heads are considerably easier to hide away than the thicker ones.

There is a type of zip which is termed 'invisible'. This is sewn in by hand or with the help of a special foot which is supplied with *some* sewing machines; alternatively, a special plastic foot can be obtained from at least one of the manufacturers of these invisible zips. This type of zip does disappear completely behind the seam when correctly applied, but as I personally find them a little stiff and awkward to operate, I rarely use them for cut-and-sew projects.

If the zip is to be a decorative feature of the garment, consider buying one of the over-sized, chunky zips, possibly in a contrasting colour. These can be obtained with fixed (closed) ends or with separating ends. Some have large ring-pulls attached. This type of zip is not intended to be hidden away.

Make sure your zip is long enough! Too many skirt and trouser zips get broken because the opening is not long enough to allow the garment to be slipped on with ease.

Sewing in a zip

Here are some guidelines to help you get it right.

1 Never sew in the zip until you are sure the fitting is right, otherwise you could have some tedious unpicking and re-stitching to do, with the added risk of snagging the knitted fabric. When trying on for fitting, simply pin the opening together along the two seamlines.

2 There is no need to stabilise the seam allowances before sewing in a zip because the zip tapes will eventually do that job. However, if the knit shows signs of stretching out of shape too easily, you could slip-stitch 6mm ($\frac{1}{4}$in) wide cotton tape to the seamlines first. Just be careful that this is not going to make the opening too bulky. It might be better to use a strip of paper which can be torn away afterwards.

3 Use pinning as a preliminary to stitching, placing the pins at right angles to the seamline, not parallel with it. This is a much more efficient way of holding everything in place than tacking.

4 Take great care not to stretch the knit when pinning it to the zip tapes. Don't gather it, either, in your efforts not to stretch it! Keep both knitted fabric and zip tapes absolutely flat together. To make this easier, do it on a table — not on your lap.

5 For cut-and-sew work, always hand-sew your zips in place initially, using matching thread. This is firmer than tacking. If you have made an error of judgment, hand-sewing is also considerably easier to unpick than small machine-stitching, especially when knitted fabrics are involved. Once you are satisfied that the zip is flat and evenly set in, you can always machine-stitch over the hand-stitching to make it more secure.

6 When hand-sewing the zip in place, use prick-stitch. This is rather like back-stitch but has less thread showing on the right side. The needle comes up from underneath the fabric and is then re-inserted only one or two threads behind where it came out; it is then carried forward, under the fabric, and re-emerges about 3mm ($\frac{1}{8}$in) to 6mm ($\frac{1}{4}$in) from the first stitch (*Fig. 67*).

7 When machine-stitching a zip in place, you must use a zipper foot in place of the normal presser foot on your machine. The normal presser foot guards the needle on both sides and so makes it impossible for the stitching to be really close to the zip teeth; a zipper foot leaves one side of the needle unguarded, making it possible to stitch very close to the zip teeth. On some types of machine, the foot is moved either to the left or to the right side of the needle; on others, the needle is moved either to the left or to the right side of the foot.

If you do not have a zipper foot with your machine, you should be able to buy one from a sewing-machine shop; if the standard ones will not fit your machine, write to the manufacturer

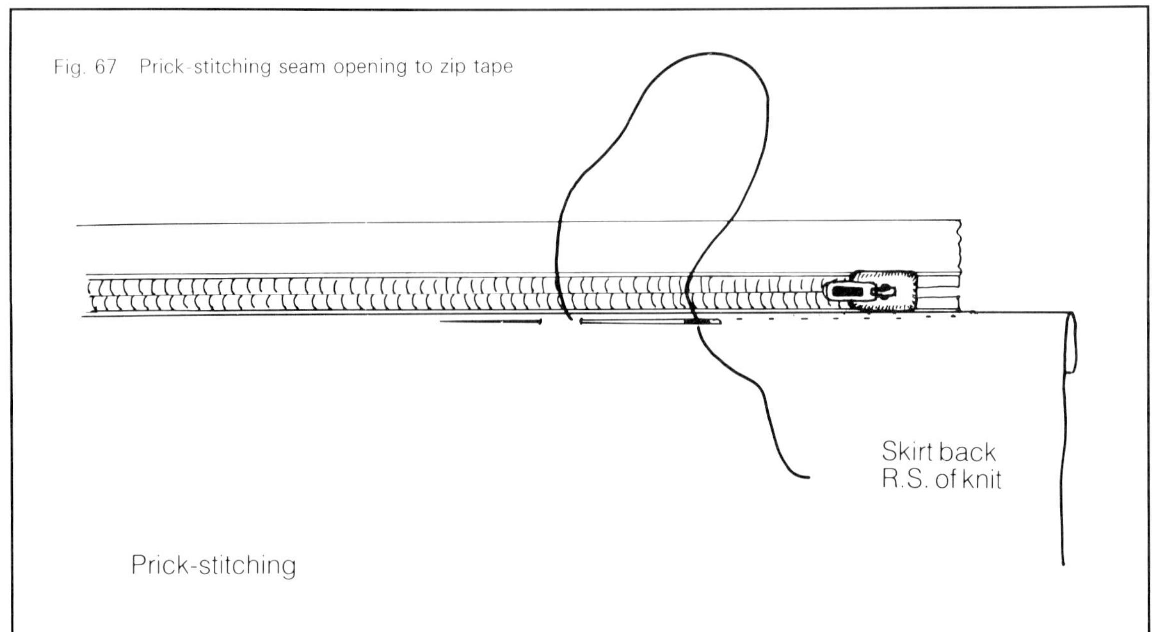

Fig. 67 Prick-stitching seam opening to zip tape

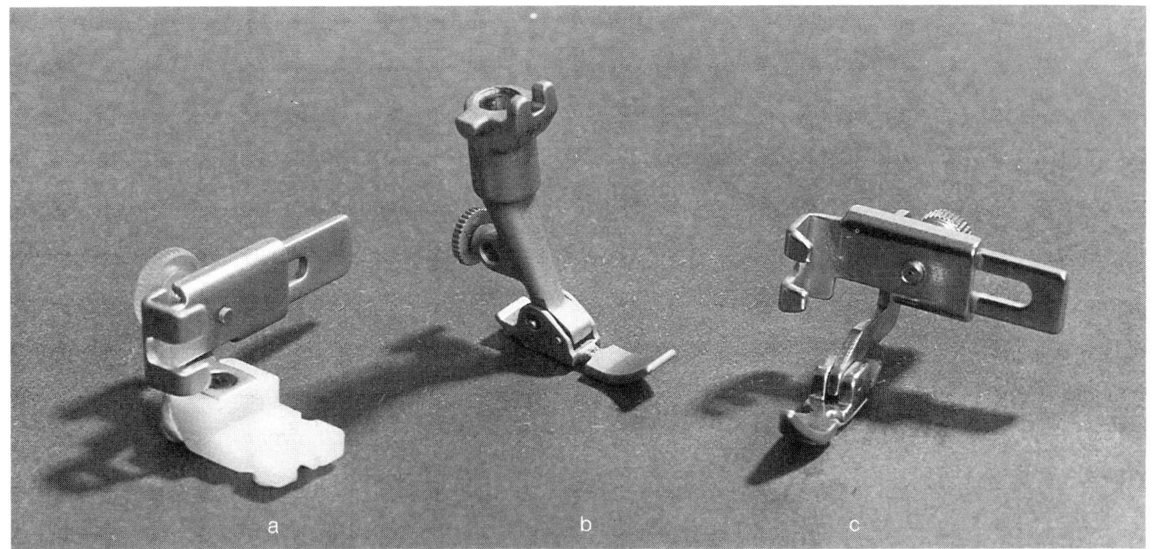

Fig. 68 Examples of zipper feet: *a* Frister Rossman, supplied with their sewing machines; *b* Bernina, supplied with their sewing machines; *c* a 'Universal' zipper foot which can be purchased to fit most sewing machines

or try one of his agents. Fig. 68 shows some examples of zipper feet.

8 Always move the zip slider away from the area on which you are actually working; never try to sew round it or you will have a wobble in the stitching-line. When stitching along the side of a zip, stop just before you get to the zip slider; with the needle *in* the fabric, raise the zipper foot, gently pull the slider past the needle until it is safely out of the way, lower the zipper foot and continue stitching.

In school dressmaking lessons (at least in my day) one was always taught to sew in a zip so that the two seamlines would meet exactly down the centre of the zip teeth; the instruction sheets given with commercial dressmaking patterns have tended to carry on this tradition. Yet this is a method which is rarely used in the world of professional garment construction; it is difficult to execute with adequate precision and practically adds a 'home-made' label to the finished garment. So, I will describe here two alternative methods, both of which I find effective in cut-and-sew work. If they are not familiar to you, try them out using odd pieces of woven fabric and old zips. Once you have mastered the techniques you will be set for success with knitted fabrics.

Lapped or semi-concealed application

Use this whenever you want a zip to be placed unobtrusively in a seamline (*example in Fig. 69*).

Employ a thin light zip in a colour which matches the fabric as closely as possible.

The instructions which follow are written as for the left side of a skirt; no matter where the zip happens to be on the garment, think of it as being on your left side and these instructions will then make sense; zips at C.B., on the left back hip, C.F., etc., can all be inserted in exactly the same way.

1 *Fig. 70a.* With the zip closed and the top of the zip slider lying 2.5cm (1in) below the top raw edges of the skirt, check that the seam is securely sewn up to a point just *above* the end stop of the zip. This will prevent strain and possible damage to the zip when the garment is put on and taken off.

2 *Fig. 70b.* On the skirt *front* turn the complete seam allowance to the W.S. Press and/or tack in position.

On the skirt *back*, tack-mark the seamline with a bright contrasting thread, finishing precisely where the sewn seam starts. This is simply to indicate exactly where the seamline lies.

3 *Fig. 70c.* On the skirt *back*, fold the seam

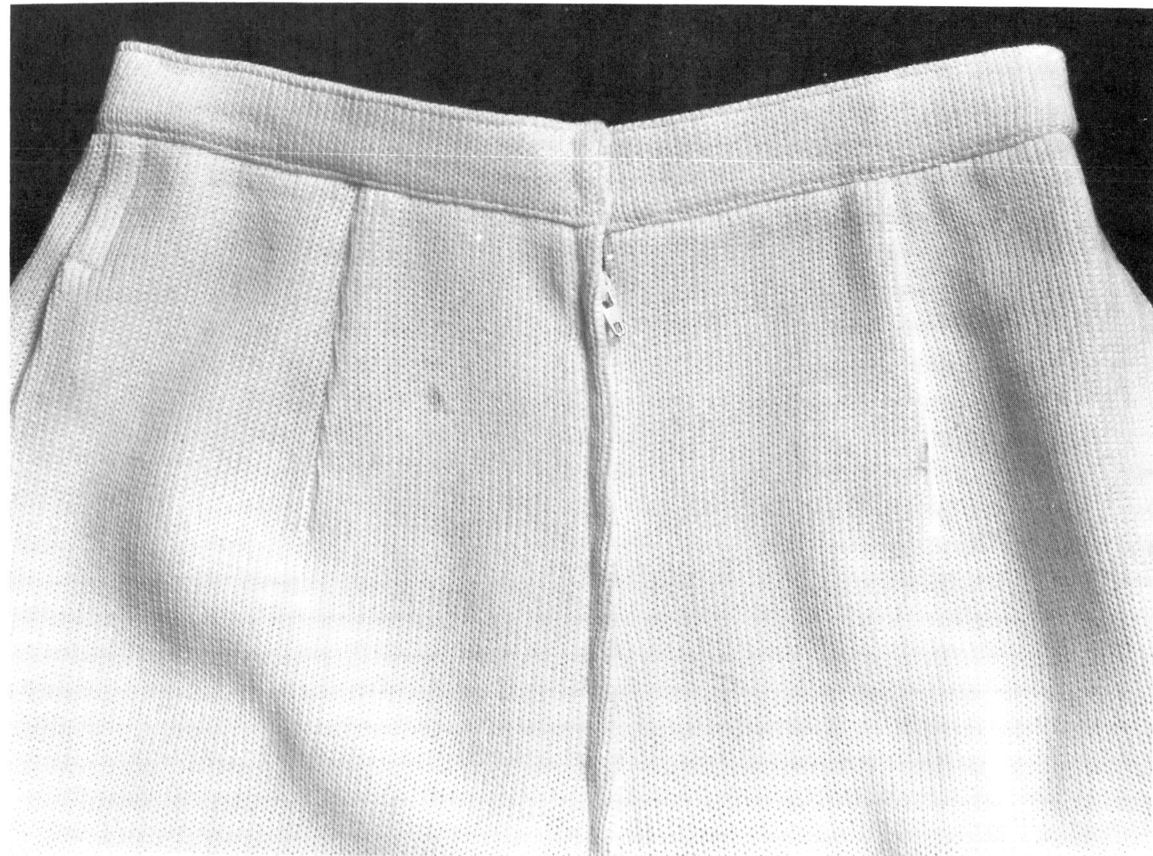

Fig. 69 Zip inserted by 'lapped' method

allowance to the W.S. along a line 3mm ($\frac{1}{8}$in) away from the tack-marked seamline, nearer to the edge of the seam allowance. Press and tack this fold in the seam allowance, *continuing on down to about 2.5cm (1in) below the point where the sewn seam starts.* Take particular care to tack, with small stitches, this 3mm ($\frac{1}{8}$in) wide fold for that last 2.5cm (1in), otherwise you can find that it has disappeared when you need it during the next stage. (If you now lay the front seamline exactly on the back seamline, you will find that you now have a 3mm [$\frac{1}{8}$in] wide underlap.)

4 *Fig. 70d.* Keeping the front of the skirt out of the way, apply the folded edge of the *back* seam allowance to the closed zip, keeping it very close to the zip teeth. Remember to keep a 2.5cm (1in) gap between the slider top and the top raw edges of the skirt. Pin the fabric to the zip tape, placing the pins, as shown, at right angles to the zip. Prick-stitch by hand, from one end of the zip tape to the other, keeping close to the folded edge and the teeth. Follow this with machine-stitching if desired. *All stitching must be completed on this side of the zip before starting on the other side.*

5 *Fig. 70e.* Position the skirt *front* so that it is level with the skirt back at the top end, and so that the folded edge of the seam allowance just covers the line of stitching you made at stage 4. (You should find that you have actually replaced the front and back seamlines exactly together.) Pin the fabric to the zip tape as shown, and prick-stitch as before. This stitching should be near but not directly up against the zip teeth, and should be an even distance from the folded

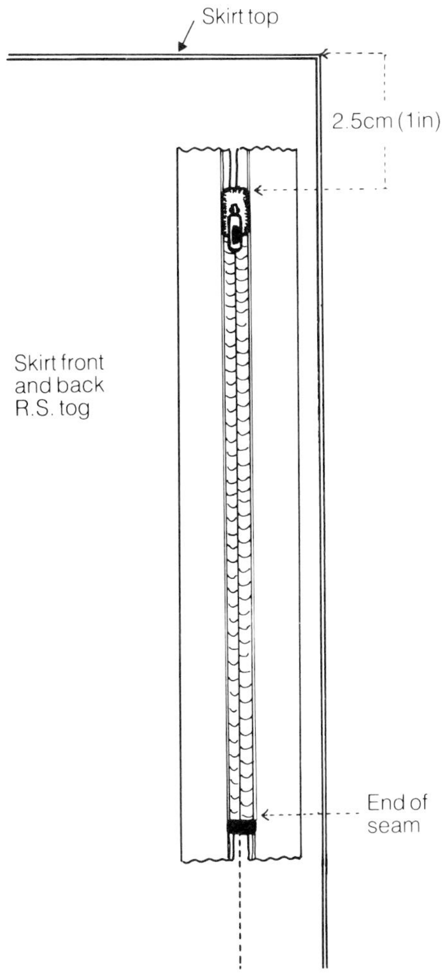

Fig. 70a Determining where seam stitching is to end

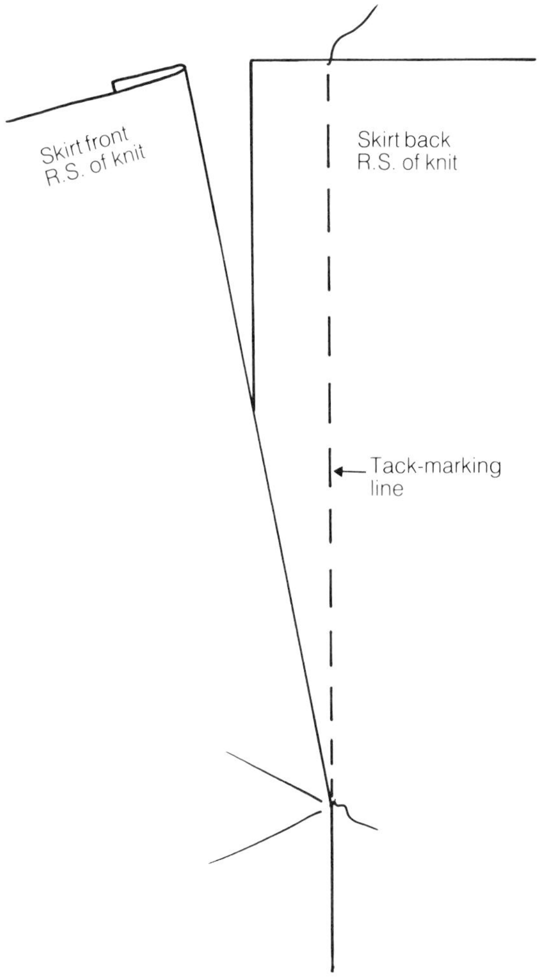

Fig. 70b Front seam allowance turned in; back seamline marked

edge for the entire length of the opening — usually about 1.2cm ($\frac{1}{2}$in) to 1.5cm ($\frac{5}{8}$in). Stitching across the lower end is optional; it sometimes seems to make an unnecessary dent in an otherwise smooth line. Reinforce with machine-stitching if there is likely to be any strain on the seam.

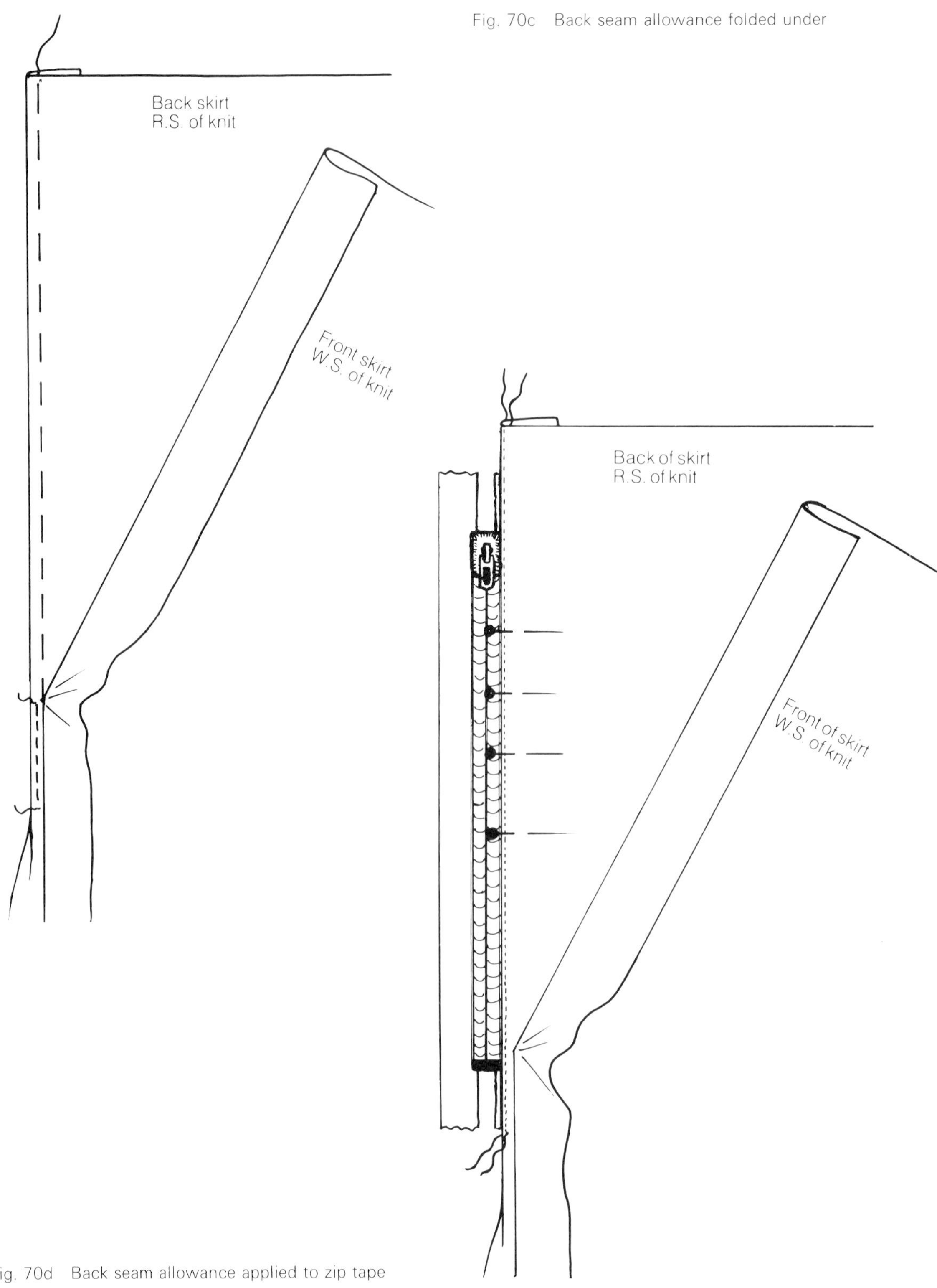

Fig. 70c Back seam allowance folded under

Fig. 70d Back seam allowance applied to zip tape

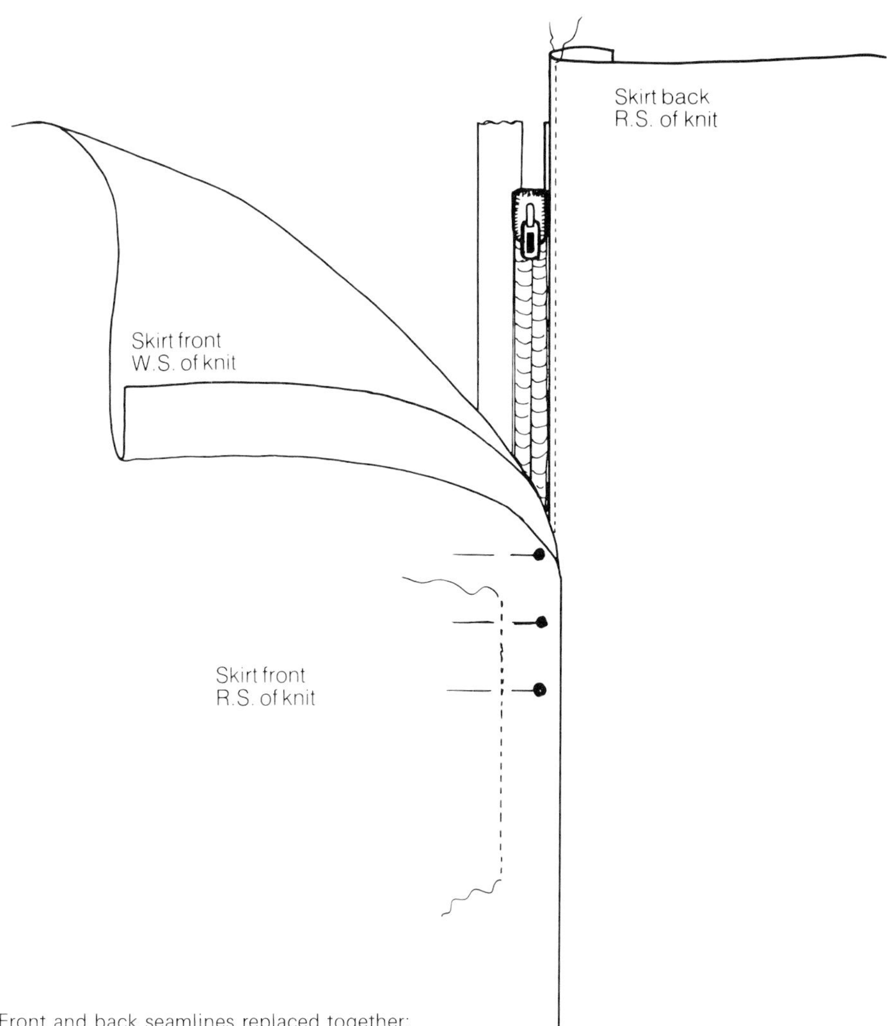

Fig. 70e Front and back seamlines replaced together; front seam allowance applied to zip tape

Visible zip application

In this case the zip teeth are completely exposed to view and can become a decorative feature of the garment. Here are two examples, with directions.

Example 1: a chunky, open-ended zip fastening the front edges of an anorak or bomber-jacket (*Fig. 71*).

1 Press the seam allowance on each side of the opening to the W.S.

2 Lay each half of the front on its appropriate half of the zip, placing the folded seamline close to the teeth. Check that the ends of the opening edges are level at top and bottom when the zip is closed. Place pins at right angles to the seamline to hold the zip in position while stitching.

3 Sew with prick-stitch close to the seamline and follow with machine-stitching to secure it.

Example 2: a zip which closes a neck opening made in a single piece of knitted fabric (*Fig. 72a and b*). In this case, no seam is involved, so the zip has to be set into a slit cut in the fabric; this slit is faced with a piece of fine woven fabric such as pre-shrunk calico, poly/cotton poplin, linen, polyester lining, etc.

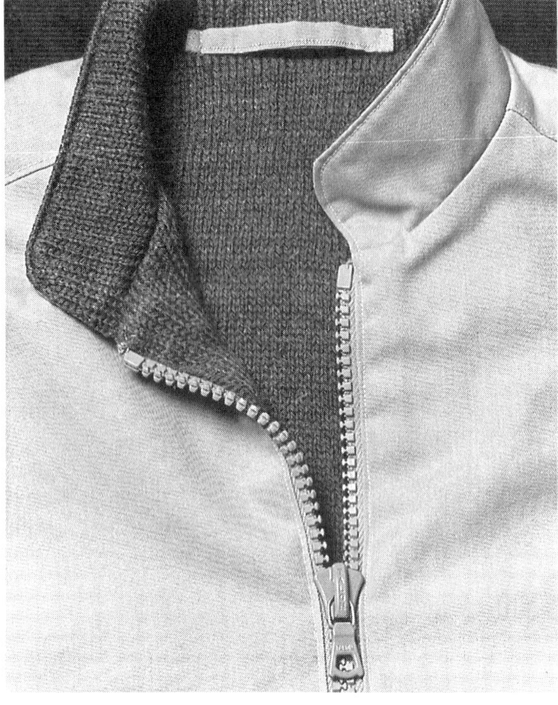

Fig. 71 Chunky zip in knit-lined showerproof anorak

1 Cut the facing, on the straight grain, to the correct size. *Note* 'length' = the length of the zip teeth (do not include the tape extensions) plus 7.5cm (3in); 'width' = the width of the zip teeth plus 10cm (4in).

Oversew, or overlock, three sides of the facing, as shown in Fig. 73a.

2 Draw the line of the proposed opening on the W.S. of the facing piece, exactly down the centre, from the top. To decide the length of the line, place the zip on the facing with the top of the zip slider 1.9cm ($\frac{3}{4}$in) to 2.5cm (1in) down from the top of the facing (the distance depends on the thickness of the knit and what you intend to do at the neck edge). Measure from the top of the facing to the end-stop.

3 Place the facing on the knitted fabric, R.S. tog., with the drawn line exactly positioned where the opening is to be. Pin in position (*Fig. 73a*).

4 Machine-stitch (short stitch length — about 1 on most machines) down one side of the

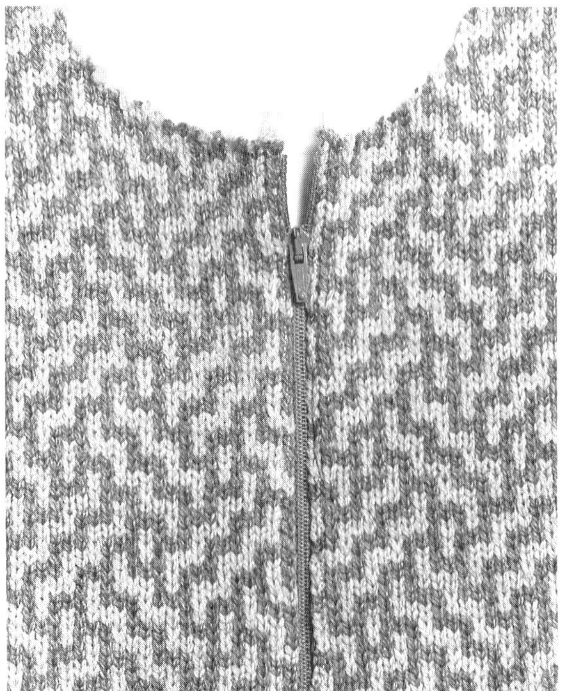

Fig. 72a Zip set into faced neck opening, R.S.

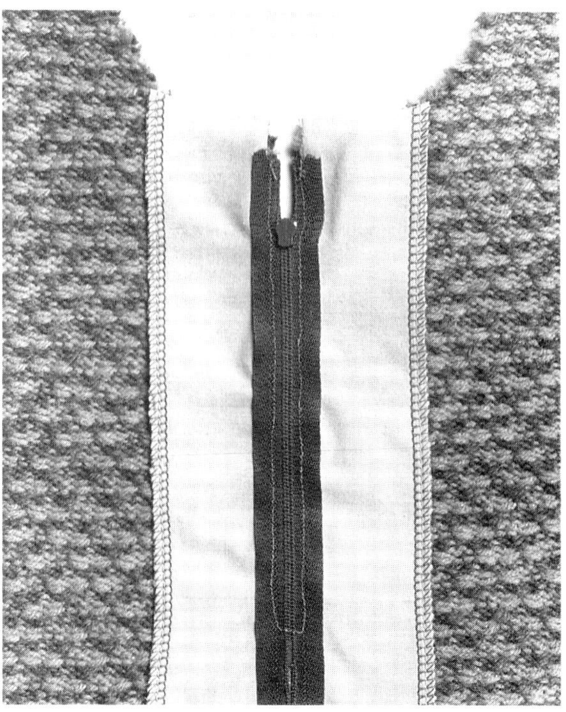

Fig. 72b Zip set into faced neck opening, W.S.

7 Blue coat/dress with shirt

8 *(inset)* Navy top with white shorts
9 Black lace dress

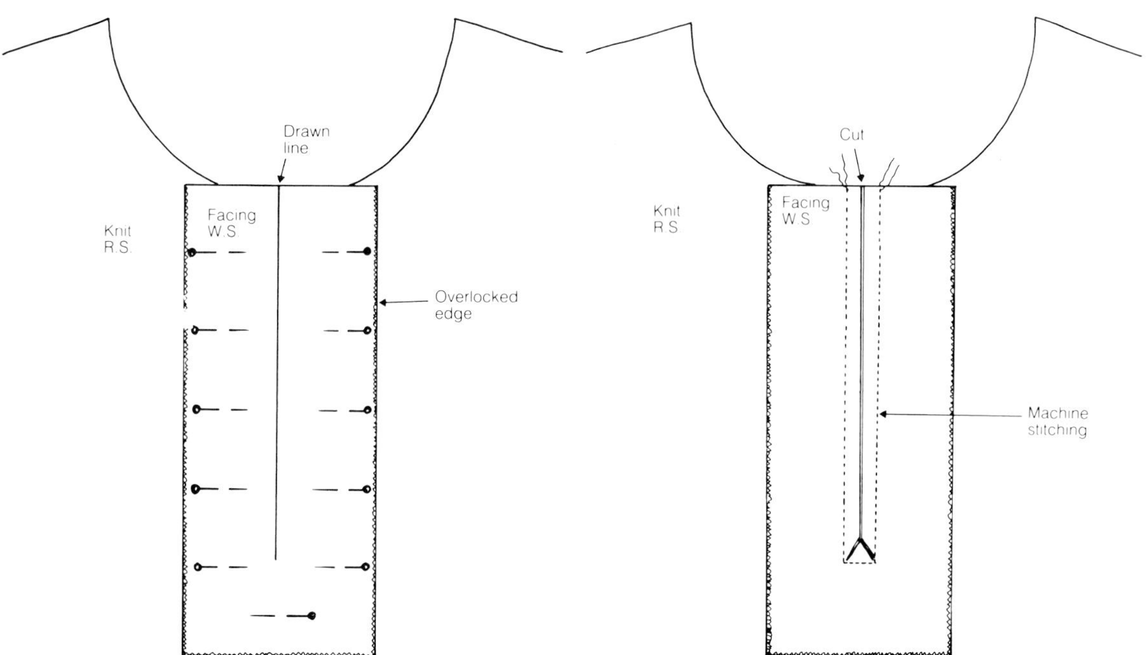

Fig. 73a Facing pinned to R.S. of garment; C.F. line has been marked and three edges overlocked

Fig. 73b Machine-stitching around marked line; cut made down centre and into both corners

drawn line, across the lower end, and up the other side. Keep the lines parallel and make the stitching across the lower end a little wider than the width of the zip teeth (*Fig. 73b*).

5 Cut precisely between the two lines of stitching, from the top to a point about 9mm ($\frac{3}{8}$in) from the lower end; then make a cut diagonally out to each corner (*Fig. 73b*).

Note You have to cut *right up to* the stitching line; if you shirk it you will inevitably have crinkles at the corners when you turn the facing to the W.S.! Providing your machine-stitching is sufficiently small, so that you have sewn all the fibres firmly in place, there should be no danger of fraying when you cut.

6 Turn the facing through to the W.S. of the knit and press the seamlines flat, rolling them slightly to the W.S.

7 Position the slit over the closed zip, keeping the top of the zip slider in its correct position (see stage 2), and the edges of the slit close up to the zip teeth. Pin in position, prick-stitch to hold, and then machine-stitch close to the edges of the slit.

This method can be adapted for making pockets (*p. 53 and Fig. 54*).

▲

Chapter nine

WAISTBANDS

A skirt must not only fit well and be the right length (and this, of course, is a fashion variable) but it must also hang properly if it is to make the figure inside look good.

As far as fitting is concerned, simply remember that any skirt made from knitted fabric must have enough ease in it to ensure that the fabric is not stretched *anywhere*. At machine-knitting conventions, where one sees more than the average number of knitted outfits being worn by their makers, regrettably the effect is too often spoiled by skirts which cling too closely, thereby revealing every curve of tummy and behind.

The main factor in making sure that the skirt hangs properly is correct alignment at the waistline of the body, i.e. the waist seamline on the skirt may need to be moved from its original position somewhere along its circumference to cope with figure peculiarities. No one likes to think that they are a freak, but it is surprising how many of us are not 'normal'! For my own part, I have a sway (hollow) back, which means that I have to move the waist seamline down about 1.9cm ($\frac{3}{4}$in) at the C.B. on every skirt I make. Many of my students have one hip slightly larger than the other; this entails moving the waist seamline down a little above the smaller hip.

Posture comes into this too; people with large tummies tend to lean backwards, whereas those with large posteriors tend to lean forwards. Unfortunately, as we grow older, these variations from the norm become more pronounced; young people, on the whole, have fewer fitting problems. Using a dressmaker's dummy does not solve the problem, simply because the dummy is unlikely to stand precisely the way you do.

Incidentally, I have often heard people say that they can wear a particular skirt (especially knitted ones) 'any way round – back-to-front, sideways, as it comes'; this may be acceptable in a casual and rather full skirt but simply is not possible in a skirt which is meant to fit.

So here is a simple programme to follow which should enable you to produce perfectly fitting skirts every time.

Note These instructions apply to fitted skirts which have an opening somewhere around the top to enable them to be slipped over the hips.

1 After the skirt pieces have been cut and the edges overlocked or oversewn in some way, any darts and all seams should be machine-tacked (or hand-tacked), leaving an opening where the zip will be. If there is no seamline at C.F. or C.B., mark these lines with a tacking thread. Do not, at this stage, sew up the lining.

2 Try on the skirt. Pin the seamlines of the opening exactly together. If your choice of pattern size was correct and you carried out any necessary adjustments to the paper pattern before cutting out, the skirt should now be fitting reasonably well. If, however, it seems obviously too big, calculate how much circumference needs to be removed, divide this amount between the number of seams and take in the skirt accordingly. If the skirt is obviously too tight, let the seams out the necessary amount, but remember that you should still retain at least 1.5cm ($\frac{5}{8}$in) seam allowance on the seam where the zip will be so that you can sew it in correctly. If the zip is on a side seam, both side seams must be at least 1.5cm ($\frac{5}{8}$in) wide, or the C.F. and C.B. points will be out of place.

3 If (or when) the fitting is reasonably good, tie a length of narrow tape firmly around the waist, fastening the ends in a bow exactly over the opening where the zip will be. Pull 1.5cm ($\frac{5}{8}$in) of the skirt up under the tape so that the tape lies exactly on the present waist seamline.

Note The tape has probably gathered the skirt fabric in a little. This is as it should be: the skirt top should be up to 4cm ($1\frac{1}{2}$in) bigger than your precise waist measurement, so that eventually it will be *eased* into the waistband rather than fitting in flat.

4 Stand in front of a long mirror and look at the seamlines and at the C.F. and C.B. lines. (To look at the C.B. line, stand with your back to the long mirror and hold a hand mirror up in front of you so that you can see the back view; do not lift your arm so much, though, that the skirt starts to lift too.) If any line or seam is hanging sideways to any degree, pull the skirt up under the tape, in the opposite direction, until the line does hang straight, at right angles to the floor. For example, if the C.F. line is leaning towards the left knee (*Fig. 74a*), the skirt will have to be lifted at the top right front to compensate (*Fig. 74b*). A large behind will probably cause the lower ends of the side seams to tilt towards the back, so the skirt top will have to be lifted at the C.F. to compensate.

Lift the skirt under the tape if and where necessary until all the lines are hanging straight.

5 Pin the tape to the skirt all round, placing the pins parallel with the tape along its centre. Doing this for yourself can be tricky; try to get someone to help, at least with the back. If there really is no help available, you will have to manage simply by feeling and by checking in a hand mirror.

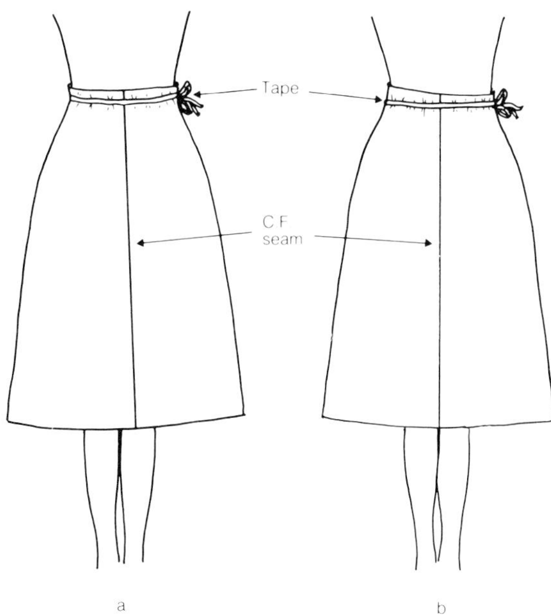

Fig. 74a C.F. line leaning towards left knee

Fig. 74b Lifting skirt over right side straightens C.F. line

6 Untie the tape and take off the skirt.

7 Trim off any surplus seam allowance, leaving precisely 1.5cm ($\frac{5}{8}$in) all round above the centre of the tape.

Note If you pin the piece you have removed, R.S. up, on to a strip of paper, and label it at the appropriate points (e.g. 'C.B.' or 'left side'), you will have a permanent record, or pattern, of the area you need to remove from every skirt you make from now onwards.

8 Make up the skirt lining, incorporating whatever alterations you made to the skirt. If you had to trim surplus fabric from the top edge of the skirt, trim exactly the same amount of fabric from the top edge of the skirt lining — but remember that the skirt lining will be worn inside out (i.e. the W.S. of the lining will face the W.S. of the skirt).

Now that your skirt is fitting correctly, put the zip in (*Chapter 8*). If you did it before marking the waist seamline, you could find that it is now too high up in the seam and will have to be unpicked and re-inserted — not to be recommended with knitted fabric.

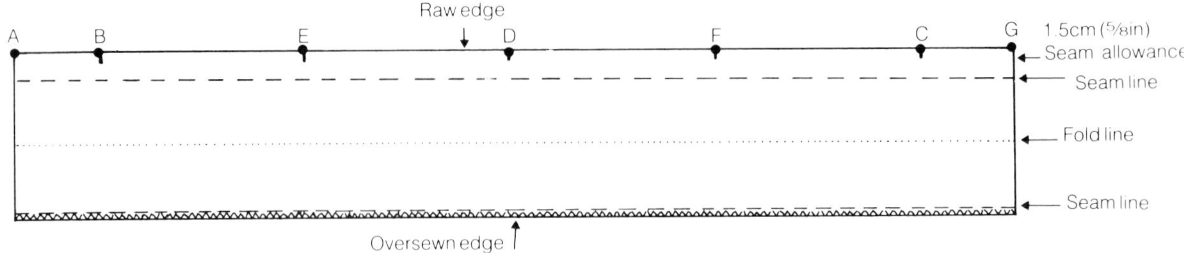

Fig. 75 Preparing the waistband

Tack the lining to the skirt, W.S. tog., all around the top. Where the darts on the skirt are pressed towards the centre, press the corresponding darts on the lining towards the sides; this avoids too much bulk at any one point.

Hem the lining to the *outer edge* of the zip tape, down both sides of the zip. If you take it too close to the zip teeth it will inevitably get caught in next time you are dressing in a hurry!

Applying a waistband

Note If your waist measurement is not exactly the same as the standard measurement for your pattern size, the paper pattern for the waistband will be wrong. It is safer to abandon it and follow the next set of guidelines.

1 Cut your waistband, using a strip cut straight *across* the knit. The knit used for the skirt will be suitable providing it is not too thick or highly textured. If necessary, knit a separate strip for the waistband using a less bulky yarn and/or a flatter stitch pattern such as stocking-stitch. If the skirt happens to be part of an outfit where the collar, facings, etc. have been cut from woven fabric, you could possibly cut the waistband from this same woven fabric.

Note 'length' = your waist measurement + 10cm (4in); 'width' = twice the intended depth of the waistband + 2.2cm ($\frac{7}{8}$in).

2 Interface the waistband strip, using either a fusible or a sew-in interfacing, to make it firmer and to reduce (or to eliminate) the stretch factor. What interfacing you use depends on whether or not you want the finished waistband to have a little 'give' or to be rigid. Here are some examples.

Fusible knitted nylon, cut lengthwise and covering the entire W.S. of the band; only suitable for narrow waistbands because it would lack the necessary firmness to stop it rolling; top-stitching would be needed as stretching could cause the two fabrics to separate.

Fusible cotton muslin, covering the entire W.S. of the band; eliminates stretch but is also not very firm.

Vilene Fold-a-Band, medium or heavy-weight; fusible, non-stretch and firm; centre the central line of slits along the foldline of the waistband; needs top-stitching to ensure that the knit adheres to it permanently.

Belt petersham, sewn-in; eliminates stretch and is also firm.

Loom elastic, tacked in; when waistband is completed, tacking stitches are removed; firm, non-roll and allows waistband to 'give' whilst retaining its grip.

3 *Fig. 75.* Overlock or over-edge stitch one long edge of the waistband. Mark off the other edge of the waistband as follows, using pins or pencil marks:

A–B is the underlap: about 6.5cm ($2\frac{1}{2}$in).
B–C should be your precise waist measurement, but allow about 1.2cm ($\frac{1}{2}$in) more for the thickness of the knit.
D is exactly halfway between B and C.
E is exactly halfway between B and D.
F is exactly halfway between D and C.
C–G is left for an overlap if required — or for letting out if you have miscalculated.

4 *Fig. 76.* Mark off the top of the skirt precisely in quarters as shown, using pins or pencil marks. Do not assume that these quarter marks will be exactly where seams occur: they might not be.

5 Place the waistband on the top of the skirt, R.S. tog., lining up the raw edges. Match and pin together the points B, C, D, E and F. Pin all around the top of the skirt, using plenty of pins and placing them across the seamline as shown in Fig. 77a. Ease the skirt in to fit the waistband.

6 *Fig. 77a.* Machine-tack along the waist seamline. Try on the skirt to check the fitting; if satisfactory, machine-stitch over the waist seamline again to secure.

7 *Fig. 77b.* Turn the waistband over to the inside of the skirt so that the oversewn edge overlaps the machined seamline by 3mm ($\frac{1}{8}$in). Pin in place temporarily.

8 Hand finish the *over* lapping end of the waistband by turning in the end and hemming in position (*Fig. 78a*). If no overlap is required, trim off the waistband so that, after hand-finishing, the end of the waistband will line up with the seamline over the zip (*Fig. 78b*). The *under*lapping end should not be turned in; simply oversew the raw edges together (*Fig. 78c*).

9 *Fig. 79a.* From the R.S., place pins as shown, so that the inside edge of the waistband is held in place. Remove any pins left on the inside of the skirt. Still on the R.S., *either* machine-stitch exactly in the seamline (*Fig. 79a*) (which is called 'stitch-in-the-ditch'), *or* top-stitch on the edge of the waistband (*Fig. 79b*). Whichever way you do it, the stitching should secure the inside edge of the waistband so that it overlaps the stage 6 stitching-line by 3mm ($\frac{1}{8}$in).

10 Apply a heavy duty hook to the underlap and a matching bar to the appropriate place on the underside of the waistband. This takes the strain of the fastening. The overlapping end can then be fastened with small invisible hooks and bars.

Alternative methods

Many women find the conventional stiffened waistband uncomfortable; here are some suggestions for alternative ways of finishing the tops of fitted skirts.

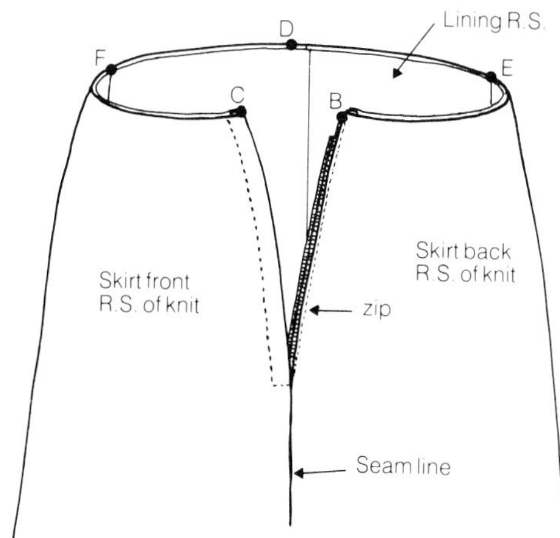

Fig. 76 Marking top of skirt in quarters

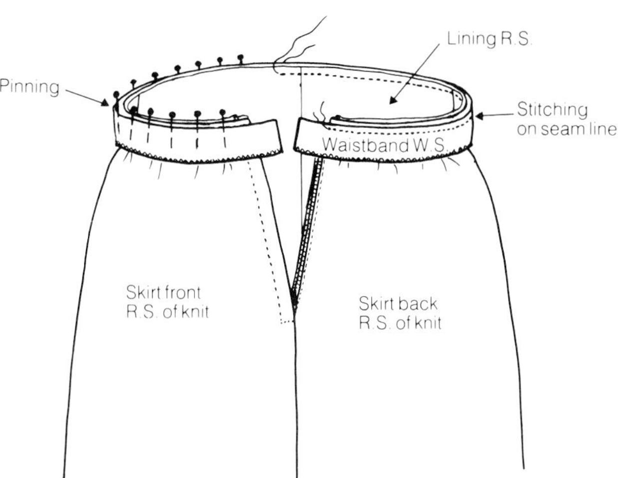

Fig. 77a Pinning and matching waistband to skirt top

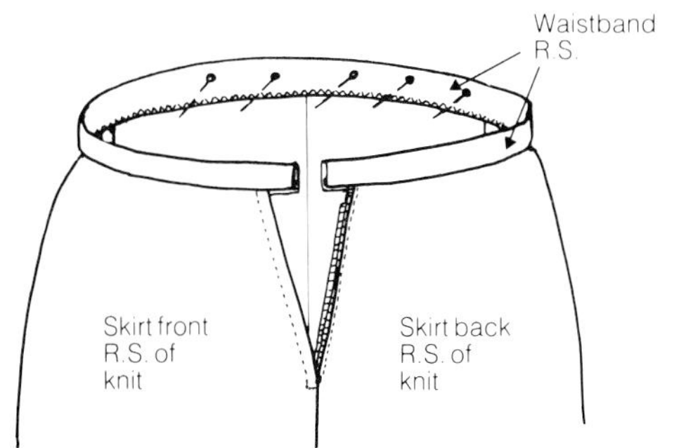

Fig. 77b Waistband folded to W.S. and pinned

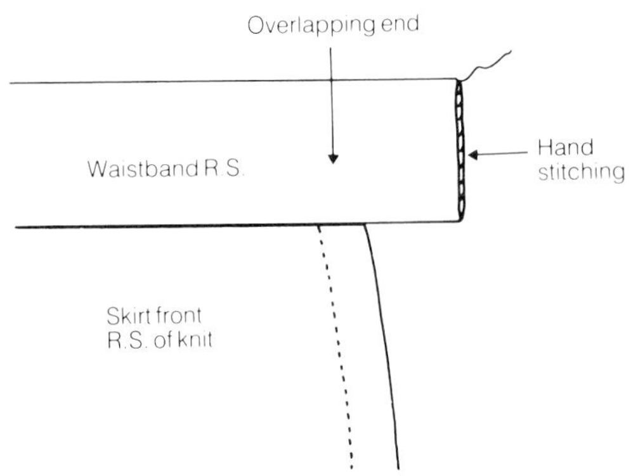

Fig. 78a Finishing overlapping end with extension

Curved petersham

After stitching the lining inside the skirt, place the inner edge of the curve of the petersham so that it overlaps the top edge of the skirt by 1.2cm ($\frac{1}{2}$in); the W.S. of the petersham faces the R.S. of the skirt. Pin and then machine-stitch parallel with, and 3mm ($\frac{1}{8}$in) from, the edge of the petersham (*Fig. 80*). Turn the band down to the W.S. of the skirt. Stitch-in-the-ditch down all seamlines and darts, through all thicknesses, to hold the band in position. Do not top-stitch around the skirt top.

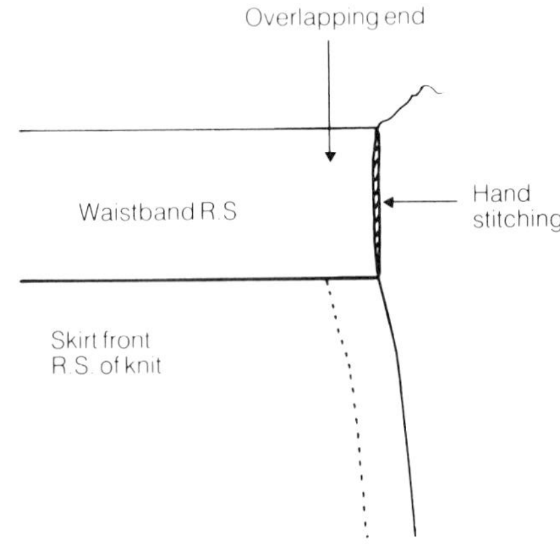

Fig. 78b Finishing overlapping end without extension

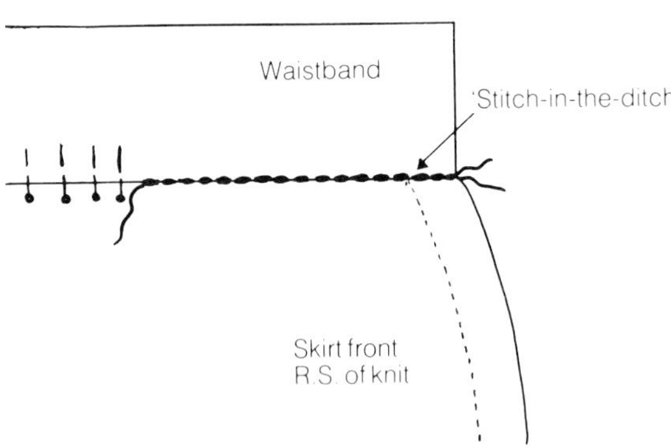

Fig. 79a Securing waistband by stitching in the seamline

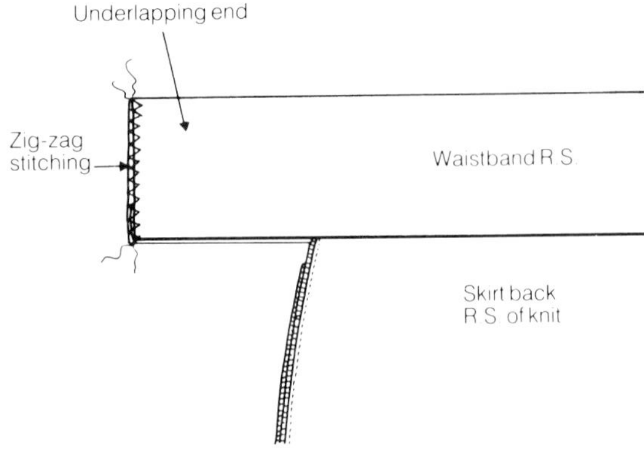

Fig. 78c Finishing underlapping end

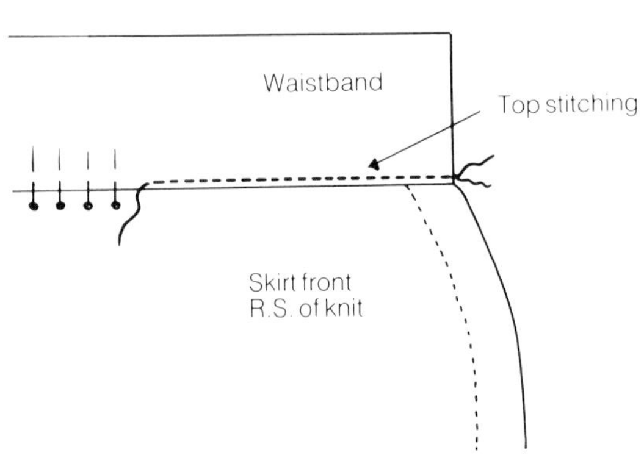

Fig. 79b Securing waistband by top-stitching

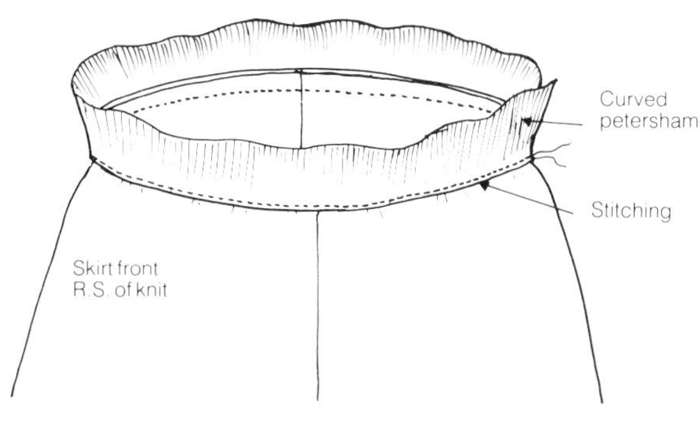

Fig. 80 Applying curved petersham to waist seamline

Loom elastic enclosed in a casing (*Fig. 81*)
Wrap a strip of the knit around the elastic, R.S. out, and machine-stitch the raw edges together, close to the edge of the elastic, using a zipper foot (*Fig. 82a*). Trim the seam allowances to 1.5cm ($\frac{5}{8}$in). Before stitching the lining inside the skirt, apply this band to the R.S. of the skirt top (*Fig. 82b*), lining up the raw edges. Machine-tack the band to the skirt, following the previous stitching-line. Place the lining on the R.S. of the skirt, R.S. tog., lining up the top raw edges; machine-stitch through all thicknesses. Turn the lining over to the W.S. This makes a neat and

Fig. 81 Skirt waistband enclosing loom elastic

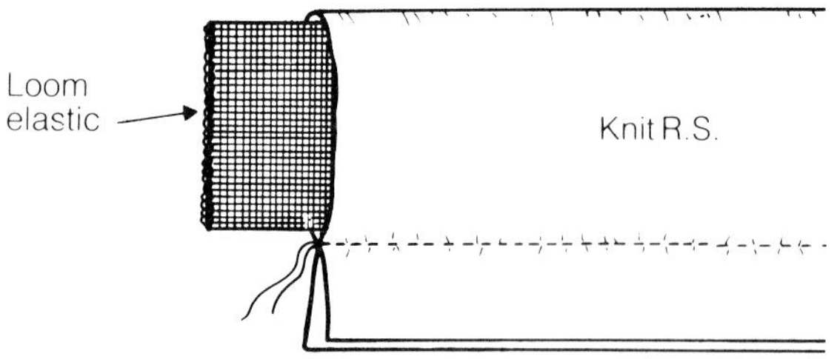

Fig. 82a Enclosing loom elastic in strip of knitted fabric

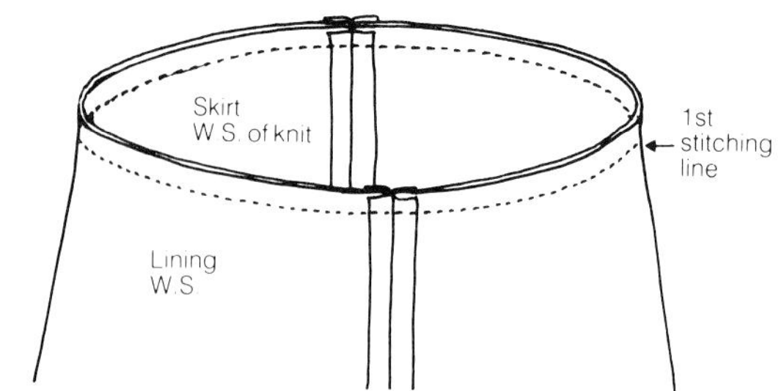

Fig. 83a Applying lining to skirt with no opening

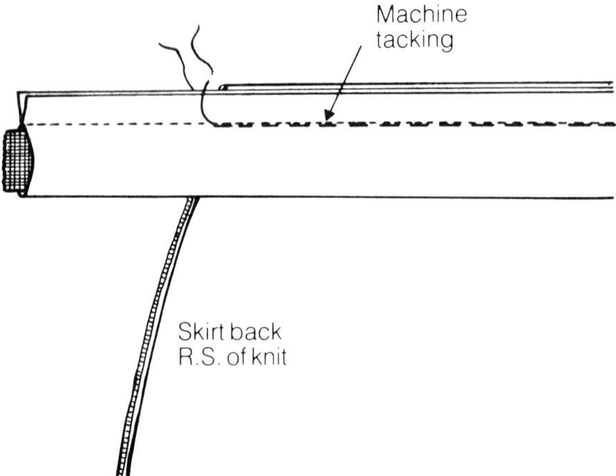

Fig. 82b Applying covered elastic to skirt top

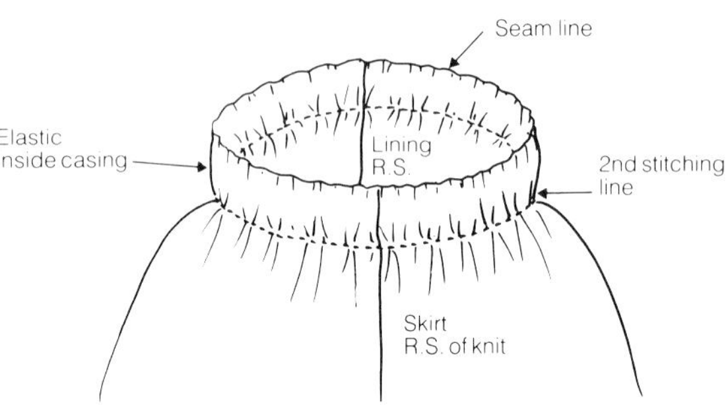

Fig. 83b Enclosing elastic between stitching lines

comfortable waistband which conveniently expands with the waistline!

Bias or straight binding

Enclose the skirt top in a narrow binding (*Chapter 10*) made from any fine woven fabric which matches or tones in with the knit. This makes a comfortable finish for the skirt top, which is acceptable providing it will always be covered by a shirt or jumper.

No waistband

Sew the lining to the skirt, R.S. tog. all around the waist seamline; it may be necessary to add tape to the seamline to prevent it stretching out of shape. Turn the lining down to the W.S. and understitch it to the seam allowances, 3mm ($\frac{1}{8}$in) from the seamline. There will be no underlap in this case, so a small hook and eye will have to be sewn just above the top end of the zip. This works well on short-waisted figures but, like the previous method, really needs to be covered by a shirt or jumper.

Skirts without openings

It is perfectly possible to make 'pull-on' skirts which have no opening at all but, of course, both the waistband and the top of the skirt must be cut large enough to slide over the hips. The waistband must then contain elastic to contract it sufficiently to fit the waist. This is perfectly feasible as long as the knit is not bulky. Use loom elastic, about 2.5cm (1in) wide, enclosed in a casing, as described on p. 79, or use narrow elastic in several parallel casings.

Alternatively, at the cutting stage, allow 4.5cm ($1\frac{3}{4}$in) extra fabric above the waist seamline, at the top of both the skirt and the lining; when the skirt and the lining are each made up, stitch them, R.S. tog., 1.5cm ($\frac{5}{8}$in) from the top raw edges (*Fig. 83a*). Turn the lining over and down on the W.S., and press the seamline. Slip the elastic between the two fabrics and, using a zipper foot, make another line of stitching close to the edge of the elastic (*Fig. 83b*).

If the skirt is to have no lining, allow an extra 6.3cm ($2\frac{1}{2}$in) of fabric above the waist seamline when cutting out. When the skirt is made up, turn 3.5cm ($1\frac{3}{8}$in) to the W.S. and stitch to enclose the elastic.

Full skirts can be gathered onto a waistband which is just large enough to slide over the hips, and which is then nipped in with elastic to fit the waist. In this case, the knit needs to be fine and soft, if the skirt is not to be too bulky.

Chapter ten

BINDINGS

Binding is an effective way of neatening and stabilising the cut edges of the knitted fabric (where these form the edges of a garment) by enclosing it in a strip of toning or contrasting fabric. Several types of binding can be employed.

You will find some illustrations of binding on pp. 95–97 of *Cut and Sew: Working with Machine-Knitted Fabrics,* and there are several more examples in this volume.

The top part of the grey two-piece shown in colour picture 6, has its softly draped collar very narrowly bound with the same polyester lining fabric that has been used as a mounting fabric for the lace knit. A close-up of this is shown in Fig. 84.

The blue vest-top shown on the back jacket has its neck and armholes bound with jade green polyester cotton to match the piped edges of the skirt pockets. A close-up of this is shown in Fig. 85.

The black lace-knit dress in colour picture 9 has a binding of bias-cut black satin around the neck and armholes.

It seemed appropriate, in this book, to enlarge on the technique, simply because it is such a useful one.

Binding with woven fabric cut on the bias

Use striped cotton or checked gingham as binding fabric, when experimenting with this process, especially if you have never done it before; the straight lines are helpful.

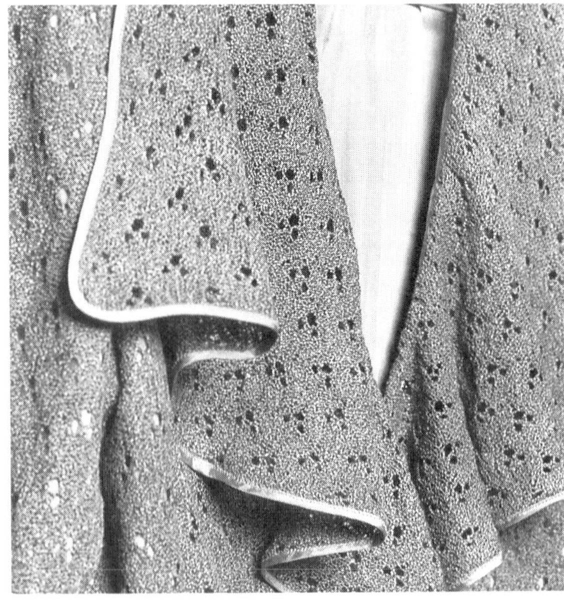

Fig. 84 Edge of draped collar bound with bias-cut polyester lining fabric (detail from colour picture 6)

Work out how much length of binding you will require and then cut one or more strips which, when joined, will produce this length.

It is possible, of course, to buy ready-made bias-binding but the process of making your own is fairly simple, and the extra effort involved is offset by having the binding made in the fabric, colour and width you personally choose.

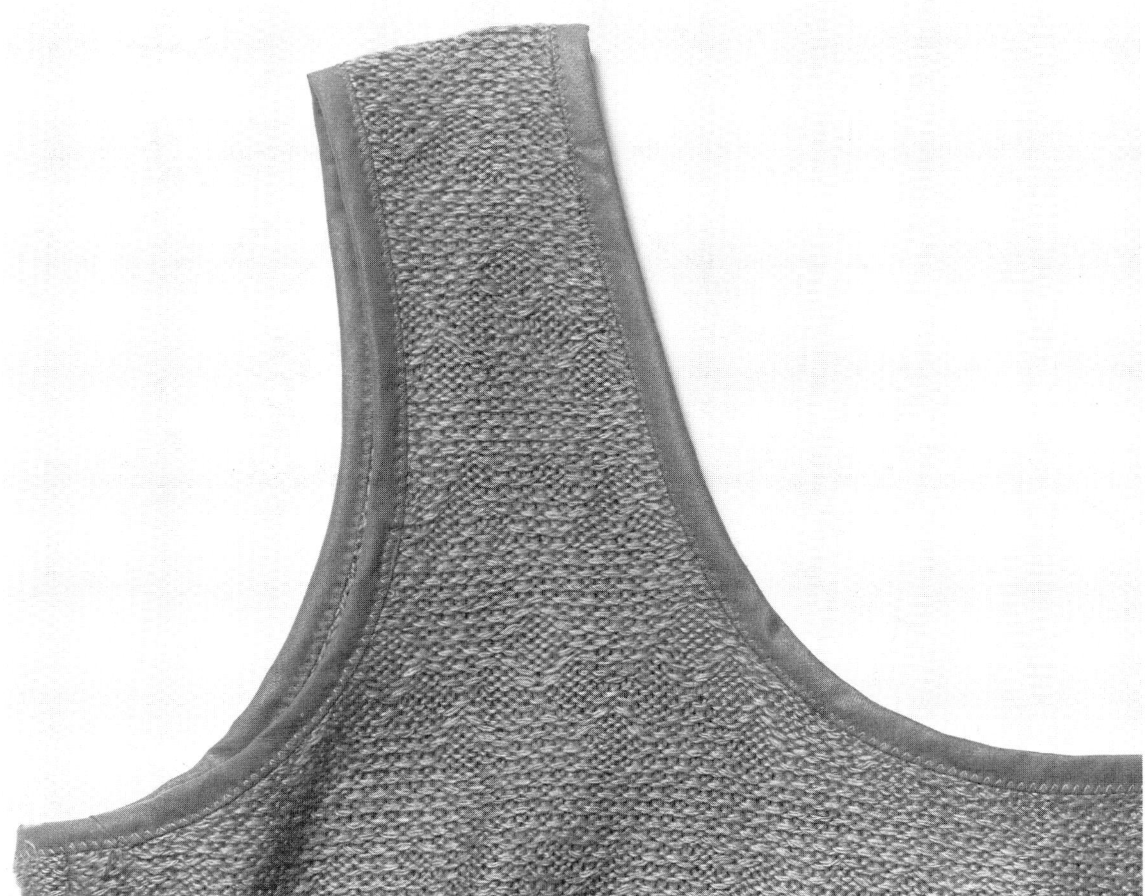

Fig. 85 Edge of pullover vest top, bound with bias-cut poly/cotton poplin (detail from back jacket)

To make the binding

1 *Fig. 86a.* Take a piece of the woven fabric, at least 30cm (12in) in length and preferably using the full width, from selvedge to selvedge. The larger the piece, the fewer the joins you will have to make (however, it is possible, by making more joins, to produce an amazingly long strip of binding from very small pieces). The cut edges of the piece should be straight with the grain of the fabric, so that a weft thread can be pulled off cleanly.

2 *Fig. 86b.* Fold the fabric so that part of the cut edge A–B lies parallel with the selvedge A–D, and the selvedge B–C is lying straight with the cut edge D–C. This sounds complicated but is really very simple. If your folding has been sufficiently exact, the foldline will be on the true bias. It *is* important to be exact because you will inevitably get crinkling in the binding if your bias-cutting is not 'true'.

3 *Fig. 86c.* Cut along the foldline and then along parallel lines, approximately 3.5cm ($1\frac{1}{2}$in) apart (possibly wider for thicker knits and fabrics) until you calculate that sufficient length will be produced when the strips are joined together.

4 Check that the ends of all the strips are actually straight with the grain. Trim them so if necessary.

5 *Fig. 86d.* Join the strips, using a 6mm ($\frac{1}{4}$in) machined seam with the stitch length set fairly small. Match the seamlines, not the cut edges. Pieces to be joined may be put under the machine foot in a continuous line, saving both thread and time (*Fig. 86e*).

6 *Fig. 86f.* Press the seams open and trim off the projecting corners.

Your binding is now ready for use.

Note If you wish the seam allowances to be pressed in, Neweys make a metal gadget which enables you to do this with amazing ease and accuracy. You simply pull the bias strip through a shaped slot, pressing with a steam iron as you go. It is available in two sizes.

To apply the binding

Note Binding is best started at some point where it is least likely to be obvious. For example, on a jacket which is to be bound all round the edge, start at the C.B. of the neck; on the lower edge of a sleeve, start at the underarm seam. Turn the diagonal end of the binding strip 1cm ($\frac{3}{8}$in) to the W.S. when commencing (*Fig. 87a*). When the circuit is completed, overlap this by 1cm ($\frac{3}{8}$in) as you finish and cut off the surplus binding on the same angle. The join is then diagonal and matches the other joins in the binding.

1 *Fig. 87a.* Place the R.S. of the bias strip to the W.S. of the knitted fabric keeping the edges level. Do this on a table, keeping the work flat. Pin in position, placing the pins *across* the seamline, i.e. at right angles to it, not parallel with it.

Take care to keep the two fabrics flat; do not stretch (or contract) either the knit or the bias strip except when a curved edge is being bound; the rule then is to *stretch* the bias strip on concave curves (such as necklines) and to *ease* the bias strip on convex curves (such as a rounded collar edge). The degree of stretching or easing depends on the degree of the curve; if you are new to this process it would be wise to do a practice piece first.

Note Angled corners will need to be mitred. You may find it easier to round-off corners on your garment before applying the binding.

2 Machine-stitch, keeping the needle 9mm ($\frac{3}{8}$in) from the edges of the two fabrics and using straight-stitch set fairly small. Remove each pin in turn just as it starts to go under the presser foot of the machine.

3 *Fig. 87b.* Turn the bias strip over to the R.S. of the knitted fabric, fold in the raw edge and pin it down (pins at right angles to the binding, not parallel with it) so that the edge of the binding just covers the machine-stitching line. Use plenty of pins: one every inch, at least, around curves. Take care not to pull the binding sideways so that it develops a crinkle. A kind of sensitivity is necessary here — let the binding lie the way it wants to! Again, use plenty of pins.

4 Machine-stitch, using either small straight-stitch very close to the folded edge of the binding, or a small, medium-width zigzag which travels on and off the folded edge.

Note If you have problems with this, try machine stitching the binding to the R.S. of the garment first and then hand hem the folded edge onto the machined line (on the W.S. of the garment) as neatly and invisibly as possible.

Binding with woven fabric cut on the straight grain

Fig. 88. This type of binding is useful for pocket tops, bands which will button-up, waistbands, etc., but remember that it is not really suitable for curved edges such as necklines or armholes unless you are expert at the tiny pleating involved.

To make the binding

1 Cut strips, straight with the grain, to the required width, i.e. twice the finished width of binding plus two seam allowances.

2 Join where necessary to produce the required length, using diagonal (bias-cut) seams.

3 Press the seams open flat and trim off any projecting corners.

To apply the binding

Use the same method as for bias-cut strips of woven fabric (*pp. 84–5*).

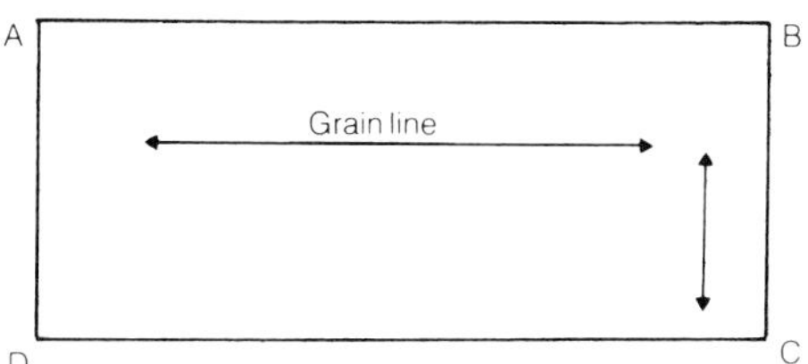

Fig. 86a Fabric piece for bias binding

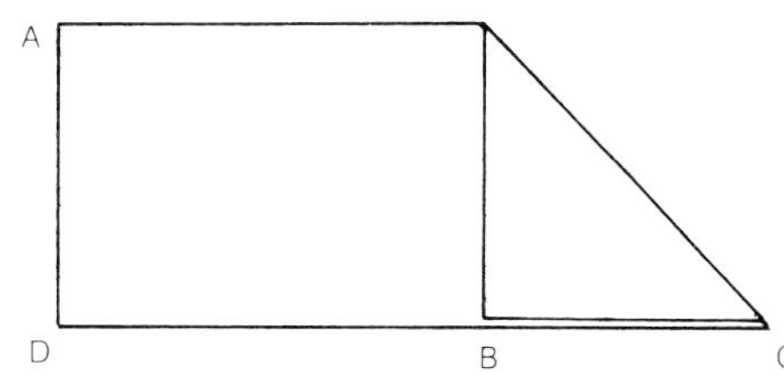

Fig. 86b Finding true bias fold

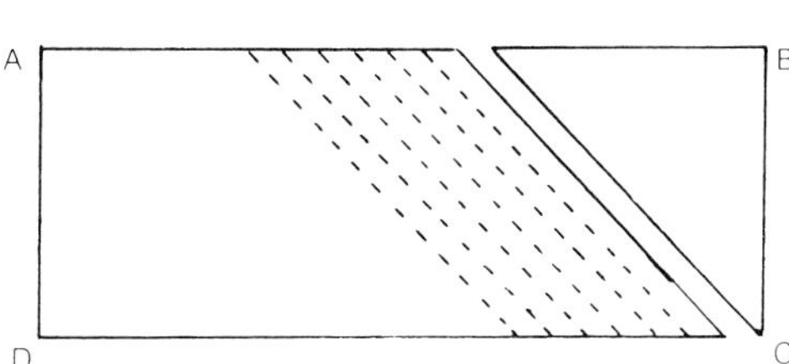

Fig. 86c Cutting bias strips

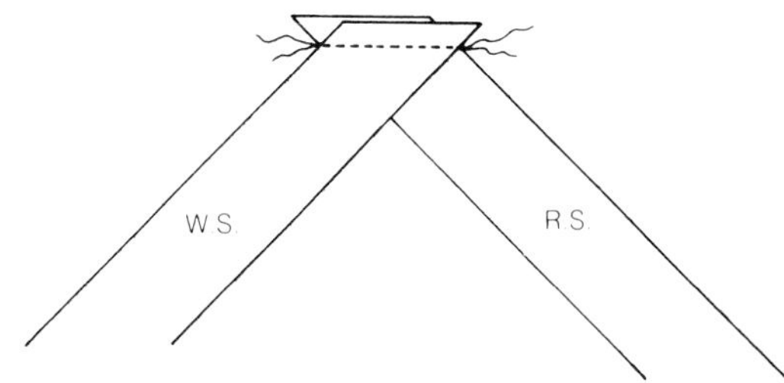

Fig. 86d Joining strips

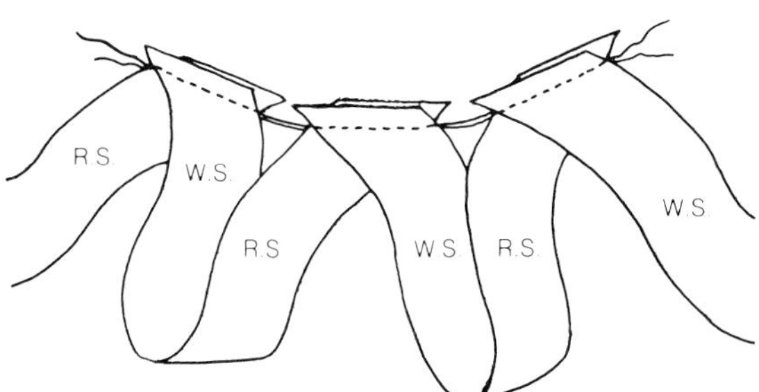

Fig. 86e Continuous joining of strips

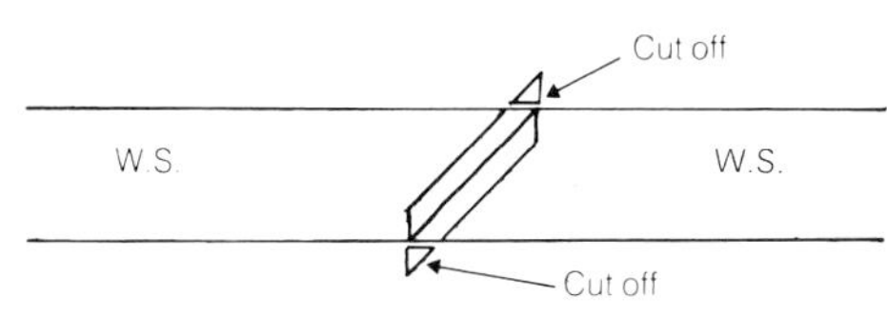

Fig. 86f Pressing seams and trimming

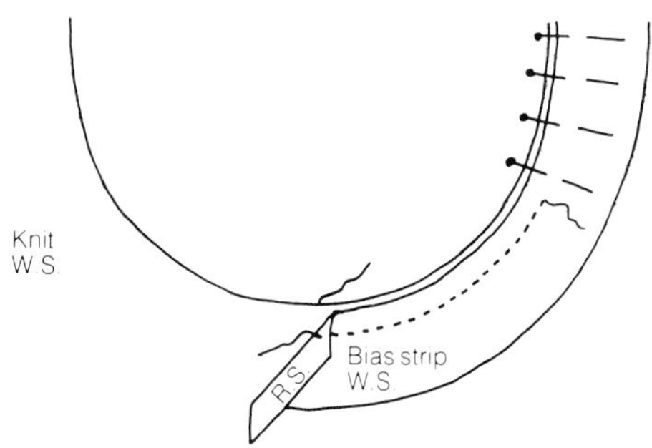

Fig. 87a Applying bias binding to garment edge

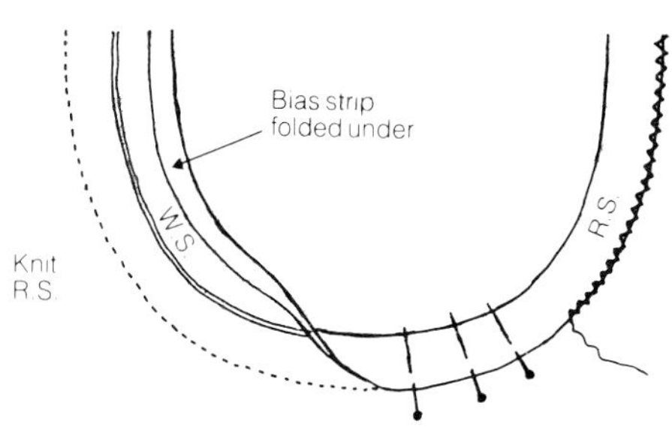

Fig. 87b Folding and stitching to R.S.

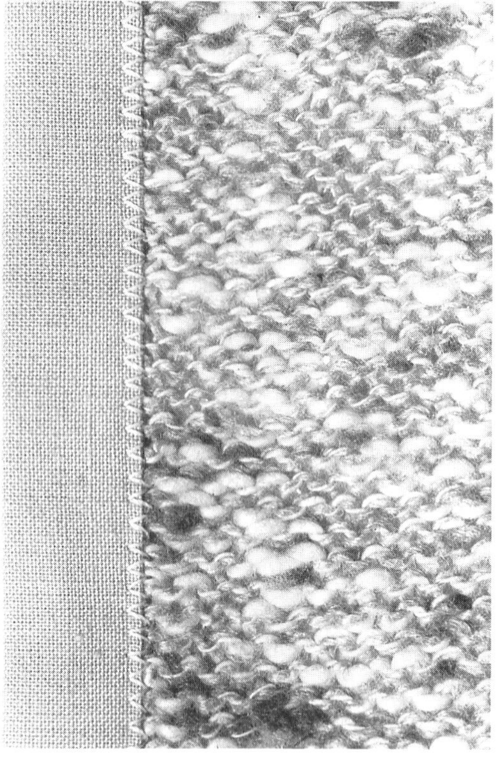

Binding with strip cut from machine-knitted fabric, on the bias

Fig. 89. Bias-cut strips for binding can be cut from the main length of knitted fabric in the same way as the garment pieces are cut. As the binding needs to be fairly firm and close in texture, avoid using lace-knits for this purpose.

To make the binding

Use the same method for cutting and joining as for bias-cut strips of woven fabric (*pp. 82–4*).

Interface if necessary, taking care to retain the stretch factor by using either fusible knitted-nylon or Vilene Superstretch; both of these should be cut straight across their width in order to make the most of their stretch quality.

To apply the binding

Use the same method of application as for woven bias binding (*pp. 83–5*).

Fig. 88 Knit bound with woven fabric cut on straight grain

Fig. 89 Knit bound with knitted fabric cut on bias grain

Fig. 90 Knit bound with knitted fabric cut on straight grain

Binding with strip cut from machine-knitted fabric, on the straight grain

Fig. 90. Straight-grain strips for binding can also be cut from the main length of knitted fabric in the same way as the garment pieces are cut. They can be cut lengthwise or across the width but great care must be taken to ensure that the strips are straight with the grain of the knitting. Remember that strips cut *across* the knitting will have more stretch than strips cut in a lengthwise direction.

Do not attempt this method with lace or rib knits because, again, the binding fabric needs to be firm and close in texture.

Interface the binding strip if necessary, retaining its stretch quality if you are binding curved edges.

Use the same method for cutting, joining and applying, as for bias-cut woven binding (*pp. 83–5*).

Binding with machine-knitted binding

To make the binding

This can be made on your own knitting machine, precisely to the correct width required, so that there is no need to turn in the edges; it can be knitted either straight or on the bias. Use a yarn which is perhaps finer than that used for the main fabric of the garment and keep the tension as tight as possible to give a firm texture. If necessary, interface the binding with a fusible interfacing, but remember that, if the binding is to fit around curves, it must retain its stretch quality, so the interfacing must stretch also.

To apply the binding

1 Press the strip exactly in half lengthwise, keeping the edges precisely together.

2 *Fig. 91.* Pin the strip to the main fabric so that the cut edge of the garment meets the inside of the crease in the binding. Use plenty of pins (at least one per 2.5cm [1in]) placed at right angles to the edge. Keep the work flat on the table whilst doing this and check that you are neither stretching nor contracting the binding too much.

3 Hand-stitch in place with a matching thread,

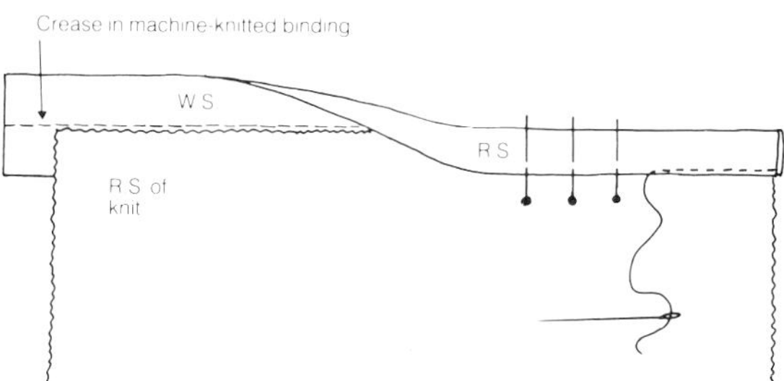

Fig. 91 Knit bound with machine-knitted binding

working on the R.S and using a half back-stitch close to the edges of the binding. Check that you are catching in the edge of the binding on the W.S.

4 Finish by machine-stitching close to the edge of the binding, using a fairly short stitch length in either straight or zigzag formation.

Note If the strip has not been knitted precisely to the correct length (and this is sometimes impossible to estimate exactly) the end will have to be cut. Here a problem arises in that, when this cut end is turned in for finishing, it promptly becomes wider than the rest of the binding. To solve this, thread a needle with matching thread and run it through one row of knitted stitches, across the width of the binding, about 1.25cm ($\frac{1}{2}$in) from the cut end (*Fig. 92*). This thread should be fastened securely at the beginning, pulled up until the width of the binding here equals the width of the rest, and then fastened off securely again.

This method works equally well when using purchased knitted or bias-woven braids.

Binding with purchased braid, (knitted or woven)

Check whether the braid you are buying is flexible or not, remembering that it needs to be flexible if it is to be applied to curved edges.

These purchased braids are sometimes already pressed in half lengthwise; if yours happens to be flat you will have to press it yourself, taking great care to keep the edges precisely together.

To apply, use the same method as for binding with machine-knitted binding.

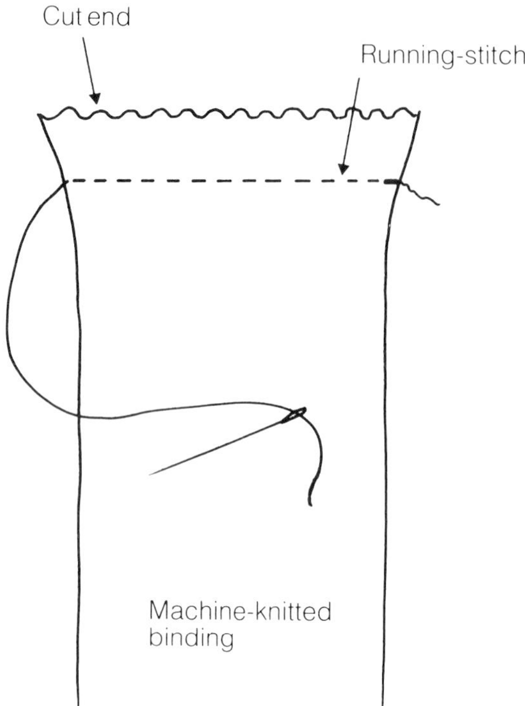

Fig. 92 Reducing stretched-out cut end of knitted or woven binding

Further suggestions for binding

Leather or suede

1 *Fig. 93.* You may be able to buy this in the form of ready-made binding strip, or you may have to cut it yourself from a skin. Avoid, in the latter case, trying to use a skin which is too heavy and which will be difficult to sew.

2 Buy washable leather if possible, otherwise the garment will have to be dry-cleaned.

3 As there is no danger of fraying, turned in seam allowances become unnecessary.

4 *Stick* the binding in place before stitching (using Copydex or a similar product), because every needle or pin which you insert will leave a mark in the leather.

5 Use special needles for leather in your sewing machine.

Vinyl or other simulated leather

This can be purchased in the form of ready-made binding strip. Make sure that it has a backing of woven cloth so that it cannot tear or split.

Depending on how much stretch the binding

Fig. 93 Knit bound with suede or leather

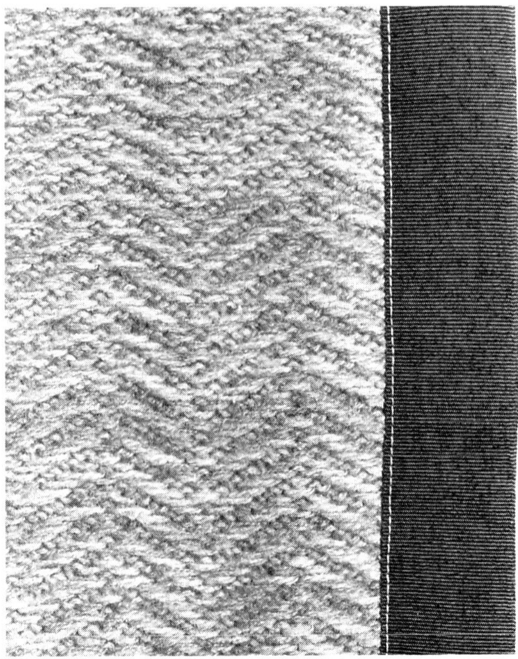

Fig. 94 Knit bound with ribbon

has, use it in the same way as binding cut from woven fabric (*pp. 84–5*) either on the bias or on the straight grain. Alternatively, interface a whole piece of vinyl by sticking some kind of thin woven fabric such as muslin to the wrong side, using Copydex or something similar; then cut strips, either on the straight-grain or on the bias.

Ribbon

Fig. 94. Because this is not flexible, use it only for binding straight edges, unless you are prepared to sew the tiny pleats involved in persuading it to go around curves. Press it exactly in half lengthwise and apply it in the same way as for binding with machine-knitted binding (*p. 87*).

Experiment using all sorts of fabrics, braids, ribbons, etc. and your leftover tension squares. You will be amazed at what expensive-looking effects you can achieve. Try bias-cut satin on a fine soft knit; bias-cut needlecord on a tweedy knit; velvet ribbon on a silky knit; gold or silver bias-cut fabric (or ribbon) on a smooth, plain-coloured knit. Consider binding a cut-and-sew jacket with the same cotton print as the dress which you will wear under it.

Binding as a means of seam finishing

This method of neatening the raw edges of seams is used mainly in the production of unlined coats and jackets. Because, I imagine, Chinese tailors made such good use of it in the production of tropical suits for taipans, it became known as the 'Hong Kong finish'.

It is extremely useful, also, as a means of making beautifully finished, unlined, cut-and-sew coats and jackets.

To make the binding

Cut 2.5cm (1in) wide bias strips of some fine woven fabric (such as pure silk or polyester lining fabric) and join to make sufficient length (*pp. 83–5*).

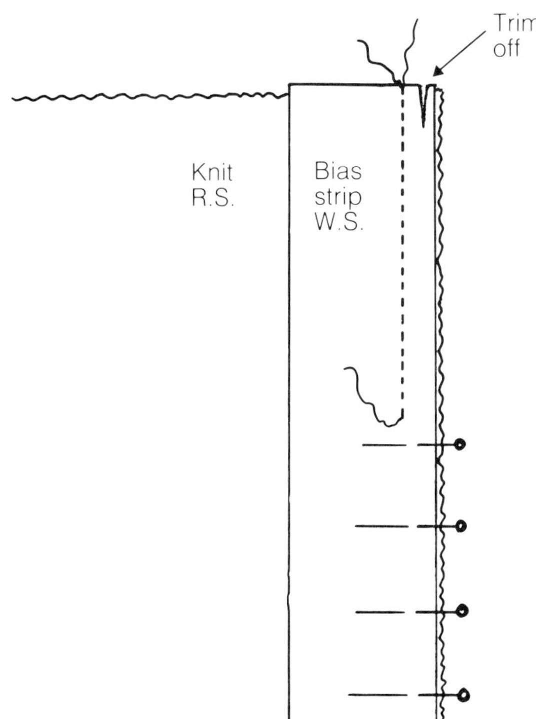

Fig. 95a Applying bias strip to edge of knitted fabric

Fig. 95b Bias strip rolled to under side and stitched

To apply the binding

1 *Fig. 95a.* Place the strip on the seam allowance, right sides of fabrics together and edges together.

2 Machine-stitch only 6mm ($\frac{1}{4}$in) from the edges, using a fairly short stitch length, so that the cut threads of the knit are securely sewn in. Take care neither to stretch nor contract the binding: keep it absolutely flat.

3 Trim the seam allowances back to 3mm ($\frac{1}{8}$in).

Note If you are using a rather thick knit, it might be wiser to start with a wider bias strip and then take a wider seam allowance when first attaching it to the knit.

4 *Fig. 95b.* Wrap the bias strip over to the wrong side of the knit seam allowance, enclosing the cut edge quite tightly.

5 Stitch-in-the-ditch from the right side, along the line where the knit and the woven fabric are joined.

6 Trim off the excess binding fabric, on the wrong side, back to 3mm ($\frac{1}{8}$in).

▲

Chapter eleven

PATCHWORK, QUILTING AND APPLIQUE

This is a 'fun' chapter — a way of adding a little touch of luxury and individuality to your cut-and-sew clothes. Although I would suggest that you perfect your basic techniques first (simply because I believe firmly that professional-looking fit and finish is more important than decoration), by all means go on from there, experimenting, playing, inventing, and using your imagination to produce clothes which are entirely your own.

Making a patchwork quilted jacket from scraps of knitted fabric

Creating a garment, such as a sleeveless vest or a short coat, entirely from left-over pieces of knitted fabric, can be satisfying and fun. This is probably one of the answers to those folk who complain that cut-and-sew is wasteful! If you have insufficient left-over pieces of knitted fabric, you will undoubtedly have some odds and ends of yarn stored away, too small to be knitted up into garments but enough to make narrow strips which can then be cut up for patchwork.

The jacket shown in colour picture 1 was simply an exercise in this field but one which proved so successful that I decided that I should describe it in this book.

Planning

1 Choose a pattern for the jacket. Keep it as simple as possible: a back (seamed down the middle), two fronts and two sleeves; these pattern pieces will be used for the patchwork, for the polyester wadding which forms the interfacing, and for the lining. You will not be using any other pattern pieces in this particular case.

2 Get all your pieces together, whether in the form of knitted fabric or of yarn still un-knitted. Sort out colours which look right together and which complement each other. This is very much a matter of personal taste and only you can know what effect you really want. It could be quiet and subdued in toning shades of one or two colours with neutrals; it could be bright and rather shocking in all sorts of contrasting hues — 'Joseph's coat of many colours', or it could be somewhere between these two extremes.

3 Decide on whether you want all your pieces in the same type of yarn and texture, or whether perhaps you might like to mix them. Remember that you can always back the thinner ones with a fusible interfacing to make them firmer where necessary. In my jacket, the pieces were in a variety of stitch patterns but all in synthetic yarns such as acrylic/nylon mixtures and bright acrylics; however, a mixture of textures, such as fluffy with flat or rough with smooth, could be even more attractive.

4 Make sure that all the pieces you are going to use are thoroughly pressed before they are cut to shape so that any alteration in size or texture takes place now and not later. See notes on

Fig. 96 Patchwork jacket, before sewing side and under-arm seams, spread out to show effect produced by joining strips (*author's photograph*)

pressing in *Cut and Sew: Working with Machine-Knitted Fabrics*, Chapter 5.

5 Interface all those pieces of fabric which need to be made firmer or less transparent. Refer to *Cut and Sew: Working with Machine-Knitted Fabrics*, pp. 54–58, for help with this, but see the Update chapter at the end of this book also. Because these pieces are relatively small (compared with, say, a whole coat front), it is reasonably safe to interface a whole section before cutting it into patchwork pieces. In my jacket I used Vilene Ultrasoft Lightweight for the pieces which needed to be made a little stiffer, and fusible knitted nylon for those which were too open and transparent.

A warning note here: beware of using too many heavy yarn textures, and of overdoing the interfacing, or you could end up with a very weighty garment.

6 Decide upon the shape and approximate size of the pieces you are going to join together. I used strips of knitted fabric which varied in width from 4cm ($1\frac{5}{8}$in) to 10cm (4in) and were however long they happened to be when I found them. You could cut a large number of squares or rectangles instead. Look at any good book on patchwork for ideas (*Appendix five*), but keep it fairly simple if this is your first attempt.

How *many* strips, squares or rectangles you are going to need is rather a matter of guesswork at this stage, but I think it is probably advisable to aim initially at a fairly short sleeveless coat which you can then extend in length, or to which you can add sleeves later on, if you find you have plenty of spare pieces. If you find that you have insufficient pieces of knitting (or yarn ends to be knitted up) you could add some woven fabric here and there, and this could give extra interest to the overall effect.

Think about what effect you are going to have at the shoulder and side seams when the front is sewn to the back. Fig. 96 shows my patchwork jacket spread out flat, before the side and sleeve seams were joined.

Making up the jacket

1 Cut the pieces. Use very sharp scissors and be exact so that you will have no trouble when you come to sew them together. If you are cutting long strips, as I did for the jacket in colour picture 1, the strips can vary in width but each strip must be even in width down its entire length. (Because I was aiming at a symmetrically patterned effect, I also took care to cut all the strips of one colour to the same width.) If you are cutting squares, it really is vital that they are all precisely the same size. Cut absolutely straight with the grain, following a row across the knit or one stitch up its length.

2 Join the pieces. Decide on what your seam allowance is to be and stick to that rigidly throughout; 1.2cm ($\frac{1}{2}$in) is normally sufficient.

Joining is fairly simply if you are using squares; just ensure that the ends of the seam match exactly every time. Pin across, at right angles to the seamline, *on* the seamline, to hold the two pieces firmly together while you stitch; remove each pin as it starts to go under the presser foot.

If you are using long strips, it can sometimes be difficult to ensure that one strip does not end up tighter than its immediate neighbour. If this happens, you end up with curved seams instead of straight ones! Avoid the problem by holding the two strips to be joined between two fingers and letting them hang down; then pin the strips together, near the end of the shorter one, exactly where they hang together (*Fig. 97*). Add more pins to hold the entire length evenly together.

Machine the seams using straight-stitch and press each seam out flat *immediately after stitching it.*

Note Any strips which are not long enough for your purpose can be joined together to make longer ones. It is better to make the joins diagonal (on the bias) rather than on the straight (*Fig. 98*).

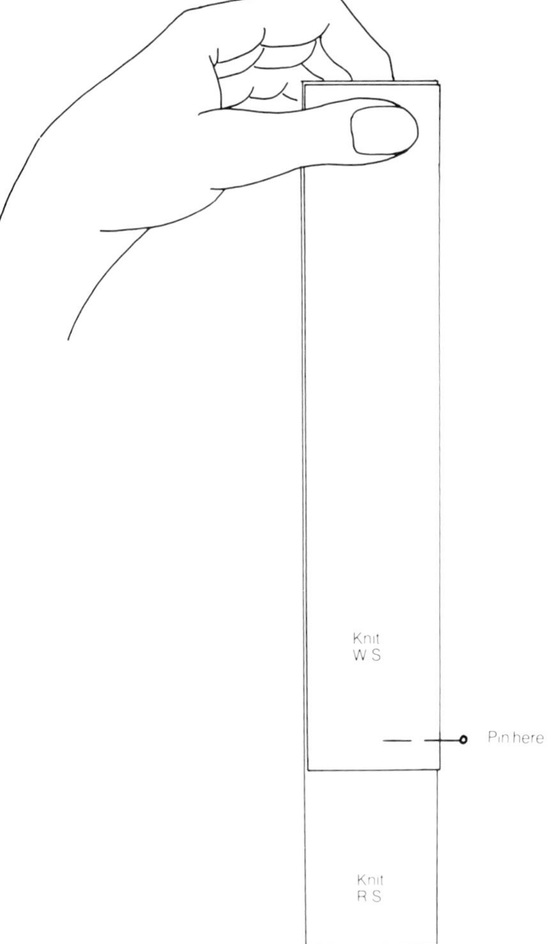

Fig. 97 Hanging strips to ascertain correct tension

3 Join enough pieces to cover the entire area of each pattern piece, *with 3.7cm ($1\frac{1}{2}$in) to spare all round.* Fig. 99 shows some examples of this.

For my jacket, I placed the straight strips using a combination of the vertical and the diagonal. I did this by first dividing my pattern pieces into two sections (A and B) and then covering each section separately (*Fig. 100a, b and c*). Before joining sections A and B, place the pattern pieces back on them and trim edges c–d and e–f to shape, leaving a 1.5cm ($\frac{5}{8}$in) seam allowance. Join by sewing the seam. Press the seam flat.

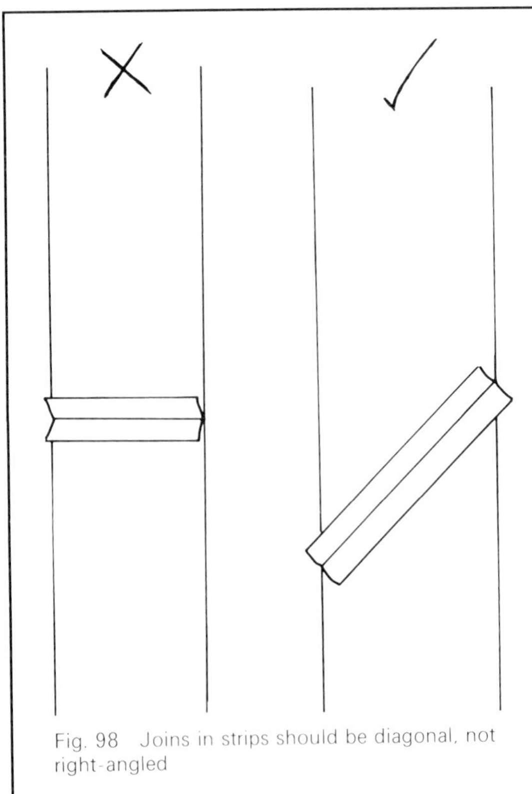

Fig. 98 Joins in strips should be diagonal, not right-angled

4 Place the pattern pieces on the polyester wadding; pin in place and cut *leaving 3.7cm ($1\frac{1}{2}$in) excess wadding all around* each pattern piece.

5 Place each patchwork garment piece on its corresponding wadding piece, W.S. tog. (*Fig. 101*). (If the filling has a 'skin', treat this as being the R.S.) Pin the two layers together all around the edge, and machine-stitch 9mm ($\frac{3}{8}$in) from the edge all round, using a fairly long straight stitch. If you are not confident about doing this successfully, then tack first by hand, but take the occasional back-stitch to prevent the layers slipping when you machine.

It is important to keep both layers flat together.

6 Quilt each separate garment piece by machining through the two layers (see the tips on quilting which follow); I did this by first following the seamlines already there and then adding more lines of stitching in each stripe (*Fig. 102*). However, there are many variations on this theme. Have a spare piece of knit, with wadding attached, and do some experimenting.

Fig. 99 Patchwork pieces joined to cover pattern area. *a* straight strips placed vertically; *b* straight strips placed diagonally; *c* squares

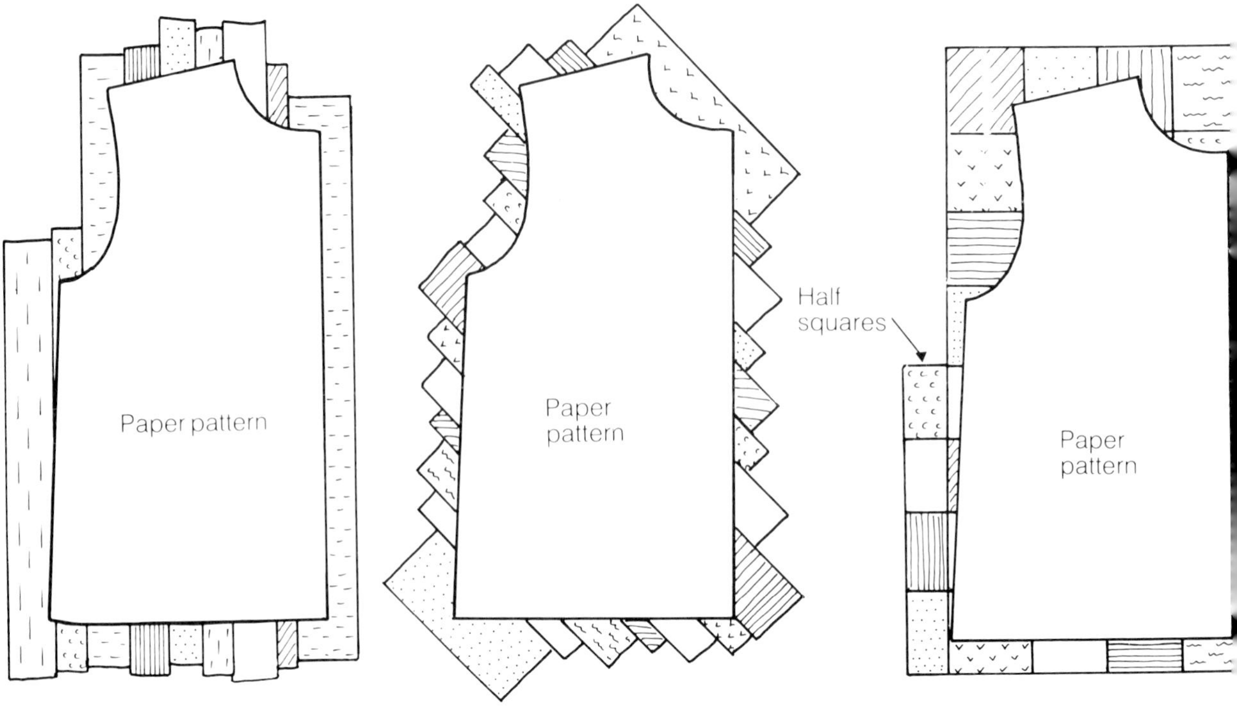

Paper pattern

Paper pattern

Half squares

Paper pattern

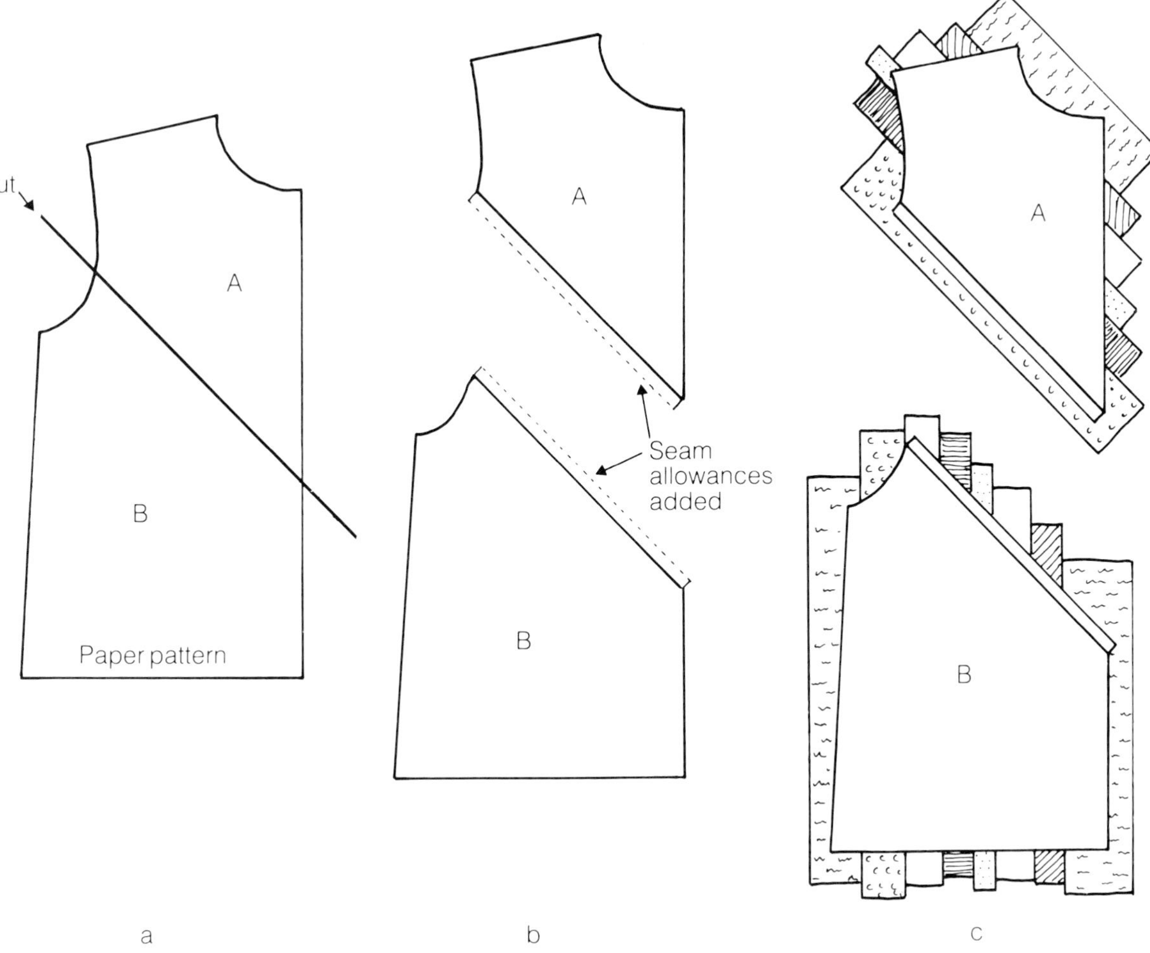

Fig. 100a Pattern piece divided by cutting

Fig. 100b Seam allowances added where cut was made

Fig. 100c Patchwork pieces joined to cover each segment of pattern

Some helpful tips on quilting
Keep the tension on both needle and bobbin threads fairly easy (but not so easy that you have loops in the stitching!); if the tension is too tight, the quilting could reduce the size of the garment pieces quite considerably.

To ensure that the two layers feed through evenly, and to avoid puckering on the top layer, pin *across* your proposed sewing-line through both thicknesses. Pin at roughly every 4cm ($1\frac{1}{2}$in) down the length of the line.

Help the process by stretching the fabrics slightly sideways, on both sides of the presser foot, as you sew.

If your quilting lines are intended to cross the seamlines, rather than simply following them, you will need some help in keeping the lines parallel. Mark the first line with a ruler and a well-sharpened piece of tailor's chalk; machine-stitch along this chalked line. Then use a quilting bar, positioned on the line you have just stitched, to enable you to keep the next line exactly parallel with it (*Fig. 103*). If the box of spare parts which came with your machine does not include a quilting bar, write to the manufacturer (or call on one of his agents) to see if you can get one; also make sure that he supplies (or you already have) a presser foot which is adapted to take a

Fig. 101 Patchwork pinned to the polyester wadding (*author's photograph*)

Fig. 102 Machine-stitched quilting through knit and wadding

quilting bar.

For short distances, simply mark the end of the line (or turning point), with a pin or a dot, and aim that mark at the needle as you stitch.

7 When all the pieces (two fronts, two half backs and two sleeves) have been quilted, place the paper pattern on each piece in turn and trim to the correct shape and size. Leaving that extra allowance all round was a safety precaution against the slight reduction in size which occurs during quilting.

8 Sew the seams at the shoulders and sides.

9 Press the seams open flat, *very lightly*. Remember that the polyester wadding can be irretrievably flattened by the heat of the iron, *so you must use a seam roller* (see *Cut and Sew: Working with Machine-Knitted Fabrics*, p. 11) to enable you to press only the seam itself and not the surrounding fabrics.

10 Cut the lining pieces for the jacket, using the same paper pattern and whatever fabric you choose for the purpose. (The back can be cut in one piece, on the fold of the fabric.) Seam these together and press the shoulder and side seams open flat.

11 If you intend to use shoulder pads, attach these now to the inside of the quilted jacket (Chapter 5).

12 Place the lining inside the quilted jacket, W.S. tog., and pin the two exactly together as follows. (Place pins at right angles to edges.)

Start at the back of the neck and match the shoulder seamlines. You may find that the back neck edge of the lining appears smaller than that of the quilted knit jacket. This is because the jacket has already stretched at this point; simply make the jacket fit the lining by easing it a little.

Pin the lining to the jacket at under-arm and top-arm points, and down each front edge. Pin the side seams of the lining to the side seams of the jacket.

Pin the lower edges of lining and jacket

10 Cream tucked dress

11 Pink acrylic knit with suede-cloth two-piece

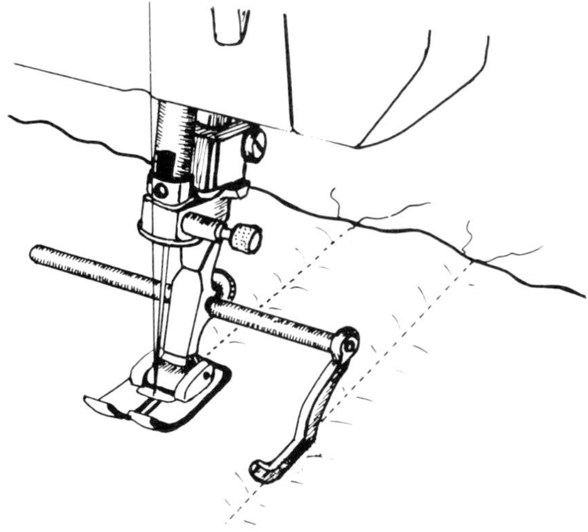

Fig. 103 Quilting bar in operation

Fig. 104 Jacket edges bound with bias-cut cotton seersucker (detail from colour picture 1)

together; take care to get these level, trimming if necessary. Put the jacket on a dummy or a coat-hanger at this stage, so that you can see exactly where they meet.

Pin the lower edges of the lining sleeves to the lower edges of the jacket sleeves, making sure that they are exactly the same length.

13 Machine-tack the jacket to the lining along all edges; keep the stitching close to the edges and remove all the pins as you get to them.

14 Bind the edge (*Fig. 104*). See Chapter 10 for notes on choice of bindings and methods of application.

I have described here the way in which I constructed the jacket shown in colour picture 1, but there are many other ideas you could pursue along similar lines. At a machine-knitted convention which I visited recently, I came across the work of Mady Gerrard, a Hungarian-born designer who has worked in Britain, Canada and the USA, and who now has a designer workshop in Bath. Many of her beautiful jackets were made entirely from square patches, set diagonally, cut from all kinds of knits intermixed with leather, suede, satin and tweed, and banding with knitted ribbing.

I once had a strong desire to try out some log-cabin patchwork as a cut-and-sew exercise, and eventually I produced the cushion shown in Fig. 105a, b. In this case, a small square of knit is applied to the centre of a much larger square of firm woven fabric (traditionally, calico is used); then narrow strips of knit, in varying tones, are applied to the edges of this small square, following each side in turn, until the square of woven fabric is completely covered. Dark tones are used on two adjacent sides of the square and lighter tones on the other two. Several completed squares are then sewn together. Consult any good book on patchwork for detailed instructions on this process (*Appendix five*). Wadding and quilting can be added if required. A complete garment made in log-cabin patchwork might well be too heavy, but a few squares used as trimming on an otherwise plain knit, could be very effective.

Fig. 105a Log-cabin patchwork cushion made from leftover strips of knitted fabric

Appliqué and machine embroidery on knitted fabrics

Any kind of motif can be applied to knitted fabrics, but do try making your own rather than buying them because they really are quite simple. They can be made from scraps of woven fabrics such as cotton gingham, silk, satin, needlecord, etc. or from leather or suede; they can be embellished with embroidery or beads.

Figs. 106 and 107 show two small, and very basic examples of what can be achieved. Simple shapes can be used, like the two leaves in Fig. 106, or these can be elaborated and extended, as in Fig. 107. It all depends on what effect you want and the shape of the garment you are working on.

It is not necessary to be able to draw. You can trace outlines from pictures in newspapers, magazines, books, birthday cards, etc.; you can even pick up fallen leaves and trace around them. Almost everybody doodles when talking on the telephone and these unplanned, unpredictable scribbles are sometimes very attactive when translated into fabric, colour and texture.

Shops and departments which sell furnishing textiles occasionally sell off their out-dated manufacturers' samples and these are often a rich source of printed motifs, such as sprays of flowers, birds or figures; see the one cut from a nursery curtain fabric shown in Fig. 108.

Fig. 105b Detail of cushion

Given a reasonably good-tempered sewing machine and good lighting, the techniques are not difficult, but, as with every other aspect of cut-and-sew, do allow time for experimenting and practising before applying these techniques to a garment.

For a more lustrous look, use proper machine-embroidery thread for the stitching rather than your normal polyester sewing-thread. This is obtainable from most good haberdashery departments, although you may have to ask for it. Use the presser foot intended for embroidery, rather than the normal presser foot with which you stitch seams.

To explain the process, we will take a simple leaf shape, cut it from a woven fabric (such as cotton poplin, calico, gingham, etc.) and apply it to a piece of well-pressed, medium-weight knitted fabric.

1 *Fig. 109a.* Draw (or trace) the leaf shape on the R.S. of the woven fabric, using a sharp pencil or a cloth-marking pen. Keep the lines thin and well-defined and, for this exercise, simple.

2 *Fig. 109b.* Cut out the leaf shape, leaving about 6mm ($\frac{1}{4}$in) of fabric outside the drawn line.

3 *Fig. 109c.* Place a sheet of Vilene Stitch'n'Tear behind the knitted fabric; pin or tack the two layers together, around the area where the leaf will be placed.

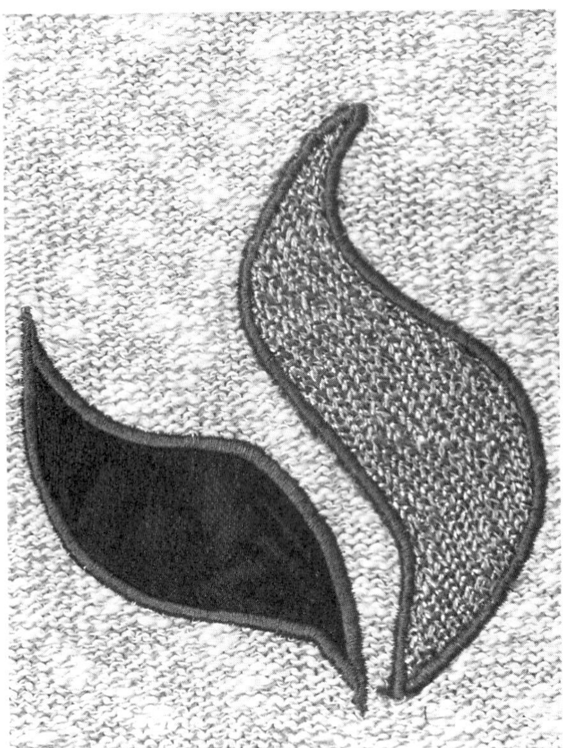

Fig. 106 Simple leaf shapes applied to knitted fabric

Fig. 107 Simple shapes elaborated and extended with added stitching

Note Vilene Stitch'n'Tear is available from most haberdashery shops and departments that stock Vilene products; it is wonderfully successful in providing a temporary means of stabilising the fabrics and thus preventing stretching and distortion. If you cannot find it and want to get on with the exercise, use typing paper instead; you will just have to take care to avoid tearing it too soon.

4 Place the leaf shape on the knitted fabric and pin in position. I find pinning more effective and safer than tacking, but you can use needle and thread, with a small running stitch, if you prefer. It is possible to stick the leaf in position, using Wundaweb, but I find that this sometimes stiffens the appliqué too much. You could try some of the textile glues which can be washed out afterwards, such as Mölnlycke Textile Glue (red pack).

5 *Fig. 109c.* Machine-stitch, following the drawn outline of the leaf, using straight-stitch *set on a very small stitch length* (about 1 on most machines). When you get to the point of the leaf, set the needle in the fabric, lift the presser foot, turn the fabric, lower the foot again and continue down the other side of the leaf. Continue stitching until you overlap the point where you started.

6 Trim off the surplus woven fabric outside the stitching line, as close as you can get to it. The best way to do this is to hold the scissors flat, i.e. horizontally, not vertically.

7 Set the machine to do a satin-stitch, i.e. a zigzag stitch with the stitch length set short enough to eliminate gaps between the threads; this is just what you do when sewing a buttonhole, so your normal buttonhole setting (on the stitch-length control) would probably be right. Adjust the stitch width until it is sufficiently wide to cover easily both the cut edge of the leaf and the straight-stitch line.

8 *Fig. 109d.* Starting on one side of the leaf, satin-stitch all around. For curved shapes, turn the fabric gently as you stitch. When you reach the point of the leaf, you have two alternatives.

You can either gradually reduce the zigzag width until you taper off into a straight-stitch, a little beyond the end of the leaf point, turn the fabric, and gradually increase the width so that it is back to its original setting when you reach the leaf point again.

Alternatively, you can keep the zigzag setting constant. When you reach the point of the leaf, stop with the needle on the *outside* of the line, pivot on the needle, turning the fabric until the second side of the leaf is lined up, and continue stitching. This makes a more blunt end to the leaf.

Note The general principle when turning any corner is that you turn the fabric, using the needle as a pivot, with the needle positioned *in* the fabric and always on the *outside* of the corner you are turning. If you turn with the needle on the inside of the corner, you will leave a gap in the stitching.

You now have lots of possibilities: you can machine-stitch lines on the leaf to simulate veining, and you can add stalks by using the same satin stitch on lines drawn directly onto the knitted fabric; you can apply more leaves (or berries, apples, clouds, birds, initials, whatever); you could even add beads for extra lustre, sewing them on by hand with a very fine needle.

When you have finished the appliqué, tear away all the Stitch'n'Tear from the back of the knitted fabric.

The fabrics used for the appliqué can vary enormously to contrast with each other and with the background knit. Try velvet, needlecord, suede-cloth, satin and lurex fabrics. Some of these may be difficult to handle because they fray badly, but never hesitate to try them out. Use also your left-over scraps of knitted fabrics, varying and contrasting stitch-patterns and textures. In Fig. 106, for example, one leaf is cut from woven slubbed silk and the other from knitted acrylic yarn.

I recently applied a huge spray of pseudo-rhododendrons to the front of a knitted track-suit top; the complete motif was cut from three pieces of printed polyester crêpe de Chine, left over from a blouse length. The fabric was actually far too thin and unstable to be used for appliqué, but proved to be perfectly suitable after Vilene Ultrasoft (lightweight) had been applied to its reverse side. You can always stabilise fabrics which are too thin or unstable in this way, but take care that the appliqué does not become too stiffened.

Fig. 108 Motif cut from furnishing fabric, applied to knitted fabric

Machine embroidery

This is an area which I have yet to explore, but having extended my applied leaves on knitted

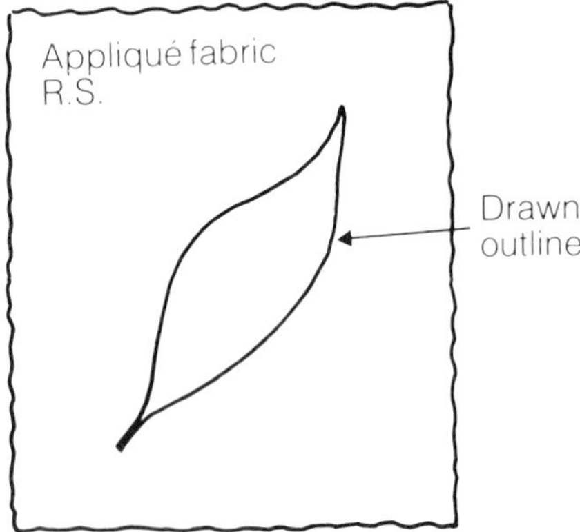

Fig. 109a Leaf outline drawn on appliqué fabric

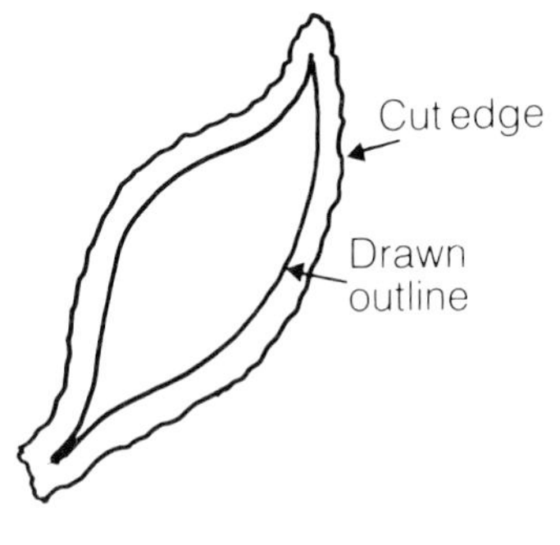

Fig. 109b Leaf cut out

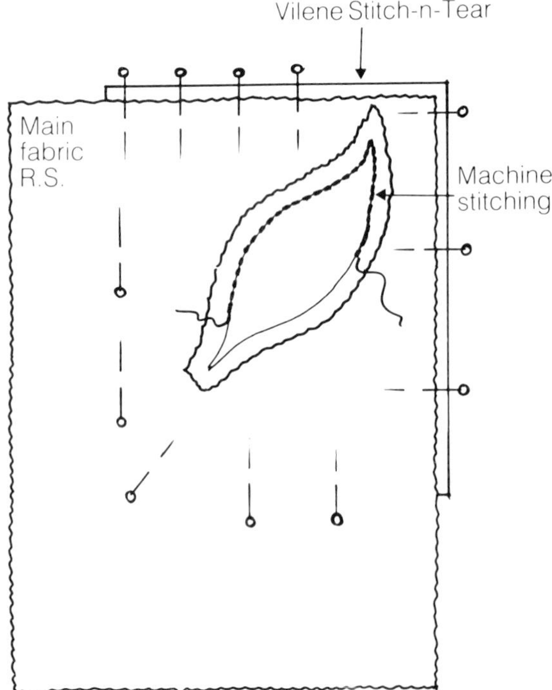

Fig. 109c Stitch'n'Tear placed behind knit and leaf, stitched through all three layers

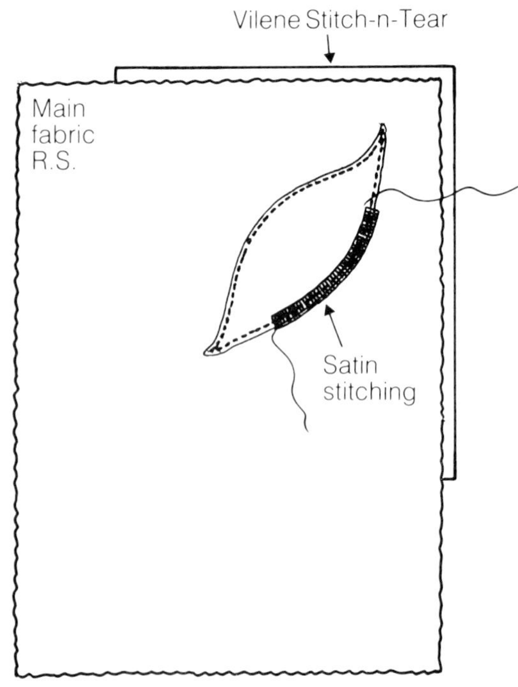

Fig. 109d Satin-stitching over machined line and raw edge of leaf

fabrics by adding satin-stitched stalks, I can see no reason why it should present any extra problems.

Vilene Stitch'n'Tear is excellent for this purpose too, used in the same way as for appliqué. The instructions given inside the packet suggest the use of an embroidery hoop; I have to confess that I have not tried this method so far but I have some fears that the knit could stretch badly and would thus distort the finished work.

There is a whole field of exploration here; you could try free-hand machine embroidery, i.e. with the feed-dog lowered and the presser foot removed. Read some of the many good books on machine embroidery, such as Christine Risley's *Machine Embroidery* and Ann Coleman's *The Creative Sewing-Machine*. Angela Thompson's *Complete Book of the Sewing Machine* has a helpful section on machine embroidery and appliqué, and Bernina have excellent sewing manuals on both techniques. See Appendix five for publishers and dates.

Chapter twelve

UPDATE

Since writing my first book on cut-and-sew techniques, I have made many more clothes in knitted fabrics, visited a large number of machine-knitting clubs, met a vast variety of knitters and dressmakers, taught classes, and discussed problems with students, teachers, designers, retailers and manufacturers. Inevitably I have modified some of my own theories, but I think I have picked up many new and useful tips as well. As with most other craft subjects, the learning process need never stop.

Also, during the interval between this book and the last, there have been a number of changes and developments in sewing and overlocking machines, in threads and in interfacings, all of which have had an improving effect on our ability to sew knitted fabrics at home.

So this final chapter consists of additional notes to those given in Chapters 2 and 3 of *Cut and Sew: Working with Machine-Knitted Fabrics.*

Sewing machines

A good sewing machine which performs well can encourage a mediocre dressmaker to become a good one; conversely, a machine which ties itself, the fabric and the operator up in knots, is ultimately totally discouraging. As a teacher of dressmaking in Adult Education classes, where the students mostly bring their own machines to work on, I have become all too aware of this.

The cost of an efficient machine is high, although I suspect that it has always been around the cost of three good coats. If you make only three or four garments a year, the machine has probably paid for itself within five years, so I personally feel that it is an excellent investment. Some very good machines are currently coming from Japan but my personal preference is for those made in Europe, particularly the Swiss and Swedish ones. However, you still have to make sure that you are buying the right machine for your needs, and this means that you have to be able to understand the current jargon.

The term 'electronic' as applied to sewing machines, is being widely used by manufacturers and by retailers and is causing some confusion amongst home-sewers. If you are thinking of buying a new machine check carefully on whether it is purely mechanical, electronically controlled, or fully electronic.

A machine which is purely mechanical loses needle-power when the speed of sewing is reduced. When sewing thick seams on jeans, for instance, the needle may seem likely to bend or even break; the motor probably hums, and you feel the need to assist it by turning the fly-wheel by hand.

'Electronically controlled' means that all the sewing parts of the machine are mechanical, but the foot control attached to it operates electronically; this enables you to sew slowly over thick layers without losing needle power.

To my mind, this has been an invaluable development because it has removed one of the most common hazards in machine sewing. Electronically controlled machines can be found in the middle-price range and are well worth saving up for, if a fully electronic machine is beyond your price range.

An electronic machine has electronic foot control and some of the sewing parts are still mechanical, but it works mainly on micro-chips in rather the same way as a computer. Needle position and stitch patterns are selected and programmed by touching buttons on a control panel. A buttonhole first sewn to a chosen length can be repeated identically as many times as required. The machine can indicate which presser foot to use for a particular stitch, and will automatically select the appropriate stitch length and stitch width.

Embroidery stitches can be programmed to repeat themselves in a certain order (e.g. a row of alternate crescent shapes and stars), to be sewn singly (one crescent alone), or to be sewn in 'mirror image' (crescents turning first one way and then the other).

In general, this means that the machine is considerably easier to use (especially when teaching beginners, or as a learner yourself) than the mechanical ones, simply because most of the decisions are made by the machine rather than by the user. Having said this, I would advise that you turn down any machine that does not allow you to over-ride its decisions on stitch length and stitch width, if and when you wish to do so; you are the boss, after all!

Examine the handbook which goes with the machine and find out how much help the retailer will give you in learning how to use the machine. It is a regrettable fact that the majority of sewing-machine manufactuers are still not giving sufficient help to buyers in the form of clear, intelligible, well-illustrated instruction books and properly informed and trained retailers. Again, my experience in Adult Education, helping students to use their own sewing machines, has brought this home to me very forcefully.

One example of how it should be done is given by Bernina, who not only produce beautifully written manuals, but also follow them up with excellent fact-sheets. They give comprehensive training to their chosen retailers, and free one-day courses (with first-class teaching) to anyone buying a new Bernina; these courses take place at their centre in London, and are available to owners of older Berninas on payment of a fee.

Many other manufacturers, unfortunately, lag behind sadly; poor illustrations, inadequate and frequently incomprehensible instructions (comic translations from the Japanese originals in some cases) abound. In two cases I have found instructions which were actually wrong. The trouble seems to be that too few manufacturers of sewing machines employ people who actually make clothes, as opposed to merely sewing samples on scraps of calico!

Cut-and-sew attachments to sewing machines

These are mechanisms which cut and oversew an edge in one operation, and which are either incorporated in the sewing machine or can be attached to the sewing machine in the form of an extra working foot. They use only the needle and bobbin threads normally used in the machine, and so should not be confused with separate, purpose-built, overlocking machines which use two, three or more threads and have no bobbin. They work well in normal dressmaking but I have not found them to be really suited to the use of domestically knitted fabrics.

Overlocking machines

While an overlocking machine is not essential for cut-and-sew work, the privileged people who own one just happen to find the whole business of sewing knitted fabrics infinitely quicker and easier. In time, I expect most of us who sew at home will accept an overlocker as a vital piece of our sewing equipment, in the same way that we have grown to expect a washing machine in the kitchen.

More and more domestic overlocking machines (or 'sergers' as they are termed in the USA) are coming on to the market and I find an increasing number of my students (both in

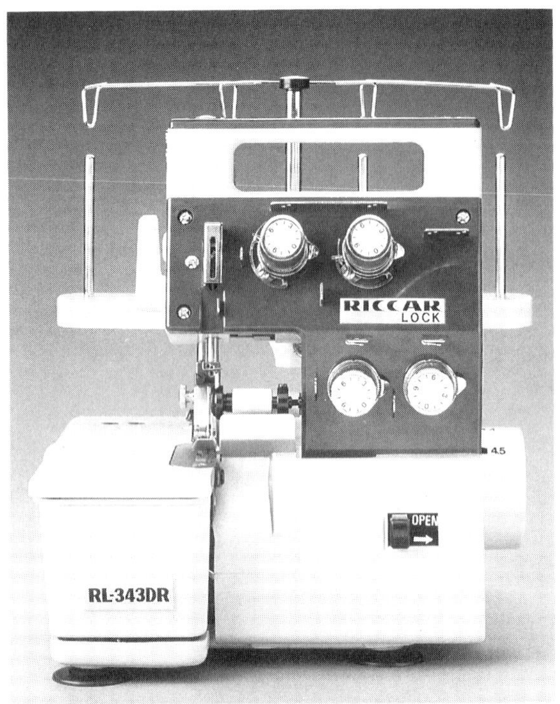

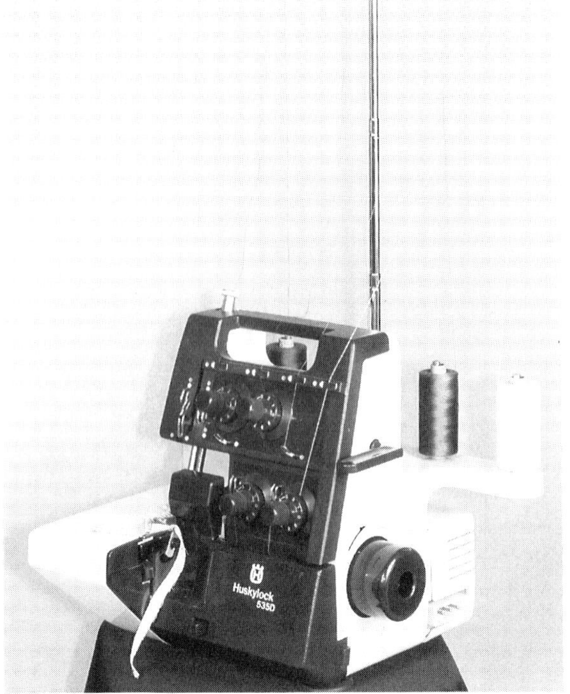

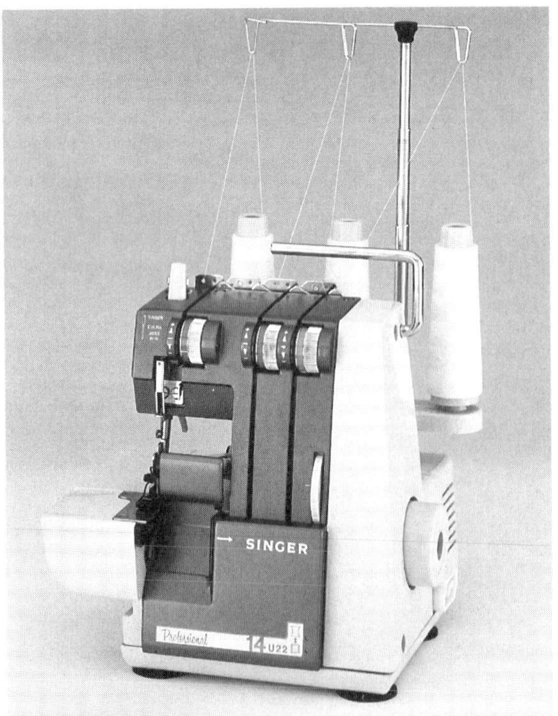

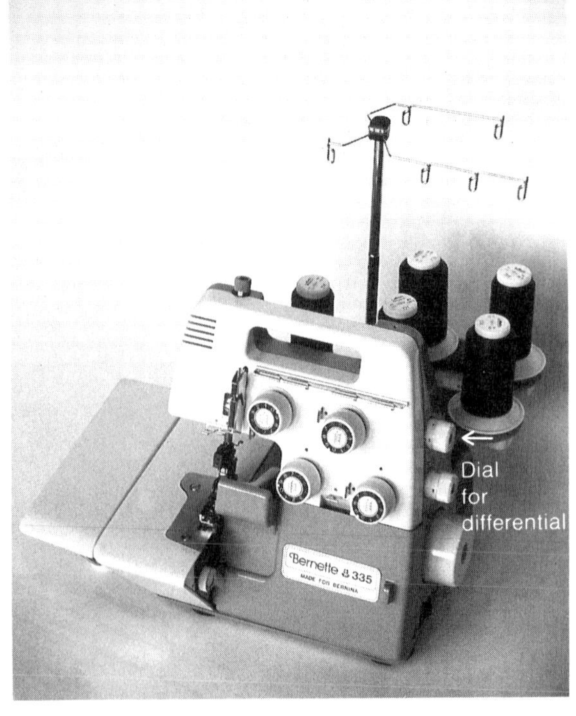

Fig. 110 Four overlocking machines which incorporate differential feed (*photographs — a Riccar (UK) Ltd; b Husqvarna Ltd; c Singer Industrial Products; d Bogod Machine Co. Ltd*)

dressmaking and in cut-and-sew) are actually using them for trimming and overlocking fabric edges in one operation. Improvements in design have been made, so that the newer machines are generally more trouble-free than their predecessors.

The most exciting development, from the cut-and-sew angle, has been the addition of *differential feed* to domestic overlockers. At the time of writing, only a few manufacturers are producing overlockers which incorporate differential feed, namely Riccar (Riccarlock 343DR, 3/4 thread [*Fig. 110a*]); Husqvarna (Huskylock 435D and 535D, 3/4 thread [*Fig. 110b*]); Singer (14U22A, 3 thread [*Fig. 110c*], and 14U23A, 4 thread) and Bernina (Bernette Mo–335, 2/3/5 thread [*Fig. 110d*]). Brother are also producing a differential overlocker, and no doubt others will follow.

I have been using the Riccarlock 343DR and have been very impressed with the results. One of the problems which I had previously encountered was that the edges of the knit tended to stretch out, especially when overlocking across the knit, parallel with the rows. By altering the differential feed ratio, I am able to eliminate this problem without having to make complicated alterations to the tension discs.

What does differential feed do?

Whereas previous overlockers have had one complete feed-dog under the presser foot (*Fig. 111a*), an overlocker with differential feed has two separate feed-dogs; one at the front and one at the back (*Fig. 111b*). When these two feed-dogs are set at different rates (i.e. the front feeding the fabric in faster than the back is taking it out) it is possible to correct the fault which frequently occurs when overlocking knitted fabrics — the stretching-out, or frilling, of the edge. Similarly, fine woven fabrics such as linings, which have tended to tighten and pucker up when overlocked, can be sewn flat by adjusting the differential feed to feed the fabric out faster than it is being fed in.

In other words, you can direct the machine either to stretch out the fabric or to contract it, and this is a tremendous advantage for cut-and-sew enthusiasts.

The means of controlling this ratio between the front and back feed-dogs, varies according to the manufacturer. Riccar have a screw (which needs a screwdriver) and Husqvarna have a lever (moved by a finger); both are hidden beneath the casing and can be moved between 0.7 and 2.0 (the higher the number, the more the fabric is contracted). Singer have a similar lever but with a clear picture next to it which shows instantly that 'up' is to stretch and 'down' is to contract (*Fig. 111b*). Bernina have a dial control placed conveniently on the right-hand side of the machine, outside the casing (*Fig. 110d*).

Buying an overlocker

Look carefully at what the machine can do and make sure that it will perform the tasks you require. Check on whether or not it has differential feed and how many threads it uses.

A 2-thread overlocker has only one needle and one looper, and so is rather limited.

A 3-thread overlocker has one needle, an upper looper and a lower looper. It can be used for seaming and overlocking in one operation, or simply overlocking, and it produces a good flexible edge.

A 3/4-thread overlocker has two needles, an upper looper and a lower looper. It can seam and overlock in one operation, the left-hand needle making a safety stitch which gives extra strength to the seam. I like to use this for simply overlocking edges on knitted fabrics because of the added insurance against fraying which the left-hand needle gives; but it can be used just like a 3-thread overlocker simply by not using the left needle. This is particularly suitable for knitted fabrics as the stitch is very flexible.

A true 4-thread overlocker uses two of its threads to overlock the edge of the fabric, and the other two to make a chain-stitch seam; by removing one needle, either of these two functions can be performed separately. The stitch made is not as flexible as that made by a 3 or 3/4-thread overlocker and would therefore seem less suitable for knitted fabrics.

The Bernette 2/4/5 thread overlocker (Fig. 110d) (I quote from a press release because at the time

Fig. 111a Overlocker without differential feed, showing single feed-dog (*photograph — Singer Industrial Products*)

of writing, this machine is not yet available) — 'is really three machines in one — a double chain-stitch machine, a 3-thread overlocker or a 5-thread overlocker, and it can cope with all types of fabric. It is particularly easy to use because all the controls are external (so you don't have to open up the machine and use a screwdriver to adjust them). There is a separate dial for stitch length, stitch width and differential feed, and a lever switches on the built-in roll hemmer'.

All overlocking machines incorporate a knife which trims the fabric edge whilst overlocking it. With the exception of the 2-thread overlockers, all can seam and overlock in one operation. Many overlockers can do blind-hemming, lace application, decorative edging, pin-tucks, etc. Remember that these functions could possibly be done at least as well, if not better, on your sewing machine, so beware of paying extra just because an overlocker has these options. Fine roll-hemming (on thin woven fabrics), however, is much better done on an overlocker than on a sewing machine.

Check on whether the machine has a built-in light. Personally I consider this absolutely essential and would reject any overlocker which does not have one.

Look at the accompanying tool box; it should contain a fine wire hook and a good pair of tweezers to help you with the threading-up process.

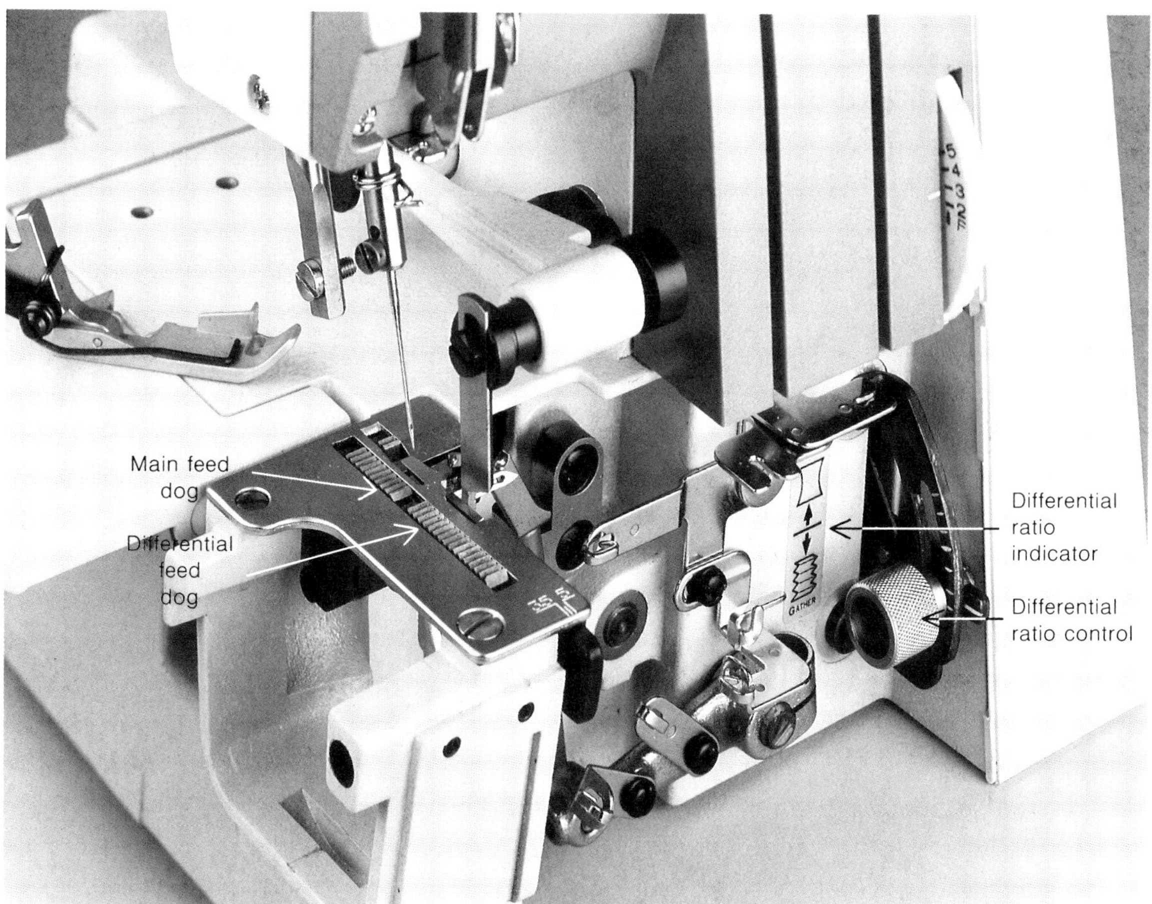

Fig. 111b Overlocker with differential feed, showing two feed-dogs (*photograph—Singer Industrial Products*)

Look at the instruction book and check on how clear the illustrations are and whether the directions are intelligible and sufficiently detailed.

Using your overlocker

Now that the pattern manufacturers are producing designs for track-suits, swimwear, sweaters, etc., all intended for knitted fabrics, there is an increased need for printed text on how to use overlockers. You will find some very helpful sheets included in many of the pattern envelopes published by Vogue and Butterick. Take the trouble to read these thoroughly; I think you will be surprised at how much useful information they contain. Also see the recommended list of books in Appendix five.

To overlock *inside* corners, stitch into the corner as far as you can without cutting into the fabric, raise the presser foot and the needles, pull the next edge towards you so that it continues in a straight line, lower the presser foot and the needles, and carry on stitching.

To overlock *outside* corners, stitch along the edge of the fabric until you have passed the tip of the corner by one stitch, lift the presser foot and the needles, turn the fabric so that the next edge is lined up, lower the foot and the needles and continue stitching.

Overlocking around curves requires a little practice. Straighten the fabric as much as possible and control the feeding of the fabric by *pulling* it towards the foot when sewing around the *outside* of a curve, and *pushing* the fabric towards the foot when sewing around the *inside* of a curve.

Changing the threads on your overlocker

Once you have threaded up the machine, in theory you need never do it again completely.

1 Cut the threads just above the spools and remove the original spools.

2 Place the new spools on the spindles and tie the thread ends together with reef knots (not 'granny' knots). Pull the knots really tight and snip off most of the remaining thread ends.

3 Make a written note of the exact position of each tension dial and then loosen them all back to O.

4 *Either* lower the presser foot and then run the machine gently and slowly until all the new threads have been worked through, *or* raise the presser foot and pull the threads through gently by hand. Take care not to bend the needles. Whichever way you do it, be prepared, if necessary, to cut off the knots on the needle threads just before they reach the needle eyes, and then to re-thread the needles by hand.

5 Re-set the tension dials.

In practice, I have to admit that things can go wrong and occasionally one has to re-thread one of the looper threads; in such a case, you will need the tweezers and wire hook which I mentioned previously, a certain amount of time and patience, and a cool head!

Threads for overlocking

While it is perfectly possible to use a variety of different threads for overlocking, some definitely produce better results than others. I have found that using threads designed specially for overlocking, particularly in the loopers, means that I have to make far fewer adjustments to the tension. Several manufacturers, including Molnlycke, Gütermann, Coates, and Tootal, are now making overlocking threads for the domestic market; Smallware, who normally distribute Mettler's threads to clothing manufacturers, now sell to the public through Bernina agents.

Finding these threads in the shops is becoming easier at last, although you may still have to shop around. See Appendix I for addresses of manufacturers and suppliers.

Cops usually contain 1500 or 2000m — anything less than 1000m is uneconomic because overlockers do use vast quantities of thread.

The colours of overlocking threads tend to be a bit limited; however, there is no need to have four cops in each and every colour because you can often get the effect you want by using several shades together.

Overlocking thread is generally not as strong as polyester sewing thread; therefore you should use your normal, matching, polyester sewing thread through one or both needles, reserving the special overlocking thread for the loopers. This is particularly important if you are seaming and overlocking in one operation, rather than simply overlocking edges.

Remember, too, that you can use bulked nylon, or even a matching fine knitting yarn, through either one or both loopers; this often gives a better covering to the edge when using knitted fabrics. Bulked polyester is now being produced by some manufacturers for retail in the shops, whereas it has previously been made purely for the clothing manufacturers (*Appendix I*).

Because developments in this field are coming thick and fast now, advice on exactly what you should use in any particular circumstance varies, and can be positively confusing. The best advice I can give is to follow the guidelines given by the manufacturer of your own overlocker; if the guidelines are not clear, write to his head office for help. The thread manufacturers themselves are also distributing some very useful leaflets, but you have to ask for them.

Interfacings

Fusible knitted nylon is still difficult to track down; retailers are reluctant to stock it because it tends to sell slowly due to limited demand. See Appendix I for several new addresses from which it can be obtained by mail order. Remember that this needs pressure with dry heat to make it stick properly, i.e. a hot iron over tissue paper or a dry cloth.

Fusible woven tailoring canvas has now appeared in some shops, whereas previously it seemed to be available only to manufacturers. See Appendix I for stockists.

Fusible cotton muslin is now being stocked more widely, in grey and white. *Vilene* have discarded the Supershape range of fusible interfacings and have replaced it with the Ultrasoft range. These still come in three weights (light, medium and heavy) and are much softer and have better draping quality than Vilene's other fusible interfacings, Soft Iron-on and Firm Iron-on. The fusing agent has been tremendously improved, so that it now sticks really well to knitted fabrics as well as to woven fabrics. Unlike the old Supershape, Ultrasoft is not intended to stretch, so has a more stabilising effect.

If you have need of a stretchy interfacing, try Vilene Superstretch; this also sticks well but allows the knit to expand a little.

Remember that all Vilene fusible interfacings need pressure with damp heat to make them stick properly, i.e. a hot iron and a damp cloth.

Shoulder pads

Due to demand, the variety of shapes and sizes available has increased. See Chapter 5 and the list of suppliers in Appendix I. Do insist on getting the correct shape of pad for the garment you are making.

Appendix one

UK suppliers of haberdashery, machines and machine parts

Bernina outlets in sewing machine shops for:
Mettler threads for sewing and overlocking; piping foot and quilting bar for Bernina sewing machines

Harlequin, Unit 25, Jubilee End, Lawford, Manningtree, Essex CO11 1UR for:
buttons and belts made from your own woven or knitted fabrics.

John Lewis, Oxford St, London (and other branches) for:
large range of shoulder pads; sewing and overlocking threads, interfacings, polyester wadding, fabrics, machine needles, zips, satin bias binding, petersham (straight and curved); large range of Coats, Newey, Tootal and Vilene products.

Kinross (Supplies), Oakhill Avenue, Pinner, Middlesex HA5 3DL for:
sewing and overlocking threads, including bulked polyester; mail order list; will match colours.

Libertys, Regent Street, London W1 for:
Molnlycke sewing threads including special overlocking thread.

MacCulloch and Wallis, 25–26 Dering Street, London W1R 0BH for:
fusible interfacings, sewing threads, piping cord, skirt level markers, machine needles, glass-headed pins, polyester wadding, etc. Personal visit or mail order catalogue.

Specialist dress fabric shops stock many of the above items. In my own area (Hampshire), notably Cozens Fabrics (Alton, Farnborough and Guildford) and Glovers of Shottermill (Haslemere).

Specialist sewing-machine shops for sewing and overlocking machines and the proper threads for these; also machine needles and spare parts such as piping feet, zipper feet, quilting bars, etc.

Appendix two

UK manufacturers and distributors

Sewing machines and overlockers (and spare parts)

Bernina. Bogod Machine Co. Ltd, 50–52 Great Sutton St, London EC1V 0DJ.
Elna Sewing Machines (GB) Ltd, Queens House, 180–82 Tottenham Court Rd, London W1P 9LE.
Husqvarna Ltd, PO Box 10 Oakley Road, Luton LU4 9QW.
Pfaff (Britain) Ltd, Pfaff House, East Street, Leeds LS9 8EH.
Riccar (UK) Ltd, Riccar House, Nuffield Way, Abingdon, Oxfordshire OX14 1RS.
Singer Industrial Products, SDL Ltd, 91, Coleman Rd, Leicester LE5 4LE.

Threads and other haberdashery

J. and P. Coats Ltd, National Distribution Centre, 39 Durham Street, Glasgow G41 1BS.
Molnlycke Ltd, Sewing Threads Division, 46 Viking Way, Bar Hill, Cambridge CB3 8EJ.
Perivale-Gütermann Ltd, Wadsworth Road, Greenford, Middlesex UB6 7JS.
Smallwares Ltd, (Mettler threads distributor), 17 Galena Rd, Hammersmith, London W6 0LU.
Tootal Sewing Products, National Sales Office, 56 Oxford St., Manchester ME0 1HJ.
The Vilene Organisation, PO Box 3, Ellistones Lane, Greetland, Halifax, W. Yorks HX4 8NJ.

Appendix three

USA suppliers and manufacturers

Bernina of America Inc., 534 West Chestnut, Hinsdale, IL 60521.

Husqvarna (*Viking*) Viking White Sewing Machine Co. 11750 Beres Road, Cleveland, Ohio 44111.

Riccar America Co., Corporate Headquarters, 14281 Franklin Avenue, Tustin, California 92680.

Riccar America Co., 4725 Fulton Industrial Blvd., Atlanta, Georgia 3036.

Singer Sewing Co., 135 Raritan Centre Parkway, Edison, N.J. 08837.

Mölnlycke Inc., 1415 Tuolumne St, Fresno, California 93706.

Gütermann of America Inc., PO Box 7387, 9800 Southern Pine Blvd., Charlotte, North Carolina 28210.

Appendix four

Overseas suppliers

Bernina

Bernina Corp., 3445 Park Ave, Montreal, H2X 2HX CANADA.

Burnells Pty. Ltd, 7–13 Queen St., GPO Box F379, Perth, W. AUSTRALIA 6001.

Bernina Sewing Machines (NZ) Ltd, 74–78 Victoria St, PO Box 30673, Lower Hutt, NEW ZEALAND.

Bernina Saskor (Pty.) Ltd, PO Box 61277, Marshaltown 2107, SOUTH AFRICA.

Frank Borda and Sons Ltd, 30–39 Jetties Wharf, Marsa, MALTA.

Husqvarna

Husqvarna Pty. Ltd, PO Box 108, North Ryde, N.S.W. 2113, AUSTRALIA.

Electrolux Ltd, PO Box 1336, Wellington, C.I. NEW ZEALAND.

Car & General, Home & Com. Appl. Div., PO Box 2000L, Nairobi, KENYA.

Muscat General Stores Ltd, 15-16 Republic Street, Valletta, MALTA.

Calvin Co., 259 Houston Centre, Kowloon, HONG KONG.

Husqvarna Vertriebs G.M.B.H., Strahlenbergerstrasse 1-3, D.6050, Offenbach 1, WEST GERMANY.

Perivale-Gütermann Ltd

Perivale-Gütermann Pty. Ltd, 64 Hotham Parade, PO Box 453, Artarmon, N.S.W. 2064, AUSTRALIA.

Perivale-Gütermann Pty. Ltd, PO Box 120 Woodlands Building, Woodlands Road, Cape Town, SOUTH AFRICA.

Joseph Borg Ltd, 30 Old Bakery St, Valletta, MALTA.

Gütermann & Co., D-7809 Gutach-Briesgau, WEST GERMANY.

Appendix five

Further reading

Sewing machines and overlockers

Make the Most of your Sewing-Machine, Ann Ladbury, Batsford, 1987.
The Sewing-Machine Handbook, Peter Lucking, Batsford, 1985.
The Sewing Machine Book, Myra Coles, Hutchinson, 1985.

General dressmaking techniques

Reader's Digest Complete Guide to Sewing. Reader's Digest Association Ltd.

Patchwork and quilting

Quilts to Wear, Virginia Avery, Bell and Hyman, 1982.
The Perfect Patchwork Primer, Beth Gutcheon, Penguin Handbooks, 1974.
Machine Appliqué, Sharon Perna, Sterling Publishing Co. Inc, New York, 1986. (Also, Blandford Press, U.K.)
Machine Embroidery, Christine Risley, Studio Vista, Cassell Ltd, London, 1973.
The Creative Sewing Machine, Anne Coleman, Batsford, London, 1979, 1986.

Articles (by the author) on Cut-and-Sew in *Machine Knitting Monthly,* available from newsagents or by subscription from Machine Knitting Monthly, PO Box 172, Maidenhead, Berkshire SL6 8XH.

Cut and Sew; working with machine-knitted fabrics, Pam Turbett, Batsford, London, 1985.

Index